Debt, Risk and Liquidity in Futures Markets

The issues of developing country debt crises, increased volatility and risk, and the determination of market liquidity are high on the agendas of policy-makers, market participants and researchers in the area of financial markets. These issues are also of major importance to regulators and exchange officials. This book contains a collection of eight papers which provide new insights into all three issues, with special emphasis on futures markets, which have received relatively little attention in the analysis of these problems.

These papers address issues which range from excess debt as a warning signal of impending financial crisis, through trading patterns in Chinese futures markets, to agricultural futures and Fourier analysis of intraday data. The book then progresses from realized volatility in thin futures markets, through forecasting and profits in currency futures, to key issues in liquidity, such as traders' perceptions of the price path in the presence of order imbalance, and the determinants of liquidity in US electricity futures.

Issues explored and findings reported in this book, have implications for policy-makers in framing recommendations to government, for government officials in shaping the regulatory structure of futures exchanges, for traders on these exchanges, and also for researchers planning future investigations. The book is relevant for postgraduate and advanced undergraduate courses on financial markets in Economics, Finance and Banking.

Barry A. Goss has a PhD from the London School of Economics, was a Reader in Economics at Monash University, Australia, from 1987 to 2004, was previously Director of the Derivatives Research Unit at Monash University and currently is director of a research company in futures markets.

Routledge international studies in money and banking

1 **Private Banking in Europe**
Lynn Bicker

2 **Bank Deregulation and Monetary Order**
George Selgin

3 **Money in Islam**
A study in Islamic political economy
Masudul Alam Choudhury

4 **The Future of European Financial Centres**
Kirsten Bindemann

5 **Payment Systems in Global Perspective**
Maxwell J. Fry, Isaak Kilato, Sandra Roger, Krzysztof Senderowicz, David Sheppard, Francisco Solis and John Trundle

6 **What is Money?**
John Smithin

7 **Finance**
A characteristics approach
Edited by David Blake

8 **Organisational Change and Retail Finance**
An ethnographic perspective
Richard Harper, Dave Randall and Mark Rouncefield

9 **The History of the Bundesbank**
Lessons for the European Central Bank
Jakob de Haan

10 **The Euro**
A challenge and opportunity for financial markets
Published on behalf of *Société Universitaire Européenne de Recherches Financières (SUERF)*
Edited by Michael Artis, Axel Weber and Elizabeth Hennessy

11 **Central Banking in Eastern Europe**
Edited by Nigel Healey and Barry Harrison

12 **Money, Credit and Prices Stability**
Paul Dalziel

13 **Monetary Policy, Capital Flows and Exchange Rates**
Essays in memory of Maxwell Fry
Edited by William Allen and David Dickinson

14 **Adapting to Financial Globalisation**
Published on behalf of *Société Universitaire Européenne de Recherches Financières (SUERF)*
Edited by Morten Balling, Eduard H. Hochreiter and Elizabeth Hennessy

15 **Monetary Macroeconomics**
A new approach
Alvaro Cencini

16 **Monetary Stability in Europe**
Stefan Collignon

17 **Technology and Finance**
Challenges for financial markets, business strategies and policy makers
Published on behalf of *Société Universitaire Européenne de Recherches Financières (SUERF)*
Edited by Morten Balling, Frank Lierman, and Andrew Mullineux

18 **Monetary Unions**
Theory, history, public choice
Edited by Forrest H. Capie and Geoffrey E. Wood

19 **HRM and Occupational Health and Safety**
Carol Boyd

20 **Central Banking Systems Compared**
The ECB, the pre-Euro Bundesbank and the Federal Reserve System
Emmanuel Apel

21 **A History of Monetary Unions**
John Chown

22 **Dollarization**
Lessons from Europe and the Americas
Edited by Louis-Philippe Rochon and Mario Seccareccia

23 **Islamic Economics and Finance**
A glossary, 2nd edition
Muhammad Akram Khan

24 **Financial Market Risk**
Measurement and analysis
Cornelis A. Los

25 **Financial Geography**
A banker's view
Risto Laulajainen

26 **Money Doctors**
The experience of international financial advising 1850–2000
Edited by Marc Flandreau

27 **Exchange Rate Dynamics**
A new open economy macroeconomics perspective
Edited by Jean-Oliver Hairault and Thepthida Sopraseuth

28 **Fixing Financial Crises in the 21st Century**
Edited by Andrew G. Haldane

29 Monetary Policy and Unemployment
The U.S., Euro-area and Japan
Edited by Willi Semmler

30 Exchange Rates, Capital Flows and Policy
Edited by Rebecca Driver, Peter J.N. Sinclair and Christoph Thoenissen

31 Great Architects of International Finance
The Bretton Woods era
Anthony M. Endres

32 The Means to Prosperity
Fiscal policy reconsidered
Edited by Per Gunnar Berglund and Matias Vernengo

33 Competition and Profitability in European Financial Services
Strategic, systemic and policy issues
Edited by Morten Balling, Frank Lierman and Andy Mullineux

34 Tax Systems and Tax Reforms in South and East Asia
Edited by Luigi Bernardi, Angela Fraschini and Parthasarathi Shome

35 Institutional Change in the Payments System and Monetary Policy
Edited by Stefan W. Schmitz and Geoffrey E. Wood

36 The Lender of Last Resort
Edited by Forrest H. Capie and Geoffrey E. Wood

37 The Structure of Financial Regulation
Edited by David G. Mayes and Geoffrey E. Wood

38 Monetary Policy in Central Europe
Miroslav Beblavy

39 Money and Payments in Theory and Practice
Sergio Rossi

40 Open Market Operations and Financial Markets
Edited by David G. Mayes and Jan Toporowski

41 Banking in Central and Eastern Europe 1980–2006
A comprehensive analysis of banking sector transformation in the former Soviet Union, Czechoslovakia, East Germany, Yugoslavia, Belarus, Bulgaria, Croatia, the Czech Republic, Hungary, Kazakhstan, Poland, Romania, the Russian Federation, Serbia and Montenegro, Slovakia, Ukraine and Uzbekistan
Stephan Barisitz

42 Debt, Risk and Liquidity in Futures Markets
Edited by Barry A. Goss

Debt, Risk and Liquidity in Futures Markets

Edited by Barry A. Goss

LONDON AND NEW YORK

First published 2008
by Routledge
2 Park Square, Milton Park, Abingdon, Oxon OX14 4RN

Simultaneously published in the USA and Canada
by Routledge
270 Madison Ave, New York, NY 10016

Routledge is an imprint of the Taylor & Francis Group, an informa business

Typeset in Times by Wearset Ltd, Boldon, Tyne and Wear
Printed and bound in Great Britain by TJI Digital, Padstow, Cornwall

British Library Cataloguing in Publication Data
A catalogue record for this book is available from the British Library

Library of Congress Cataloging in Publication Data
A catalog record for this book has been requested

ISBN10: 0-415-40001-5 (hbk)
ISBN10: 0-203-94015-6 (ebk)

ISBN13: 978-0-415-40001-5 (hbk)
ISBN13: 978-0-203-94015-0 (ebk)

Contents

List of figures ix
List of tables xi
List of charts xiii
List of contributors xiv
Acknowledgements xviii

1 **Editor's introduction: optimal debt and aspects of risk and liquidity** 1
BARRY A. GOSS

2 **Asian crises: theory, evidence, warning signals** 18
JEROME L. STEIN AND GUAY C. LIM

3 **The development of futures markets in China: evidence of some unique trading characteristics** 46
ANNE E. PECK

4 **Issues and research opportunities in agricultural futures markets** 75
PHILIP GARCIA, RAYMOND M. LEUTHOLD AND THORSTEN M. EGELKRAUT

5 **Currency futures volatility during the 1997 East Asian crisis: an application of Fourier analysis** 103
VANESSA MATTIUSSI AND GIULIA IORI

6 **Distributional properties of returns in thin futures markets: the case of the US$/AU$ contract** 123
VOLKER SCHIECK

7 Simultaneity, forecasting and profits in the US dollar/Deutschemark futures market 150
BARRY A. GOSS AND S. GULAY AVSAR

8 Perceptions of futures market liquidity: an empirical study of CBOT and CME traders 171
JULIA W. MARSH, JOOST M.E. PENNINGS AND PHILIP GARCIA

9 Simultaneity and liquidity in US electricity futures 191
S. GULAY AVSAR AND BARRY A. GOSS

Index 208

Figures

2.1	The medium run and long run real exchange rate NATREX	26
2.2	Optimal ratio debt/net worth f^* curve *US*, when there are no liquidation costs and curve *U'S'*, with liquidation costs	30
3.1	Production, price, and year-end stocks of wheat in China 1986–2003	50
3.2	Production, price, and imports of soybeans in China 1986–2003	52
3.3	Volume of trading on China's futures markets 1993–2003	55
3.4	Volume of trading in China's soybean, wheat, aluminum, and copper futures markets 1998–2003	57
3.5	Average pattern of trading in soybean futures at DCE 1998–2003	59
3.6	Average pattern of trading of wheat futures at ZCE 2002–03	60
3.7	Average pattern of trading of copper futures 1999–2003	60
3.8	Average pattern of trading of aluminum futures 1999–2003	61
3.9	Wheat futures prices of ZCE vs. cash prices of China Zhengzhou grain wholesale market	67
5.1	Squared diffusion coefficient $\hat{\eta}^2 r^{2\hat{\gamma}}(t)$ as simulated by model (5) and estimated trajectory via Fourier method	109
5.2	One simulated path of $\sigma^2(t)$ by model (7) and volatility reconstruction with Fourier method	110
5.3	Fourier correlation and Pearson correlation between two simulated asset prices according to model (8)	112
5.4	Times series of the tick prices and of the log returns for the future contracts under study	115
5.5	Estimated volatility via Fourier method for the S&P 500, the AU$–US$ and the JPY–US$ futures over the period April–December 1997	116
5.6	Weekly correlation estimated via Fourier method over the period April–December 1997	118
6.1	Empirical density graph of March 1997 contracts' realized variances and logarithmic standard deviation series	133

6.2 Empirical density graph of March 1997 contracts' raw and standardized return series 138
6.A.1 Empirical kernel densities of realized variances 143
6.A.2 Empirical kernel densities of realized logarithmic standard deviations 144
6.A.3 Empirical kernel densities of returns 145
6.A.4 Empirical kernel densities of standardized returns 146
8.1 Shapes of price path due to order imbalances (slippage) 177
8.2 Traders' price path perceptions due to order imbalances 179
8.3 Index contract traders associated with perceptions of the shape of the price path 184
8.4 Difference in price path perceptions between corn and soybean traders 187
9.1 The US index of industrial production 200

Tables

2.1 The Asian Crisis 1997–98 19
2.2 Macroeconomic variables 1975–85 and 1986–96 21
2.3 Net private capital flows to Asia 22
2.4 Measure of "sustainability" 23
2.5 Debt service/export ratios 23
2.6 Summary of warning signals analysis for 1997–98 crises 36
3.1 Seasonal variations in trading on Chinese futures exchanges 62
3.2 Studies of pricing linkages with China's futures markets 64–5
6.1 Descriptive statistics of realized variances and logarithmic standard deviations 132
6.2 Results from the normality tests of the realized variances' and logarithmic standard deviations' distributions 135
6.3 Descriptive statistics of return and standardized return series 137
6.4 Results from the normality tests of the returns' and standardized returns series' distributions 139
7.1 Unit root tests: Phillips-Perron 156
7.2 Johansen maximum eigenvalue test 156
7.3 Coefficient estimates: equations 1 to 4 158–9
7.4 Diagnostic tests on residuals 160
7.5 Post-sample simulation of exchange rates 160
7.6 Post-sample forecasts of spot exchange rate 162
7.7 Simulated trading: summary of results 162
7.8 Simulated trading: US$/DEM futures rates of return: 7 day positions 163
7.9 Simulated trading: US$/DEM futures rates of return: 1 month positions 164
8.1 Types of traders in survey (n=408) 178
8.2 Differences between a small and large order imbalance 180
8.3 Perceptions of the speed of price changes and shape of price path 180
8.4 Price path perceptions associated with trader characteristics 181
8.5 Price path perceptions associated with trader characteristics by market 183
8.6 Major contracts and the perceptions of the price path 186

9.1 Unit root tests: calculated test statistics 199
9.2 System estimates: equations 2, 4 and 6 201
9.3 Diagnostic tests on residuals: equations 2, 4 and 6 202
9.A.1 Single equation estimates: equations 2, 4 and 6 204–5

Charts

2.1	Indonesia	37
2.2	Korea	38
2.3	Malaysia	39
2.4	The Philippines	40
2.5	Thailand	41

Contributors

S. Gulay Avsar is a graduate in economics from the Middle East Technical University, Turkey, and has a PhD from Monash University, Australia. Currently she is a Lecturer in Economics, Central Queensland University, Sydney International Campus, and previously she has been a Lecturer in Mathematical Economics and Econometrics at Victoria University of Technology, Australia, and a Research Fellow in Economics at Monash University. Her research interests include price determination and forecasting in spot and futures markets for commodities and currencies, and liquidity in futures markets. She has published papers in international journals and as book chapters with leading international publishers.

Thorsten M. Egelkraut was born in Rostock, Germany, and currently is an Assistant Professor of Agri-Business/Marketing at Oregon State University. He has a Master of Science in Agronomy from the University of Georgia, a Master of Science in Finance from the University of Illinois at Urbana-Champaign (UIUC), and a PhD in Agricultural and Consumer Economics also from UIUC. He has worked on contract development at the Chicago Board of Trade, and as a post-doctoral fellow at the Office for Futures and Options Research at UIUC. His research interests focus on forecasting volatility with options price data.

Philip Garcia is the Thomas A. Hieronymus Distinguished Chair in Futures Markets and the Director of the Office of Futures and Options Research (OFOR) at the University of Illinois at Urbana-Champaign (UIUC). Dr Garcia is recognized for his research and teaching in agricultural commodity market and price analysis. He has made major contributions to the field of commodity futures and options markets, particularly in the areas of market efficiency, cash and futures price relationships, and the usefulness of marketing strategies.

Barry A. Goss is Director, Futures Markets Research Associates Pty Ltd, Melbourne, Australia, and has a PhD from the London School of Economics. Previously he was Reader in Economics and Director of the Derivatives Research Unit at Monash University, Australia. His research interests include simultaneous determination of spot and futures prices, liquidity in futures markets and the development of new futures contracts. He has published papers in international journals, and his books include *The Theory of Futures Trading* (1972), (with B.S. Yamey) *Economia Dei Mercati a Termine* (1980), (ed.) *Futures Markets: Their Establishment and Performance* (1986), (ed.) *Rational Expectations and Efficiency in Futures Markets* (1992), and (ed.) *Models of Futures Markets* (2000). He edited (with J.L. Stein) special issues of *Economic Record* and *Australian Economic Papers* relating to futures markets. He has been a consultant to the World Bank on futures markets, and wrote the feasibility study for the establishment of the Hong Kong Futures Exchange.

Giulia Iori has a PhD in Physics from the University of Rome, and currently is Professor of Economics at City University, London. She has conducted research in theoretical physics at various institutions including the CEA-Saclay (Paris) and the University of Barcelona. Previously she was Lecturer in Finance at the University of Essex, and Lecturer in Financial Mathematics and then Reader in Applied Mathematics at King's College London. Her research embraces physics, applied mathematics, finance and economics. Her current research interests include market microstructure, risk modeling and management, option pricing, economic networks and high-frequency financial time series analysis. She has published papers in international journals in Economics and Physics, and has been a referee for the British Council, the Engineering and Physical Science Research Council, and the European Commission.

Raymond M. Leuthold is the Thomas A. Hieronymus Professor of Futures Markets Emeritus, Department of Agricultural and Consumer Economics at the University of Illinois at Urbana-Champaign (UIUC). He also was previously Founding Director of the Office for Futures and Options Research at UIUC, where he has taught graduate and undergraduate courses, and conducted research on futures markets since 1967. He has published widely in many academic journals, and is a co-author of the textbook *The Theory and Practice of Futures Markets*. He has been a visiting scholar at Stanford University, USA, IGIA in France, and the Chicago Mercantile Exchange, USA.

Guay C. Lim is a Professorial Research Fellow at the Institute of Applied Economic and Social Research, University of Melbourne. Her research interests are primarily in the area of quantitative macroeconomics with emphasis on the design of time-series models for forecasting, and dynamic stochastic general equilibrium models for policy analysis. Her current research focuses on the financial and monetary aspects of macroeconomics, and her papers have been published in leading journals including *Journal of Applied Econometrics*, *Journal of Business and Economic Statistics*, *Journal of International Money and Finance*, *Journal of International Economics*, and *Journal of Banking and Finance*.

Julia W. Marsh received her Master of Science in Agricultural and Applied Economics from the University of Illinois at Urbana-Champaign, where she was Jonathon B. Turner Fellow. She also has degrees from Virginia Tech in Agricultural and Applied Economics and Interdisciplinary Studies. She has delivered papers at the Applied Commodity Price Analysis, Forecasting, and Marketing Risk Management Conference and for futures traders in Chicago. Previously Julia has interned with the Foreign Agricultural Service and the Chicago Board of Trade. Currently she works for Southern States Cooperative as the analyst for Strategic Planning and Business Development. Many of her current projects involve geographic information systems, including the creation of a new retail pricing system.

Vanessa Mattiussi is currently a PhD student at City University, London, and has a BSc in Mathematical Statistics from the University of Padua, a MSc in Financial Mathematics from King's College London, and a Diploma in Applied Statistics and Operational Research from Birkbeck College, London. She has held appointments as an analyst with Banca Intesa and J.P. Morgan, and her current research focuses on dependency measures for portfolio hedging and optimal trading strategies in limit order markets.

Anne E. Peck is the Holbrook Working Professor of Commodity Price Studies Emerita, Stanford University. Her research focuses principally on the evaluation of market performance. In previous studies she has examined inter alia the role of futures markets in grain price stabilization, adequacy of margins, the delivery terms of the Chicago Board of Trade grain and oilseeds contracts, and the development of futures exchanges in China and Kazakhstan. She also has been a Fulbright Scholar at the Kazakhstan Institute for Management, Economics and Strategic Planning, where she lectured on commodity markets and undertook research on the grain exchange in that country. In addition, Anne Peck has been an advisor to the governments of Kazakhstan and Uzbekistan. Her papers have appeared in leading international journals, and she has published several books on futures and commodity markets as author or editor, including *Readings in Futures Markets* (5 vols); *Futures Markets: Their Economic Role*; *Futures Markets: Regulatory Issues*; and most recently *Economic Development in Kazakhstan: the Role of the Large Enterprises.*

Joost M.E. Pennings is a Professor in the Department of Agricultural and Consumer Economics, Marketing and Decision Sciences Group at the University of Illinois at Urbana-Champaign and the AST Professor in Marketing at Wageningen University in the Netherlands. Dr Pennings' research deals with understanding *revealed* economic behavior by studying the decision-making behaviour of *real* decision-makers (market participants, consumers, managers, etc.). Special attention is given to decision-making under risk and uncertainty. The understanding of revealed economic behaviour is utilized to advance product development and public policy. The research is quantitative and rooted in economics, finance, management sciences, and psychology theory. Dr. Pennings' research has been published in among others *American Journal of Agricultural Economics*, *Economics Letters*, *International Journal of Research in Marketing*, *Journal of Agricultural Economics*, *Journal of Banking & Finance*, *Journal of Bioeconomics*, *Journal of Business*, *Journal of Business Research*, *Journal of Economic Psychology*, *Journal of International Money and Finance*, *European Financial Management*, and *Management Science*.

Volker Schieck was born in Emmerich, in the German state of North Rhine-Westphalia. He received his Master's degree from the University of Maastricht, completing the Econometrics and Operations Research Programme, and a minor in European Studies with distinction. With a grant from the European Union's Erasmus Programme, he studied at the Libera Università degli Studi Sociali (LUISS) in Rome from 2004 to 2005. Volker has worked for the BMW Group in Munich, and has worked on interest rate related projects for Montesquieu Finance and Treasury in Maastricht. In addition to econometrics, his areas of interest include international relations, strategic studies, as well as international finance.

Jerome L. Stein is Visiting Professor (research) in the Division of Applied Mathematics, Emeritus Professor of Economics and Eastman Professor of Political Economy at Brown University, USA. He has been Associate Editor of the *American Economic Review*, *Journal of Finance* and *Journal of Banking and Finance*. His research interests include macroeconomics, economic growth, futures markets, and international finance. His current research focuses on the application of stochastic optimal control/dynamic programming to international finance and debt crises. His books include *Economic Growth in a Free Market* (1964), *Money and Capacity Growth* (1971), *Monetarism, Keynesian and New Classical Economics* (1982), *The Economics of Futures Markets* (1986), (with P.R. Allen) *Fundamental Determinants of Exchange Rates* (1995), and *Stochastic Optimal Control, International Finance and Debt Crises* (2006). He received the degree Docteur Honoris Causa from the Université de la Mediterranée, Aix-Marseille II.

Acknowledgements

The Editor would like to thank World Scientific Publishing Co. for permission to reprint the paper "Asian Crises: Theory, Evidence, Warning Signals" by Jerome L. Stein and Guay C. Lim which was published in *The Singapore Economic Review*, Vol. 49, No. 2 (2004) pp. 135–161, and which appears as Chapter 2 in this book. All others papers published here were prepared specifically for this volume and are previously unpublished. Thanks are due also to Jerome Stein, Ray Leuthold, Heather Anderson, Gulay Avsar, Giulia Iori and Thorsten Egelkraut for comments on parts of the manuscript, and to participants at the Symposium on Risk Management in Less Developed and More Developed Countries, hosted by Monash University at Grand Hyatt Melbourne, November 2004, for comments on earlier versions of papers by Peck (Chapter 3) and Garcia, Leuthold and Egelkraut (Chapter 4). None of these persons, however, is responsible for any remaining errors or omissions. The Editor also is indebted to the editorial staff at Routledge, particularly Robert Langham, Terry Clague, Taiba Batool and Sarah Hastings, for encouraging and facilitating the preparation of this volume, and to Simon Kear and Gary Smith for their input to the production process. The Editor wishes to express his appreciation for the help of Lendriani Thursfield, who prepared the manuscript for this volume to her usual meticulous standards.

1 Editor's introduction

Optimal debt and aspects of risk and liquidity

Barry A. Goss

This book is divided into three sections: first, developing country debt; second, volatility and risk; and third, liquidity. Each of these areas has important unresolved issues regarding financial markets in general, and futures markets in particular. Moreover, in each case the futures markets aspects of these issues appear to have received relatively less attention than their spot market counterparts. Indeed, there are reasons to expect futures markets to behave differently compared with spot markets, because of important asymmetries between spot and futures markets, and within futures markets. An example of the first type of asymmetry is that futures markets operate on margin, whereas spot market transactions typically require payment in full. An example of the second type of asymmetry is that within futures markets, delivery, if possible, is only at seller's option.

The papers included in this volume have been selected because each provides new insights into an open question in the area of, or pertinent to, futures markets. These papers discuss the following issues:

- debt in excess of the optimal as a warning signal of impending financial crises[1]
- trading characteristics of Chinese futures markets
- recent contributions to the literature on performance of agricultural futures markets
- Fourier analysis of intraday data, which avoids homogenization
- realized volatility in a thin currency futures market
- forecasting and profits in currency futures
- traders' perceptions of the price path in the presence of order imbalance
- simultaneous relationships between liquidity, volume and volatility in US electricity futures markets.

Optimal debt in East Asia 1994–96

Conventional indicators of macroeconomic performance, such as inflation rate, ratio of budget deficit to GDP and ratio of current account deficit to GDP, failed to anticipate the Asian crises of 1997–98. The same is true also of the reports of sovereign credit rating agencies. Yet some researchers have wondered whether there was information in the market, if one only knew how to identify and extract it, which could be used to predict the onset of such an event. In Chapter 2 Stein and Lim provide an answer to this question. The information is that the exchange rates of some Asian countries were misaligned, and for some Asian countries the ratio of debt to net worth, relative to net risk-adjusted returns, was excessive. These two pieces of information suggested that a currency and/or debt crisis were likely if a random shock were to occur.

The analysis in Chapter 2 is based on Stein's (1995) theory of the Natural Real Exchange Rate (NATREX) and the stochastic optimal control theory of foreign debt of Fleming and Stein (2001), which was used by Stein and Paladino (2001) to analyse foreign debt of inter alia African, South American, Asian and Eastern European countries. These two theories recently have been brought together in Stein (2006). Stein's (1995) NATREX is an equilibrium medium and long term real exchange rate, which assumes internal balance (e.g. capacity utilization is at its long run mean) and external balance (e.g. equality between domestic and foreign real interest rates, and no speculative capital flows).

The NATREX is expressed as $R[Z(t)]$, where R is the real exchange rate, and is quoted as units of foreign currency per unit of domestic currency (raise is an appreciation of domestic currency), Z represents fundamentals and other exogenous variables and t is time. The actual real exchange rate at time t is $R(t)$, and the difference between the actual and equilibrium rates is

$$\Phi_t = R(t) - R[Z(t)] \tag{1}$$

where Φ_t is a measure of misalignment of the actual rate relative to NATREX. If $\Phi_t > 0$ this indicates overvaluation of the domestic currency, and suggests that depreciation or possibly a currency crisis[2] is probable. Conversely, if $\Phi_t < 0$ this indicates undervaluation of the domestic currency, and suggests that inflationary pressure will likely follow in the presence of a pegged nominal rate. Stein (2006, p. 11) suggests that a difference between the actual real rate and NATREX may be due to interest differentials, cyclical factors and/or speculative capital flows.

The optimal debt ratio f^*, of Stein and Lim in Chapter 2, is that which maximizes a HARA (hyperbolic absolute risk aversion) expected utility function of discounted consumption, subject to the constraints that consumption and net worth (X) are always positive. In this model, which is based on Fleming and Stein (2001) and summarized in Stein (2006, pp. 20–24, 28–37), the current external debt (L_t) is expressed as a ratio (f_t) of net worth, which is defined as capital (K) minus debt.[3] Thus

$$X_t = K_t - L_t \tag{2}$$

$$f_t = L_t / X_t \tag{3}$$

A measure of excess debt is the difference between the current debt ratio and that which is optimal

$$\Psi_t = f_t - f^* \tag{4}$$

The optimal debt ratio can be expected to vary inter alia with the mean net rate of return adjusted for risk $(b-r)/\sigma$, where $b = Y/K$ is the productivity of capital ($Y = GDP$), r is the real rate of interest and $\sigma^2 = var\ (b-r)$. In this model there are two stochastic variables, Y and r, which are both assumed to follow Brownian motion with drift.

The implications of this analysis are threefold. First, if the domestic currency is overvalued relative to NATREX ($\Phi_t > 0$), this acts as a warning signal that a devaluation, or possibly a currency crisis, is likely. Second, if the current debt ratio exceeds the optimal ($\Psi > 0$), this acts as a warning signal that a debt crisis is likely if a random shock occurs. Third, there may be interaction between a misaligned exchange rate and excess debt, which can increase the probability of a currency and/or debt crisis. For example, if mean net returns fall due to a decline in domestic productivity, capital outflow may occur, which can lead to devaluation. This devaluation will likely make it more difficult for the domestic economy to service external debt, which, if denominated in US dollars, implies a shock to the real rate of interest, and can lead to default.[4]

In Chapter 2 Stein and Lim estimate the NATREX for five Asian economies (Indonesia, Korea, Malaysia, the Philippines and Thailand) for the period 1982–2000. They find that

- Thailand had prolonged exchange rate misalignment 1990–96
- there was minor misalignment for Korea 1995–97
- there was no misalignment for Indonesia, Malaysia or the Philippines.

The authors then estimate the time paths of the ratio of external debt to GDP and net return on investment $(b-r)$ for these five economies. They argue that if returns are falling but the debt ratio is not declining, then the probability of default increases. This is because it becomes more difficult to service the debt without reducing consumption. Stein and Lim found inter alia that both Thailand and Korea exhibited warning signals of excess debt: there was a rise in the debt/GDP ratio, and a fall in relative returns 1994–96 in both cases. The authors then compare the forecasts of the NATREX and excess debt models, and their interaction, with the events in east Asia 1997–98.

Volatility and risk

Volatility, in the view of Poon and Granger (2003, pp. 481, 492), is a latent variable, and, unlike price, cannot be observed, but needs to be estimated, if inferences about volatility are to be drawn. This would appear to contrast, to some extent, with the view of Andersen, Bollerslev, Diebold and Labys (2003) (henceforth ABDL), who, in proposing their concept of realized volatility, claim that empirically, they are "treating volatility as observed rather than latent" (ABDL, p. 581), although realized volatility (RV) still needs to be estimated. In any case, volatility is not identical to risk: while a sample standard deviation can be employed as an estimate of volatility, an inference about risk requires that this estimate be attached to a statistical distribution, either theoretical or empirical. Poon and Granger (2003) agree that volatility can be interpreted as uncertainty, although they believe that in such cases there is usually an implicit assumption about the distribution of returns (Poon and Granger, 2003, p. 480).

This section of the Introduction deals with five papers which address a range of issues in the areas of volatility and risk. Chapter 3 deals with the trading characteristics of instruments for managing and taking risk on China's futures exchanges, while Chapter 4 surveys recent contributions to the literature on these instruments in agricultural economics. Chapter 5 discusses the application of Fourier analysis to intraday data, which are not evenly spaced in time, to avoid problems from homogenizing and synchronizing the data. Chapter 6 discusses the distributional properties of realized volatilities estimated from intraday data for a thinly traded currency futures market, while Chapter 7 is concerned with the development of a model to produce risk-adjusted returns with data from a leading currency futures market.

Recent developments in Chinese futures markets

A developed cash market and a system of warehouse receipts, both important foundations for the support of futures markets in agricultural commodities, were late developments in China. Nevertheless, the China Zhengzhou Commodity Exchange (CZCE), acting on advice from the Chicago Board of Trade, opened a wholesale market in 1990, and futures trading began on CZCE in May 1993. By the end of 1993 there were more than 30 futures exchanges operating in China, although this number was reduced by Chinese regulatory authorities to 14 by the end of 1995, and to three in 1998, namely CZCE (known as the Zhengzhou Commodity Exchange or ZCE since 1998), the Dalian Commodity Exchange and the Shanghai Futures Exchange (Peck, 2001, pp. 445, 452–454). Futures trading on these three exchanges, which is all electronic, centred on commodities, especially mungbeans at ZCE, soybeans at Dalian and copper at Shanghai. Trading activity on China's futures exchanges reached a peak in 1995 of 667 million contracts (see Chapter 3) or approximately ten trillion yuan (Peck, 2001, p. 454), and thereafter declined until around 2000, from which time there has been a revival. New futures contracts, mostly listed since 2000, have played an important part in the recovery in trading volumes on China's futures exchanges in 2005 and 2006. These commodities include especially strong gluten wheat, white sugar and cotton on ZCE, corn, soybean oil and meal on Dalian, and aluminium, rubber and fuel oil on Shanghai. Of the commodities which previously were strong performers on these exchanges, mungbeans have faded into oblivion at ZCE, although soybeans were a strong performer at Dalian in 2005, as was copper at Shanghai in the same year (http://english.czce.com.cn www.dce.cn www.shfe.com.cn all accessed August 18, 2006).

In a previous paper Peck was able to point to the speculative interest and activity by commercials on ZCE prior to 1998. This was in contrast to trading in wheat futures in Kazakhstan, which was in decline. The comparative success of ZCE, which was the most successful of the Chinese exchanges up to that date, Peck attributed in no small part to the managerial ability of the exchange officials (Peck, 2000, p. 54).

In Chapter 3, Peck discusses trading patterns and aspects of the performance of Chinese futures exchanges which have received little attention in the literature. Trading on China's futures exchanges typically reaches a maximum some five to seven months prior to maturity. This is true of soybeans at Dalian, of wheat at Zhengzhou, and of copper at Shanghai (the peak for aluminium at Shanghai is three to four months prior to maturity). Moreover, open interest follows the same course. This is in contrast to trading volume in the US, the UK, continental Europe and most other places, where the most active future is typically two to three months from maturity. Peck refers to a study which claims that the Chinese characteristic is due to the rules of Chinese exchanges, which require greater margins and smaller position limits in the month prior to delivery. Peck also seeks evidence of seasonality in Chinese trading patterns, and finds some surprising contrasts compared with US exchanges, especially for grains.

In Chapter 3, Peck also reviews the literature on performance of China's futures markets, including studies of the links between futures and cash prices in China, and between Chinese and US futures prices, for commodities which are traded in both countries. She finds contrasting results for soybeans at Dalian and wheat at Zhengzhou, and seeks reasons for these contrasts.

Futures market performance: a survey

Previous surveys of the literature on futures markets were published by Gray and Rutledge (1971) and Goss and Yamey (1976, 1978). Those surveys, however, preceded many important developments in futures markets, such as the dominance of financial futures, the consolidation of clearing and/or ownership among major exchanges, the almost universal switch to screen trading and the significant increase in the importance of hedge funds and other managed funds. In Chapter 4, Garcia, Leuthold and Egelkraut provide a survey of the literature on selected topics, with emphasis on agricultural futures markets, in which they not only review the contributions to the extant literature, but also make suggestions for future research.

Issues emphasized in the review in Chapter 4 include risk management, price relationships, informational efficiency, electronic trading and liquidity. In the discussion of risk management the reader's attention will be drawn to factors which may cause actual hedge ratios to diverge from those which are optimal, such as the distinction between maximum utility and minimum risk. In the discussion of price relationships the reader may be surprised to find that the issue of whether the convenience yield can explain backwardation in the presence of scarce stocks is still unresolved. The reader will note the asymmetry between backwardation (limited only by expectations, in the view of Keynes, 1930, pp. 142–144) and contango, which is constrained by storage costs, and she may like to consider the interpretation of these price spreads for non-storables, such as live cattle and electricity.

Chapter 4 reviews an extensive literature on weak-form and semi-strong form tests of the efficient market hypothesis for agricultural commodities, and the issue of informational efficiency may appear to be closed. Yet where is the literature on strong form tests in futures markets? Strong form efficiency means that all information, including private information, is impounded in price, and Ito, Lyons and Melvin (1998) inferred that the higher lunchtime variance in the JPY/US$ and DEM/US$ spot rates, when the Tokyo foreign exchange market is open, is due to private information.

Lyons (2001, pp. 87–88, 271) describes how dealers in spot foreign currencies impound private information into prices, and it would seem that the data for strong form tests in futures are potentially available in intraday order flow and price information. (A trader with private information is termed an "informed trader", and is to be distinguished from an "insider" who is an employee of a corporation and who possesses private information about that corporation (see Grossman, 1986, p. S130).)

The section on prices in Chapter 4 includes a discussion of volatility, where the authors remind us of the direct relationship between seasonality and volatility, which is important for agricultural markets, and of the need for volatility forecasts. The review in Chapter 4 concludes with a discussion of factors which impact price discovery and the trading environment, such as electronic trading and liquidity. While evidence from agricultural markets is scarce on the effect of electronic trading on price discovery, Anderson and Vahid (2001) find *inter alia*, with Sydney stock index data, that futures returns led stock returns before the switch to screen trading, and afterward this lead increases. While the review in Chapter 4 emphasizes the neglect of the time dimension and forecasts of liquidity, discussion of the liquidity topic will be delayed until the introductions of Chapters 8 and 9, both of which deal with liquidity.

Fourier analysis with high frequency data

Not all information relevant to the determination of asset prices is publicly known. Some information is private, as, for example, when a foreign exchange dealer receives an order for central bank intervention, or even a private client order, before the information is known to other market participants. Dealers can learn about this private information, not from direct access to the pieces of information held by the parties which initiate the transactions, but by observing the order flow. Moreover, because order flow is predictive of future price changes, dealers can be expected to respond to this information, for example, by taking market positions, either of a speculative or a risk management nature, or by adjusting the bid–ask spread (Lyons, 2001, pp. 4–8, 13–14, 21–27). The microstructure approach takes these processes, which will impact on price, into account.

High frequency data have been found to be more revealing of some microstructure processes, such as order flow, than low frequency data. Intraday data, however, are not evenly spaced in time, and the implementation of conditional volatility models requires that data are homogenized, for example, by linear interpolation, which can induce bias in volatility estimates, or by previous tick, which tends to introduce spurious autocorrelation among estimated returns (Barrucci and Renò, 2002, pp. 371–378). Similarly, standard correlation measures can not be applied to data which are produced by non-synchronous trading, and if the data are synchronized by interpolation this can introduce bias.

Recently, a method has been developed, based on Fourier analysis, which permits correlation statistics to be obtained, or volatility to be estimated, without incurring the penalties imposed by attempts to homogenize and synchronize the data (see Malliavin and Mancino, 2002). In contrast, the Fourier method can be applied directly to raw data, and is based on integration of the time series, rather than interpolation. The Fourier integrals can be obtained through integration by parts, and these will permit the volatility to be reconstructed (e.g. Barrucci and Renò, 2002) or the correlation statistics to be obtained (e.g. Precup and Iori, 2005). For example, if $S_i(t)$ is the price of asset i at time t and $p_i(t) = \ln S_i(t)$, the Fourier coefficients of dp_i are:

$$a_o(dp_i) = \frac{1}{2\Pi}\int_0^{2\Pi} dp_i(t) \tag{5}$$

$$a_k(dp_i) = \frac{1}{2\Pi}\int_0^{2\Pi} \cos(kt)dp_i(t) \tag{6}$$

$$b_k(dp_i) = \frac{1}{\Pi}\int_0^{2\Pi} \sin(kt)dp_i(t)\ k = 1 \tag{7}$$

where the time window for asset prices $[0, T]$ is normalized to $[0, 2\,\Pi]$. It has been shown that the Fourier coefficients of the volatility $\sigma^2(t)$ can be computed from the Fourier coefficients of the dp_i (Malliavin and Mancino, 2002, pp. 49–61). A similar procedure will yield the Fourier correlation matrix ρ_{ij} for two assets i, j (Precup and Iori, 2005).

The Fourier method has been employed by Barrucci and Renò (2002, pp. 371–378), who estimated the volatility of a diffusion process with high frequency data, and found inter alia that the Fourier volatility estimator has smaller bias and smaller variance than volatility estimates provided by cumulative squared intraday returns. The authors also found that a GARCH(1,1) model provided superior forecasts when volatilities obtained by the Fourier method were employed, as compared with volatilities computed by cumulative squared intraday returns. The Fourier method also has been employed by Precup and Iori (2006), who estimated correlation coefficients for two pairs of stocks on the

New York Stock Exchange with intraday data, and found that the Fourier estimates were more stable and more robust to variations in trading rates than estimates provided by the Pearson method and an extension to the Pearson method that allowed for "covolatility weighting". In Chapter 5 Mattiussi and Iori employ the Fourier method to analyse volatilities and correlation of returns with intraday data from the Chicago Mercantile Exchange (CME) on futures contracts for S&P500 Index, US dollar/Japanese yen and US dollar/Australian dollar, for the period April to December 1997, which includes the onset of the Asian crisis.

Realized volatility in thin markets

Representation of the behaviour of intrasample volatility requires that the model proposed is able to account for key stylized facts, including that

- daily returns are leptokurtic
- time series of returns exhibit volatility clustering
- returns are negatively skewed (e.g. Franses and van Dijk, 2000, pp. 5–17; Poon and Granger, 2003, p. 481).

Nevertheless, Poon and Granger (2003, p. 479) hold the view that the success of a volatility model is to be measured in terms of its post-sample forecasting power. ABDL (p. 580) argued that since "standard" volatility models (e.g. GARCH models) cannot fully utilize the information in intraday data, a new approach was necessary. To address this perceived deficiency they proposed their realized volatility (RV) approach. They note first that while raw returns are leptokurtic, returns standardized by RV are approximately normal. Second, they note that while distributions of RV are positively skewed, logarithms of RV are approximately normal (ABDL, p. 581).

Post-sample VAR volatility forecasts based on RV for one and ten day horizons appear to outperform rival forecasts by models based on absolute returns, autoregressive models and GARCH type models (ABDL, pp. 603–612). In the ranking of volatility models by Poon and Granger (2003, pp. 508–535), according to their ability to forecast post-sample, and evaluated by a range of criteria, RV forecasts are ranked highly. Implied volatility forecasts derived from option pricing models also are highly ranked by Poon and Granger (2003). In option pricing models, such as Black-Scholes, the option price is a function of asset price, strike price, risk-free rate of interest, time to maturity and volatility. Since the first five variables are observable, the implied volatility can be obtained by inverting the pricing model. Option price data also can be employed to find implied forward volatility between two non-overlapping maturities (e.g. Egelkraut and Garcia, 2006). Implied volatility is a market expectation of average volatility until expiration, and Poon and Granger (2003, pp. 486–489, 499) point out that a test of forecasting performance of an implied volatility model is a joint test of option market performance and validity of the option pricing model.

The distributional results for returns standardized by RV and log realized volatilities obtained by ABDL (pp. 581, 598–600) refer to large samples of spot foreign currency data (3045 days intrasample, 596 days post-sample, with 30-minute returns derived from several million quotes at an average of approximately 4500 per day (ABDL, pp. 591–593 and n. 17)). In Chapter 6 Schieck explores the extent to which these properties hold for the more thinly traded US dollar/Australian dollar futures contract at the Chicago Mercantile Exchange. Schieck calculates realized volatilities for ten-minute returns for the near future with maturities from March 1997 to December 1999.

Forecasting and profits in currency futures

Meese and Rogoff (1983) found that traditional economic models of exchange rates, such as the monetary model, could not outperform a random walk, in post-sample forecasts of the spot rate for the period 1976–81, for three key exchange rates against the US dollar. Among the reasons suggested for this relative lack of success were simultaneous equations bias and misspecification (Meese and Rogoff, 1983, pp. 12–13, 17–19). This criticism was re-emphasized by Isard (1987), Meese (1990) and others. Perceived deficiencies of traditional models included undue reliance on single equation methods, inadequate representation of expectations and insufficient attention to capital flows (Isard, 1987, pp. 1, 3, 15–16; Meese, 1990, p. 117).

In a world where models which could outperform a random walk were extremely rare, Goss and Avsar (1996) developed a simultaneous model of the Australian dollar/US dollar rate which forecasts the spot rate out of sample with a per cent root mean square error (RMSE) one quarter that of a random walk, albeit with only ten post-sample months of forecasting in a thin market (Goss and Avsar, 1996, pp. 171–172). Goss and Avsar (2000) developed a simultaneous model of the US dollar/German deutschemark futures market, which was the most active currency futures market on the Chicago Mercantile Exchange prior to the introduction of the Euro, and this model outperforms a random walk in 34 months of post-sample forecasts of the spot rate with per cent RMSE less than one fifth that of a random walk (Goss and Avsar, 2000, pp. 77–79).

It has not been shown, however, that the model of Goss and Avsar (2000) could be employed to produce risk-adjusted profits. Moreover, that model assumed an exogenous risk premium, an assumption which is unduly restrictive, because the risk premium is likely to vary inter alia with the time-varying volatility of the market under review. In Chapter 7 Goss and Avsar redevelop and re-estimate their model of the USD/DEM spot and futures markets (endogenization of the risk premium requires respecification of the error terms, and re-estimation of the mean and variance equations). The respecified model contains functional relationships for short hedgers, long hedgers, net short speculators in futures, and for traders with unhedged spot positions. Conditional variances of the hedging and speculation equations are modelled as EGARCH (p, q) processes (Nelson, 1991) to capture the likely asymmetrical financial innovations.

The redeveloped model again significantly outperforms a random walk in post-sample forecasts, and as the foundation for a simulated trading program in DM futures, it produces significant risk-adjusted profits for a holding period of seven days, while the average profits are positive but not significant if the positions are held for one month. This result may be interpreted as evidence against informational efficiency in the very short term. While this outcome may appear inconsistent with the concept of rational expectations, which is employed to represent expectations in this model, the authors provide two lines of reconciliation to this apparent conflict. The first is the presence of a significant risk premium (since the efficient market hypothesis is a joint hypothesis, embodying the assumptions of risk neutrality and rational expectations). The second avenue of reconciliation is the evidently greater power of the hypothesis tests based on post-sample forecasts, compared with those based on intrasample tests of significance of estimated coefficients.

Liquidity

Order imbalance and liquidity relationships

Liquidity can be defined as the ability to buy or sell the desired quantity of a security at the market price in a short period of time. Liquidity has value, so that securities with a greater liquidity tend to have higher prices than less liquid securities, other things being equal (Amihud *et al.*, 2006, pp. 1–9, 49–51). The issue of determination of liquidity is important in the economics of futures markets, because the cost of liquidity is a major cost of transacting (Ding, 1999, p. 308; Wang *et al.*, 1997, p. 759). Liquidity also has value to exchanges, in the sense that an exchange which trades a given security with greater liquidity than rival exchanges can expect to attract volume at expense of rivals. Previous research has identified key variables in the determination of liquidity, especially volume and volatility, and several studies have investigated the relationships between cost of liquidity and volume, between volume and volatility, as well as between cost of liquidity and volatility (e.g. Fleming, 1997; Wang *et al.*, 1997; Hartmann, 1999; Bollerslev and Melvin, 1994; Goss and Avsar, 1998).

While no ideal measure of liquidity has been proposed, the bid–ask spread is a popular measure, although as Fleming (2003, p. 85) has emphasized, this measure represents the cost of executing a small trade and is valid for only a short time period. This measure of cost of liquidity has been supplemented by measures of market depth, such as quote size (the quantity of securities to which the bid or offer refers) or trade size (the quantity of securities traded). Fleming (2003, p. 85) argues that such measures tend to underestimate market depth, because they do not indicate the quantity of securities which could have been traded at the quoted price. Distinctions have been drawn between "nominal" and "effective" bid–ask spreads, where the effective spread is the difference between prices of a dealer's buy (sell) and sell (buy) transactions for a security, which may be separated in time (e.g. Grossman and Miller, 1988, p. 628; Smith and Whaley, 1994, pp. 438–439; Ding, 1999, pp. 309–310).

Futures markets do not have official market makers like some equities markets, such as the New York Stock Exchange, where "specialists" declare simultaneously the bid and offer prices at which they are willing to trade (i.e. provide "immediacy": see Grossman and Miller, 1988, p. 628). In futures markets with open outcry, such as the Chicago Mercantile Exchange (CME), bid and offer quotes are provided, possibly by different persons, possibly separated in time (some futures contracts at CME now utilize electronic and open outcry side-by-side trading). In futures markets with screen trading, such as the London International Financial Futures Exchange, bid and offer prices are matched by computer to effect transactions.[5]

Previous research has distinguished four components of the bid–ask spread, each of which is influenced inter alia by volume and/or volatility:

1 Dealer's inventory cost, which represents essentially the dealer's risk from holding inventory, is a direct function of volatility, and varies inversely with volume.
2 Asymmetric information cost, which gives rise to a compensation to the dealer from dealing with better informed traders. This component may vary directly with volume if the dealer perceives that orders are being placed by traders with private information, and is likely a direct function of volatility if increased volatility generates information driven orders.
3 Unit direct costs of order execution, which are likely to be negatively related to volume, due to the presence of fixed costs in the short run (Grossman and Miller, 1988, p. 629) and economies of scale in the long run[6] (Ding, 1999, p. 313; Hartmann, 1999, pp. 803–804).
4 Market power of the dealer is likely to decrease with competition among dealers, and hence to be negatively related to volume (Fleming, 1997; Wang *et al.*, 1994; Glosten, 1987; McInish and Wood, 1992; Hartman, 1999). This component could be measured by the difference between dealer's price and marginal cost or by the number of dealers trading in the pits (Wang *et al.*, 1997, p. 762). In a market with official market makers, Lyons (2001, p. 40) points out that the market maker's monopoly power is limited by the limit order book, because in matching a market order, the market maker's bid or ask quotes must be compared with the order book.

Previous research has studied the relationship between pairs of the three variables: liquidity, volume and volatility. In the cost-of-liquidity volume relationship, an increase in volume will reduce the cost-of-order execution due to spreading fixed costs (short run) and economies of scale (long run), as discussed above. Moreover, an increase in volume will make it easier for a dealer to sell from inventory, thus reducing inventory cost, and also will likely reduce the dealer's monopoly power if more dealers are active. These three influences will tend to reduce the bid–ask spread. In contrast, if the dealer believes that new orders are driven by private information, then asymmetric information cost will increase, which will widen the bid–ask spread. While in theory the sign of this relationship is ambiguous, an increase in volume is generally thought to reduce the cost of liquidity, and empirically the relationship usually has been found to be negative (Hartmann, 1999, p. 805; Wang *et al.*, 1997, pp. 761–762, 765–773; McInish and Wood, 1992, pp. 753–754; Copeland and Galai, 1983, p. 1463; Goss and Avsar, 1998, pp. 106–108).

Some authors have argued that, in theory, volume varies directly with volatility, while others regard the sign of this relationship as ambiguous. In the model of Epps and Epps (1976), for example, volatility (as measured by the conditional variance of price changes) varies directly with volume, through increased disagreement between buyers and sellers following the arrival of new information. In comparison, in the model of Tauchen and Pitts (1983), price variability and volume are directly related, given the number of traders. An increase in the number of traders, however, reduces the variance of price changes through a reduction in the differences between traders. Hence, in the model of Tauchen and Pitts (1983), the sign of the volume–volatility relationship is indeterminate (Tauchen and Pitts, 1983, pp. 487–490). From the liquidity viewpoint, an increase in volatility contains information which will likely lead to increased volume as traders respond to this information. To the extent that dealers perceive new orders are being placed by traders with private information, there will be an increase in asymmetric information cost, and an increase in the bid–ask spread, which will tend to reduce volume. Moreover, increased volatility represents increased uncertainty, which will increase the dealer's inventory risk, which also will tend to increase the bid–ask spread. Hence the sign of the volume–volatility relationship is ambiguous (see French and Roll, 1986; Ito *et al.*, 1998; McInish and Wood, 1992, p. 754; Wang *et al.*, 1994, p. 838, n. 1). Empirically, the sign of this relationship is typically found to be positive (see e.g. Clark, 1973, pp. 143–145; Wang *et al.*, 1997, pp. 765–773; Fleming, 1997, p. 18; Goss and Avsar, 2006, pp. 44–45). Volume can also impact upon volatility (see Bessembinder and Seguin, 1993, pp. 23, 30–33).

The relationship between cost of liquidity and volatility is positive. Increased volatility contains new information, and to the extent that dealers perceive that the resulting orders are driven by private information, there will be an increase in asymmetric information cost, and hence in the bid–ask spread. Moreover, increased volatility also implies increased uncertainty, which will raise the dealer's inventory cost, and hence raise the bid–ask spread (see McInish and Wood, 1992, p. 764; Fleming, 1997, pp. 21–23; Bollerslev and Melvin, 1994, pp. 356, 370–371; Wang *et al.*, 1994, p. 838).

Dealers will know public information, and while they will not know the private information possessed by informed traders, they can learn about private information from (signed) order flow (negative for sales). Indeed, dealers can use order flow to forecast price movements. Moreover, because dealers hold inventory, a client order can result in disequilibrium in the dealer's portfolio. A dealer can be expected to respond to the arrival of private information, as revealed by order flow, by undertaking risk management and/or spec trading activity (Lyons, 2001, pp. 4–8, 13–14, 21–27). Pennings *et al.* studied the price path due to order imbalance as a measure of market dep the number of contracts needed to change price by one tick: Kyle, 1985, p. 1319) and found evidence of a non-linear price path. In Chapter 8 Marsh, Pennings and Garcia survey the perceptions of the price path due to order imbalance of more than 400 traders at the Chicago Board of Trade (CBOT) and CME. The nature of this price path is critical to the cost of liquidity, and the authors argue that perceptions drive the behaviour of traders. Marsh, Pennings and Garcia find considerable heterogeneity in traders' perceptions of the price path due to small and large order imbalances, and the question is whether the variation in perceptions is related to characteristics of the traders themselves (e.g. scalping or spreading) or to aspects of market microstructure. The authors present evidence that the answer is to be found in microstructure, particularly in differences in market characteristics such as the extent to which trading is open outcry or electronic, and whether contracts traded are agricultural or financial. They also find differences in traders' perceptions, between contracts within the agricultural and financial groups, and these differences possibly reflect inter alia differences in trading systems and contract specification.

Previous research on relationships between the variables cost of liquidity, volume and volatility has employed, almost exclusively, single equation methods (Wang *et al.*, 1997, is a rare exception). Nevertheless, in practice, these relationships are determined simultaneously, and this should be taken into account in empirical research. This is especially true of relationships between pairs of the three variables liquidity, volume and volatility, because if these relationships are estimated as regression functions, each equation will contain an endogenous regressor. The residuals and the regressors, therefore, will be contemporaneously correlated, so that ordinary least squares estimates will be biased and inconsistent. Furthermore, the residuals of these equations are likely to exhibit time-varying volatility and volatility clustering, i.e. heteroskedasticity, so that inferences drawn from conventional hypothesis tests likely will be invalid. Indeed, the necessity for a simultaneous approach to the analysis of liquidity is suggested in Andersen and Bollerslev (1998, p. 220). Although Wang *et al.* (1997) develop a two-equation model to analyse the simultaneous determination of cost of liquidity and volume, this model does not endogenize volatility.

While liquidity in futures markets has received some attention in previous research, liquidity in electricity futures markets has virtually been ignored. This is unfortunate because competitive electricity markets are in an early stage of development, and an understanding of liquidity in these markets will be of increased importance as deregulation of electricity markets proceeds in Europe, North America, Asia and Oceania. Indeed, given the substantial volatility and price spikes observed in US markets, it is clear that effective risk management tools are essential in deregulated electricity markets (see Stoft, 2000; Avsar and Goss, 2001, pp. 480–481). In Chapter 9 Avsar and Goss develop and estimate a three-equation simultaneous model of the relationships between each pair of the variables cost of liquidity, volume and volatility. This model is estimated by three stage least squares with data from California–Oregon Border electricity futures contracts, which was one of the first two electricity futures contracts introduced in the US, and the most active during the sample period from April 1996 to December 1999. Three stage least squares (3SLS) is an appropriate estimator for this model, given the characteristics of liquidity relationships described above, and the likely covariation of the residuals of the individual equations. Single-equation estimates of these relationships are provided for comparison, and to estimate the ARCH-in-mean terms for the simultaneous model, and they also act as starting values for the 3SLS estimates. The reader will observe that the systems estimates are generally larger, and are more supportive of the theoretical foundations of the model, than the single equation estimates.

Notes

1 Although this paper (Chapter 2 by Stein and Lim) does not employ futures market data, it is pertinent to futures markets, first because reform of East Asian financial architecture is an important policy issue for major international institutions (see Woo *et al.*, 2000, pp. 4–11), and futures markets can be expected to play a role in any revised financial arrangements in East Asia. Second, it has been shown that activity in East Asian derivatives markets increased during the Asian crisis (see Zhang, 2004, pp. 159–173, 211–220).

2 Goldstein *et al.* (2000, p. 19) define a currency crisis as follows: "A currency crisis is defined as a situation in which an attack on the currency leads to substantial reserve losses, or to a sharp depreciation of the currency – if the speculative attack is ultimately successful – or to both." This definition is helpful for the present discussion.

A debt crisis in the sense of Stein (2006, p. 226) occurs "if the attempt to service the debt requires a drastic decline in consumption". Stein (2006, p. 227) argues, however, that a drastic reduction in consumption is unlikely, and that default is the likely outcome of such a situation.

Goldstein *et al.* (2000, p. 20) also define the events which they believe mark the beginning of a banking crisis. Although banking crises do not play an explicit role in the model of Stein and Lim in Chapter 2, they are nevertheless relevant, because as Goldstein *et al.* (2000, pp. 2, 13) argue, a banking crisis may precede a currency crisis, for example by leading to a loss of international reserves.

3 Stein (2006, chapter 1) can be accessed at www.oup.co.uk (search <Jerome Stein>, download <sample>).

4 An alternative warning system of banking and currency crises, which involves 24 indicators, is developed by Goldstein *et al.* (2000, pp. 21–43, 55–71).

5 Some futures exchanges now have market makers for electronic trading. For example, Chicago Board of Trade introduced an Electronic Market Maker Program in November 2005 for options on its two-year US Treasury Note Futures Contract. In October 2006 Chicago Mercantile Exchange introduced a market maker program for its Eurodollar options. Under this program firms could compete for benefits (see www.cme.com, accessed 13 July 2007).

6 The merger between the Chicago Mercantile Exchange and the Chicago Board of Trade, announced 17 October 2006 (see www.cme.com; www.bot.com; *The Economist*, 21 October 2006, p. 78), is consistent with the hypothesis of economies of scale of order execution, and with the view, expressed in Goss and Avsar (1998, pp. 105–109), that there are increasing returns to liquidity. Indeed, paragraph two of the merger announcement refers to the combined company as providing "One of the

world's most liquid market places, with average daily trading volume approaching 9 million contracts per day" (available at: www.cme.com).

References

Amihud, Y., H. Mendelson and L. Pedersen (2006), *Liquidity and Asset Prices*, Boston and Delft: Now Publishers Inc.

Andersen, T.G. and T. Bollerslev (1998), "Deutsche Mark–Dollar Volatility: Intraday Activity Patterns, Macroeconomic Announcements, and Longer Run Dependencies", *Journal of Finance*, 53(1), 219–265.

Anderson, H. and F. Vahid (2001), "Market Architecture and Nonlinear Dynamics of Australian Stock and Futures Indices", *Australian Economic Papers*, 40(4), 541–566.

Anderson, T., T. Bollerslev, F. Diebold and P. Labys (2003), "Modelling and Forecasting Realized Volatility", *Econometrica*, 71(2), 579–625.

Avsar, S.G. and B.A. Goss (2001), "Forecast Errors and Efficiency in the US Electricity Futures Market", *Australian Economic Papers*, 40(4), 479–499.

Barrucci, E. and R. Renò (2002), "On Measuring Volatility of Diffusion Processes with High Frequency Data", *Economics Letters*, 74, 371–378.

Bessembinder, H. and P. Seguin (1993), "Price Volatility, Trading Volume, and Market Depth: Evidence from the Futures Markets", *Journal of Financial and Quantitative Analysis*, 28, 21–39.

Bollerslev, T. and M. Melvin (1994), "Bid–ask Spreads and Volatility in the Foreign Exchange Market", *Journal of International Economics*, 36, 355–372.

Clark, P. (1973), "A Subordinated Stochastic Process Model with Finite Variance for Speculative Prices", *Econometrica*, 41(1), 135–155.

Copeland, T. and D. Galai (1983), "Information Effects on the Bid-Ask Spread", *Journal of Finance*, 38(5), 1457–1469.

Ding, D.K. (1999), "The Determinants of Bid–Ask Spreads in the Foreign Exchange Futures Market: A Microstructure Analysis", *Journal of Futures Markets*, 19(3), 307–324.

Egelkraut, T.M. and P. Garcia (2006), "Intermediate Volatility Forecasts Using Implied Forward Volatility: The Performance of Selected Agricultural Commodity Options", *Journal of Agricultural and Resource Economics*, 31(3), 508–528.

Epps, T.W. and M.L. Epps (1976), "The Stochastic Dependence of Security Price Changes and Transaction Volumes: Implications for the Mixture-of-Distributions Hypothesis", *Econometrica*, 44(2), 305–321.

Fleming, M.J. (1997), "The Round-the-Clock Market for US Treasury Securities", *Federal Reserve Bank of New York Economic Policy Review*, July, 9–32.

Fleming, M.J. (2003), "Measuring Treasury Market Liquidity", *Federal Reserve Bank of New York Economic Policy Review*, September, 83–108.

Fleming, Wendell H. and Jerome L. Stein (2001), "Stochastic Inter-temporal Optimization in Discrete Time", in Negishi, Takashi, R. Ramachandran and K. Mino (eds), *Economic Theory, Dynamics and Markets: Essays in Honor of Ryuzo Sato*, Boston: Kluwer.

Franses, P.H. and D. van Dijk (2000), *Non-Linear Time Series Models in Empirical Finance*, Cambridge: Cambridge University Press.

French, K.R. and R. Roll (1986), "Stock Return Variances", *Journal of Financial Economics*, 17, 5–26.

Glosten, L. (1987), "Components of the Bid-Ask Spread and the Statistical Properties of Transaction Prices", *Journal of Finance*, 42(5), 1293–1307.

Goldstein, M., G. Kaminsky and C. Reinhart (2000), *Assessing Financial Vulnerability: An Early Warning System for Emerging Markets*, Washington, DC: Institute for International Economics.

Goss, B.A. and S.G. Avsar (1996), "A Simultaneous, Rational Expectations Model of the Australian Dollar/US Dollar Market", *Applied Financial Economics*, 6, 163–174.

Goss, B.A. and S.G. Avsar (1998), "Increasing Returns to Liquidity in Futures Markets", *Applied Economics Letters*, 5, 105–109.

Goss, B.A. and S.G. Avsar (2000), "A Simultaneous Model of the US Dollar/Deutschmark Spot and Futures Markets", chapter 4 in B.A. Goss (ed.), *Models of Futures Markets*, London: Routledge, 61–85.

Goss, B.A. and S.G. Avsar (2006), "Liquidity, Volume and Volatility in US Electricity Futures: The Case of Palo Verde", *Applied Financial Economics Letters*, 2, 43–46.

Goss, B.A. and B.S. Yamey (eds) (1976), *The Economics of Futures Trading*, London: Macmillan, second edition 1978.

Gray, R.W. and D.J.S. Rutledge (1971), "The Economics of Commodity Futures Markets: A Survey", *Review of Marketing and Agricultural Economics*, 39, 3–54.

Grossman, S.J. (1986), "An Analysis of the Role of 'Insider Trading' on Futures Markets", *Journal of Business*, 59(2), S129–S146.

Grossman, S.J. and M.H. Miller (1988), "Liquidity and Market Structure", *Journal of Finance*, 43, 617–633.

Hartmann, P. (1999), "Trading Volumes and Transaction Costs in the Foreign Exchange Market: Evidence from Daily Dollar–Yen Spot Data", *Journal of Banking and Finance*, 23, 801–824.

Isard, P. (1987), "Lessons from Empirical Models of Exchange Rates", *International Monetary Fund Staff Papers*, 34(1), 1–28.

Ito, T., R.K. Lyons and M.T. Melvin (1998), "Is There Private Information in the FX Market: The Tokyo Experiment", *Journal of Finance*, 53(3), 1111–1130.

Keynes, J.M. (1930), *A Treatise on Money*, vol. 2, London: Macmillan.

Kyle, A.S. (1985), "Continuous Auctions and Insider Trading", *Econometrica*, 53, 1315–1335.

Lyons, R.K. (2001), *The Microstructure Approach to Exchange Rates*, Cambridge, MA: MIT Press.

Malliavin, P. and M. Mancino (2002), "Fourier Series Method for Measurement of Multivariate Volatilities", *Finance and Stochastics*, 6(1), 49–61.

McInish, T. and R. Wood (1992), "An Analysis of Intraday Patterns in Bid/Ask Spreads for NYSE Stocks", *Journal of Finance*, 47(2), 753–764.

Meese, R. and A. Rogoff (1983), "Empirical Exchange Rate Models of the Seventies: Do they Fit out of Sample?", *Journal of International Economics*, 14, 3–24.

Meese, R. (1990), "Currency Fluctuations in the post-Bretton Woods Era", *Journal of Economic Perspectives*, 4(1), 117–134.

Nelson, D. (1991), "Conditional Heteroskedasticity in Asset Returns: A New Approach", *Econometrica*, 59, 347–370.

Peck, A.E. (2000), "The Development of Commodity Futures Exchanges in Kazakhstan and China", in B.A. Goss (ed.), *Models of Futures Markets*, London: Routledge, 42–60.

Peck, A.E. (2001), "The Development of Commodity Exchanges in the Former Soviet Union, Eastern Europe, and China", *Australian Economic Papers*, Special Issue on Financial Markets, 40(4), 437–460.

Pennings, J.M.E., W.E. Kuiper, F. ter Hofstede and M.T.G. Meulenberg (1998), "The Price Path Due to Order Imbalances: Evidence from the Amsterdam Futures Exchange", *European Financial Management*, 4, 27–44.

Poon, S-H. and C.W.J. Granger (2003), "Forecasting Volatility in Financial Markets: A Review", *Journal of Economic Literature*, 41(2), 478–539.

Precup, O. and G. Iori (2006), "Cross-correlation Measures in the High-frequency Domain", *The European Journal of Finance*, 12, November.

Smith, T. and R.E. Whaley (1994), "Estimating the Effective Bid/Ask Spread from Time and Sales Data", *Journal of Futures Markets*, 14, 437–455.

Stein, J.L., Polly Reynolds Allen and Associates (1995), *Fundamental Determinants of Exchange Rates*, Oxford: Oxford University Press.

Stein, J.L. (2006), *Stochastic Optimal Control, International Finance, and Debt Crises*, Oxford: Oxford University Press.

Stein, J.L. and G. Paladino (2001), "Country Default Risk: An Empirical Assessment", *Australian Economic Papers*, Special Issue on Financial Markets, 40(4), 417–436.

Stoft, S. (2000), "PJM's Capacity Market in a Price-Spike World", Working Paper PWP-077, University of California Energy Institute, Berkeley CA 94720–5180.

Tauchen, G.E. and M. Pitts (1983), "The Price Variability–Volume Relationship on Speculative Markets", *Econometrica*, 51(2), 485–506.

Wang, G.H.K., R.J. Michalski, J.V. Jordan and E.J. Moriarty (1994), "An Intra-day Analysis of Bid-spreads and Price Volatility in the S&P 500 Index Futures Market", *Journal of Futures Markets*, 14, 837–859.

Wang, G.H.K., J. Yau and T. Baptiste (1997), "Trading Volume and Transaction Costs in Futures Markets", *Journal of Futures Markets*, 17(7), 757–780.

Woo, W.T., J.D. Sachs and K. Schwab (2000), *The Asian Financial Crisis: Lessons for a Resilient Asia*, Cambridge, MA; London, England: MIT Press.

Zhang, P.G. (2004), *Chinese Yuan Renminbi Derivative Products*, Singapore: World Scientific Publishing Co.

2 Asian crises

Theory, evidence, warning signals

Jerome L. Stein and Guay C. Lim[1]

Abstract

In July 1997, the economies of East Asia became embroiled in one of the worst financial crises of the postwar period. Yet, prior to the crisis, these economies were seen as models of economic growth experiencing sustained growth rates that exceeded those earlier thought unattainable. Why did the market not anticipate the crises? To this end, we review the Asian financial crisis from two related perspectives – whether the crisis was precipitated by a failure of the real exchange rate to be aligned with its fundamental determinants and/or whether the crisis was precipitated by a divergence of the foreign debt from its optimal path. The first perspective is based on a coherent theory of the equilibrium real exchange rate – the NATREX model – that shows how "misalignments" lead to currency crises. The second perspective is based on a model of optimal foreign debt ratio – derived from stochastic optimal control – which shows why "divergences" lead to debt crises. The important point here is that these models suggest important variables which may serve as warning signals to predict crises.

Key Words: Asian crises, optimal debt, equilibrium exchange rates, NATREX, stochastic optimal control, warning signals of crises, exchange rate misalignment

JEL classification: F3, F31, F32, F34, F4.

Aims of the study

In July 1997, the economies of East Asia became embroiled in one of the worst financial crises of the postwar period. Yet, prior to the crisis, these economies were seen as models of economic growth experiencing sustained growth rates that exceeded those earlier thought unattainable. Table 2.1 describes the situation for ASEAN4 and Korea before and after 1997. The high growth from 1986–96 was suddenly followed by a collapse of the real economy, with negative growth in 1998. In 1997, the exchange rates depreciated by double digits and, for some countries, the depreciation continued into 1998.

Table 2.1 The Asian Crisis 1997–98

Country	*GDP: annual growth rate %*		*Exchange rate depreciations %*	
	1986–96	*1998:1–1998:6*	*1997*	*1998:1–1998:6*
Indonesia	7.4	–12.0	–52.0	–50.0
Korea	8.6	–5.0	–43.0	6.0
Malaysia	7.8	–5.0	–33.0	–1.0
The Philippines	3.7	–12.5[a]	–29.0	–5.0
Thailand	9.1	–8.0	–44.0	16.0

Source: IMF, Oct. 1998, tables 3.11, 3.12.

Note
a 1997:4–1998:2.

What went wrong? What caused the financial crisis? With hindsight, there is now a consensus as to what went wrong with the Asian countries. Dean (2001)[2] briefly describes the consensus as follows. The Asian growth was generated by high investment and saving. The difference was financed by capital inflows, made possible when the economies were liberalized in the early 1990s. Since these economies generally had fixed exchange rates, the capital inflows led to increases in the money supply. There was inflation of asset prices, speculative bubbles, but not inflation of prices of goods and services. The investment was poorly intermediated and misallocated.

The capital inflows produced a high ratio of external debt and debt service obligations relative to export earnings. With the bursting of the speculative bubble in asset prices, the former capital inflows turned to outflows. The countries faced a dilemma. If interest rates were raised to stem the outflow, the debt service burden to domestic borrowers would be raised. If the interest rates were not raised, devaluation would have to occur; and the debt service burden on the foreign currency denominated debt would rise. The net result was a financial collapse and exchange rate depreciation.

But why did the market not anticipate the crises?[3] Could it be that the market and credit rating agencies failed to anticipate the crisis because there were no useful warning signals? More importantly could it be that the range of qualitative and quantitative indicators normally monitored (for example, per capita income, growth rates, inflation rates, ratios of foreign debt to exports, history of defaults, level of economic development, government budget deficits, ratio of current account deficits to GDP) were not helpful because these measures were assessed in an ad hoc manner?

We contend that it would be more useful to derive warning signals based on concepts derived from a coherent theoretical framework which can predict the crisis. Hence our aim is to present a coherent theory which may be used to generate operational warning signals. To this end, we review the Asian financial crisis from two related perspectives – whether the crisis was precipitated by a failure of the real exchange rate to be aligned with its fundamental determinants and/or whether the crisis was precipitated by a divergence of the foreign debt from its optimal path. The first perspective is based on a coherent theory of the equilibrium real exchange rate which shows how "misalignments" lead to currency crises. The second perspective is based on a model of optimal foreign debt ratio which showed why "divergences" lead to debt crises. The important point here is that these models suggest important variables which may serve as warning signals to predict crises.

The chapter is organized as follows. In the second section of the paper we discuss some traditional warning signals. The third section provides an overview of the Natural Real Exchange Rate (NATREX) approach to the determination of the equilibrium real exchange rate and the measure of misalignment that may serve as a warning signal for currency crises. This section also describes the stochastic optimal control/dynamic programming (SOC/DP) approach to derive the optimal foreign debt ratio and shows how the deviation of the actual debt from this benchmark measure of performance may serve as a sufficient condition for a debt crisis. In the fourth section we explore the explanatory value of our theoretically-based warning signals all *utilizing only available information* to explain and predict the Asian crises. Concluding remarks are contained in the final section.

Traditional warning signals

This paper is concerned with two types of crises. The first is a *currency crisis*, which results from an "overvalued" exchange rate, and the second is a *debt crisis*, which occurs when the country cannot service its foreign debt. In both cases, the likely outcome is a dramatic currency devaluation or depreciation.

A common view associated with currency crises is that they result from "unstable macroeconomic policies". Consequently the early warning measures are the state of key macroeconomic variables and the response to a currency crisis is to implement restrictive monetary and fiscal policies.[4] The first sub-section below explains why the crises in Asia could not be explained by "unstable macroeconomic policies". Debt crises are associated with "unsustainable" external debt and the second sub-section below reviews a few traditional measures of "unsustainability".

Warning signals have two components. (a) What variables are considered? (b) What periods are compared? In this section, we focus primarily upon International Monetary Fund WEO reports that organized the data in forms (a) and (b) above: variables and comparison periods. For example, Table 2.2 is based upon the IMF's presentation. We show the limitations of the standard approaches.

Was there macroeconomic instability?

It is now well-documented that the Asian crises were not preceded by increases in "macroeconomic instability". Table 2.2 compares some macroeconomic indicators for the pre-crisis period 1986–96 with the earlier tranquil period

Table 2.2 Macroeconomic variables 1975–85 and 1986–96

Country	*Inflation % p.a.*		*Fiscal balance/ GDP %*		*Current account/ GDP %*	
	1975–85	*1986–96*	*1975–85*	*1986–96*	*1975–85*	*1986–96*
Hong Kong	8.2	8.0	1.1	2.1	3.0	5.6
Indonesia	13.4	8.2	0.3	–0.5	–2.0	–2.8
Korea	13.5	5.7	–2.2	–0.1	–3.7	0.9
Malaysia	4.8	2.6	–5.3	–2.4	–3.2	–2.6
The Philippines	15.6	8.9	–2.0	–2.3	–5.1	–2.6
Singapore	3.4	1.9	1.9	9.1	–7.2	9.5
Taiwan	6.3	3.0	0.3	–0.5	4.3	7.8
Thailand	7.2	4.5	–3.7	2.1	–5.5	–4.9

Source: International Monetary Fund, October 1998, Table 3.11.

1975–85. Inflation declined, and there were no significant increases in fiscal deficits or current account deficits. By the usual standards of macroeconomic performance the Asian economies were doing very well. In fact, prior to the crises, according to the International Monetary Fund (October 1998, ch. III, pp. 82ff.), the successful economic performance of these East Asian countries can be attributable to their emphasis on stability oriented macroeconomic policies such as maintaining low rates of inflation, avoiding overvalued exchange rates, and sustaining high rates of physical and human capital accumulation and export oriented production. This evidence leads one to reject an assertion that the crises were produced by monetary and fiscal mismanagement.

However, the currency did collapse and that leads one to question the usefulness of the above macroeconomic variables as warning signals of vulnerability. In the third section, we suggest that it may be more useful to look at the behavior of the fundamental determinants of the real exchange rate to predict the probability of a currency crisis. Our warning signals are based on a theoretically justifiable concept and measure of exchange rate misalignment.

Was the foreign debt sustainable?

Since the crises could not be attributed to "macroeconomic instability", the focus turned to the role of the external debt[5] and to the weaknesses in the financial structure as explanations of the crises. For the Asian economies, the banking system was the means by which foreign lending was intermediated through the corporate sector. Equity markets played a limited role, and fixed income money and bond markets were less developed and liquid. Table 2.3 describes the net private capital flows to Asia.

Table 2.3 shows the volatility in total capital flows. Net foreign direct investment was the main component of the capital flows, 55 percent in 1996, and was relatively steady. The highly volatile element was the category of bank loans,

Table 2.3 Net private capital flows to Asia

$ billion	*1990*	*1991*	*1992*	*1993*	*1994*	*1995*	*1996*	*1997*	*1998*
Total investment	19.6	34.1	17.9	57.3	66.4	95.1	100.5	3.2	–55.1
Net foreign direct	9.3	14.4	14.8	33.0	45.3	49.8	55.1	62.6	50.0
Net portfolio; bond and equity	–2.7	1.4	7.8	21.0	9.4	10.9	12.6	0.9	–15.4
Bank loans, investments	13.0	18.4	–4.7	3.3	11.7	34.4	32.8	–60.3	–89.7

Source: IMF, *International Capital Markets*, September 1999a, Table 3.1.

which was about 33 percent in 1996. It switched from an inflow of $32.8 billion in 1996 to an outflow of $89.7 billion in 1998. What caused the turnaround? Clearly the outflow reflected a reaction to a perceived weakness in the nature of the foreign debt. Can we identify some features which may be used as indicators of financial stress?

Consider first, an assessment of financial vulnerability from a perspective on the composition of debt. The Fund considers countries with high levels of short term debt, variable interest rate debt and foreign currency denominated debt as being particularly vulnerable to internal and external shocks and thus as susceptible to financial crises.[6] Was the Fund's view correct? Arteta (2003) investigated two questions. First, does high dollarization of deposits and credits increase the likelihood of banking crises and currency crashes and second does the dollarization make these crises and crashes more costly? He used a comprehensive dataset on deposit and credit dollarization for a large number of developing and transition economies and based on extensive econometric estimation finds little evidence of any particular link between high bank dollarization and the likelihood of banking crises or currency crashes.

Next consider a macroeconomic aggregate approach based on a widely used measure of "solvency" or "sustainability" to assess the excessiveness of foreign debt.[7] The measure of *solvency* is the net resource transfer (that is the trade surplus) that an indebted country must have to keep the ratio of external liabilities to GDP a constant. The argument is that the greater is the long term resource transfer, the greater is the probability of a debt crisis. More specifically, the "sustainability" argument asks what will be the value of the steady state debt/GDP (in this paper denoted as h^*) if current policy as measured by the current account deficit/GDP were to continue at the current growth rate? *The standard argument is that the greater is the equilibrium value of the debt* h^* *based upon current policy, the greater is the probability of a crisis.*

To empirically apply this concept, the standard approach is to calculate h^* as the ratio of current account deficit/GDP divided by the growth rate of GDP. This is because in the steady state, when the ratio of debt/GDP has stabilized, the ratio of the current account deficit to the debt is equal to the growth rate. Hence h^* is as defined below. Table 2.4 presents the average value of h^* over two sample periods, the pre-crisis period 1986–96 and the corresponding 1975–85 tranquil period, for the Asian countries that experienced crises.

Table 2.4 Measure of "sustainability"

Country	*h* = (Current account deficit/GDP)/growth rate*	
	1975–85	*1986–96*
Hong Kong	–0.37	–0.89
Indonesia	0.35	0.38
Korea	0.49	–0.10
Malaysia	0.51	0.33
The Philippines	1.76	0.68
Singapore	1.0	–1.13
Taiwan	–0.52	–1.01
Thailand	0.83	0.54

Note
Positive values of h^* are debtor positions.

As shown in Table 2.4, for Indonesia, there was no significant change in the "sustainable debt" measure; for Korea, the pre-crisis policies would have led to a creditor rather than to a debtor situation. Similarly, Malaysia, Philippines and Thailand would have become less of a debtor. In other words, the current account deficit/GDP ratios in the pre-crisis period, were the same or less than what they were a decade earlier for the ASEAN4 and Korea. In other words, these measures of sustainability would have failed to signal problems ahead for the Asian countries affected by the crisis.

The failure of the above "sustainability" approach arises because, as explained in Stein and Paladino (2001), the growth rate is simply related to the current account without taking into account the purpose of the foreign borrowings. If the current account deficit finances productive investment, then present current account deficits will generate future growth. The latter can make the economy more competitive and increase future trade balances. Moreover, another point to note here is that the actual debt to GDP ratio by itself is also *not* a relevant variable in predicting a debt crisis. For example, the ratio of debt service payments/exports for the Asian countries did not rise in the years before the crisis, as seen in Table 2.5 below.[8]

Summary of market anticipations

The International Monetary Fund, International Capital Markets (September 1999, Chapter V and annex V) contains a comprehensive analysis of market

Table 2.5 Debt service/export ratios (%)

	1989	*1990*	*1991*	*1992*	*1993*	*1994*	*1995*	*1996*
Asian countries	20.9	17.7	17.3	18.1	17.8	16.0	15.7	16.1
Developing countries	24.5	21.3	22.7	23.8	23.8	23.1	22.0	23.1

anticipations prior to the Asian crises. We draw upon and paraphrase the analysis contained there to evaluate the "early warning signals" used.

Global securities markets became important sources of funding for many emerging market countries in the period of the 1990s. The portfolio preferences of the major institutional investors became key determinants and conditions of capital flows. Credit rating agencies had great influence upon the effective cost of capital charged by international lenders to the borrowers in the emerging market countries. In many cases, intuitional investors are constrained to hold securities that have been classified by rating agencies as investment grade. Therefore, the cost of capital is effectively reflected in the ratings of the agencies and/or the bond spread. These two variables should reflect the market anticipation of crises, whereby the debtor may experience difficulties in servicing the debt.

Although the rating agencies stress that they do not use a specific formula to derive their ratings, empirical researchers explained the ratings as a weighted average of key indicators. Warning signals used by the international market are reflected by low credit ratings. The statistically significant variables to explain a high rating were: high per capita income, more rapid growth, low inflation, low ratio of foreign currency debt/exports, absence of a history of defaults and high level of development. The recent history of budget surplus/GDP and current account surplus/GDP were not statistically significant.

The conclusion drawn by the International Monetary Fund study is that: "spreads as well as market analysts – as represented in Institutional Investor and Euromoney ratings – provided signals similar to those of the credit rating agencies. They failed to signal the Asian crises in advance;[9] they down-graded these countries after their crises" (p. 195).

In summary, with hindsight it is clear that neither the market nor the credit rating agencies anticipated the Asian crises. It is also clear that there is an inadequacy in the standard theories to provide warning signals that identify weaknesses early enough to guide policy makers in either the prevention of crises or in making a rational response to them.

The object of our paper is to provide a coherent theory, which implies quantitatively measurable warning signals of a crisis based upon available information. We draw upon two relatively recent theoretical developments to provide an operational theory to answer:

a *Was a currency crisis produced by an **overvalued** real exchange rate?*
b *Was a debt crisis produced by an **"excessive/unsustainable"** external debt?*
c *What was the **interaction** between the two?*

The phrases in bold letters must be given theoretical and operational content. We use the NATREX model of equilibrium real exchange rates to evaluate whether the exchange rate is misaligned – that is whether the actual exchange rate deviates significantly from its "equilibrium" value thereby precipitating a currency crisis. We use a Stochastic Optimal Control/Dynamic Programming

(SOC/DP) approach to derive the optimal foreign debt ratio and we then evaluate the divergence of actual debt from optimal to see whether the economy is vulnerable to a debt crisis. Both NATREX and SOC/DP have proved to have explanatory power. The aim of this paper is to apply these techniques and concepts to explain the Asian crises, and thereby provide early *warning signals* of a crisis.

Currency and debt crises: an overview

Currency crisis

A currency crisis is generated by an overvalued exchange rate. In order to determine whether a rate is overvalued, we need a definition of an "equilibrium" real exchange rate. We use the concept of the natural real exchange rate (NATREX)[10] which is the rate that satisfies the four conditions (C1)–(C4) below.

(C1) Internal balance prevails where the rate of capacity utilization is equal to its long run stationary mean.

(C2) External balance exists where there are no speculative capital movements or changes in reserves, and domestic and foreign long-term real rates of interest are equal.

(C3) The ratio of net foreign liabilities/GDP is constant.

(C4) As a result of market forces, the actual exchange rate converges to a distribution whose conditional mean is the "equilibrium" rate.

The NATREX theory can be presented graphically. In Figure 2.1, the current account CA is negatively related to the real exchange rate R. An appreciation of the currency – rise in R – raises domestic production costs and prices relative to foreign production costs and prices. Competitiveness is reduced and the trade balance declines. The saving less investment curve SI is positively related to the real exchange rate, because an appreciation of the real exchange rate adversely affects investment. Insofar as goods are sold in the world market, an appreciation of the real exchange rate lowers the Tobin q-ratio, which lowers investment. Hence an appreciation of the real exchange rate increases saving less investment. The intersection of the CA and SI lines gives the determination of the real exchange rate R_0 when conditions (C1) and (C2) are satisfied. We call this the medium run NATREX and it is described algebraically in equation (1)

$$R_0 = [R \mid I - S + CA = 0] \quad (1)$$

In this case, net savings is negative (the current account deficit is A in Figure 2.1) and hence the foreign debt is rising. Stability is achieved if the rise in the foreign debt stimulates saving, and shifts the SI curve to the right. For example, the government may react to a rising public debt by increasing the primary surplus.[11] As saving rises, in response to the accumulation of the debt, the SI curve shifts to the right towards SI^*. However, the rise in interest payments on the debt shifts the current account curve to the left towards CA^*. In the long run equilibrium, the real exchange rate converges to R^* in Figure 2.1, where the ratio of debt/GDP is constant. Condition (C3) implies that the *equilibrium* trade balance to GDP ratio (denoted B^*) divided by the *equilibrium* debt/GDP ratio (h^*) is equal to $(r-g^*)$ the real interest rate (return on financial assets) less the *equilibrium* growth rate g^*. This term must be positive if present values of assets are finite. The *long run* NATREX satisfies conditions (C1)–(C4) and is described by equations (1) and (2).

$$B(R^*; Z) = (r - g^*)h^* \tag{2}$$

Where R^* is the long run NATREX, h^* is the equilibrium debt to GDP ratio. The elements of vector Z are the fundamental determinants underlying the S-I and CA functions. They are productivity (θ) and time preference (ρ) measured as the ratio of social consumption/GDP. In Figure 2.1, the current account/GDP is denoted as $E<0$ and the debt to GDP has stabilized at h^*.

In the short run, the uncovered "interest rate" parity theory states that the real exchange rate R_t will exceed (be less than) its longer run equilibrium value R^* if the domestic real rate of return on assets i_t exceeds (is less than) the corresponding foreign rate i_t^*.[12] This is denoted as R_t in Figure 2.1 and mathematically in equation (3). Coefficient α is a speed of response.

$$\log(R_t) = \log(R^*) + \alpha(i_t - i_t^*) \tag{3}$$

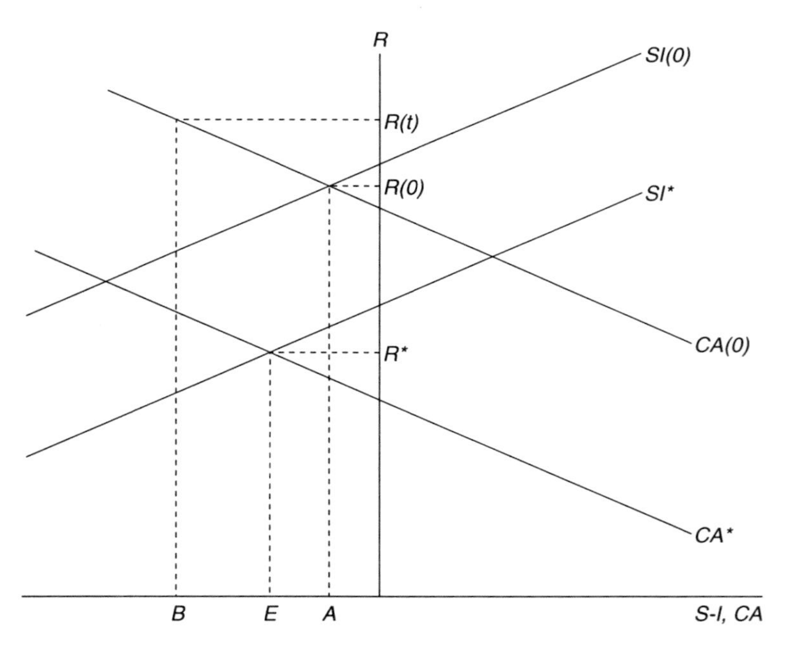

Figure 2.1 The medium run and long run real exchange rate NATREX.

If there is a speculative bubble in asset prices, then the domestic anticipated return i_t rises relative to the foreign rate i_t^*. There is a speculative capital inflow, which appreciates the real exchange rate to R_t above R_0 the medium run equilibrium value. We can think of this inflow as the bank loans and investments in Table 2.3 during the period 1993–96. The net effect is that the current account deficit rises to $B>A$, and the external debt rises at a faster rate.

Real exchange rate R_t is not sustainable for several reasons. First, it can only persist as long as there is a speculative capital inflow. The latter is generated by the differential in rate of return on assets. Insofar as the higher rate of return is generated solely by anticipated capital gains – where asset prices are rising without a corresponding rise in earnings generated – debt service payments are increasing relative to earnings. The bubble must burst, sooner or later. Second, as long as there is a current account deficit (for example point *B* in Figure 2.1) due to speculative capital inflow, the debt/GDP and interest payments/GDP will rise. The rise in the debt service reduces the current account, and shifts the *CA* curve to the left along the initial saving less investment curve *SI(0)*. The decline in the current account relative to saving less investment depreciates the real exchange rate.

A measure of misalignment ($\Phi_t = R_t - R_t^*$) is the deviation of actual real exchange (R_t) from the equilibrium value (R_t^*). A large value of Φ_t is clearly a warning signal of an impending currency crisis. Furthermore, since the equilibrium value (R_t^*) is related to the set of fundamental variables Z_t, we can also explain the cause of the misalignment. In the fourth section, we examine how well this measure identified periods of overvaluation, and hence how well this measure served as a warning signal of a currency crisis for the Asian countries.

Debt crisis

A currency crisis is likely to result when the actual real exchange rate exceeds the benchmark exchange rate – the NATREX – for a considerable period of time. Similarly, a debt crisis is likely to occur when actual external debt is excessive or "unsustainable". In order to assess whether the debt is "unsustainable" we need a concept of an optimal debt as our benchmark. Excess debt can then be measured as the deviation of the actual debt from the optimal debt. Our concept of an optimal debt draws upon our recent work on stochastic optimal control/dynamic programming analysis of optimal debt.[13]

The country will have a debt crisis if the attempt to service the debt requires a decline in consumption below a tolerable level, or requires a drastic decline in consumption. To see this first consider equation (4) which describes the change in the debt dL_t, where L is the real external debt.

$$dL_t = (I_t - S_t)dt = (C_t + I_t + r_t L_t - Y_t)dt \tag{4}$$

It arises because consumption C_t plus investment I_t plus the debt service $r_t L_t$ exceeds Y_t the GDP. Alternatively, the change in the debt is $(I_t - S_t)dt$ investment less saving over the period. In the Latin American countries the debt has risen due to high consumption and/or low social saving by the public plus the private sectors. In the Asian countries, the high investment has produced the external debt. For example, there were speculative bubbles in asset prices for land and/or equity that raise the anticipated returns. The differential investment less saving leads to a capital inflow and an increase in the external debt.

The external debt has to be serviced and that would clearly affect consumption. We can see this by writing consumption at some time after t, say at time $s=t+\Delta t$, equation (5) below.

$$C_s dt=(Y_s-r_s L_s-I_s)dt+dL_t \qquad (5)$$

Consumption is equal to the GNP, which is equal to the GDP less the debt service $(Y_s-r_s L_s)$, less investment I_t plus new borrowing dL_t.

Focus now on the behavior of the two stochastic variables – real GDP and real interest rate. If bad shocks reduce the GDP and raise real interest rates, and investment falls to a minimum level $I_s=I_{min}$ then consumption may have to be reduced – unless there is new borrowing to offset the decline.[14] In the event that new borrowing is not forthcoming, we may expect a debt crisis because it is more likely that the *country would renegotiate its debt than reduce consumption.*

To formalize the discussion we model the two sources of uncertainty which affect consumption. The first source of uncertainty is the growth of GDP described in equation (6) below.

$$dY_t/Y_t=(bI_t/Y_t)dt+\sigma_y dw_y \qquad (6)$$

Real growth dY_t/Y_t has two components: a deterministic component bI_t/Y_t where b is the mean return on investment times I_t/Y_t the ratio of investment/GDP, and a stochastic component involving the variance of output $\sigma_y^2 dt$. This stochastic part may be viewed as arising from variations in the terms of trade, the conditions of aggregate demand and the composition and quality of the investments.

The second source of uncertainty concerns the real interest rate required to service the external debt L_t. The real interest rate in terms of consumer goods r_t has three components. The first is the real interest rate on US Treasury long term debt. The second is the premium on dollar denominated debt charged to sovereign borrowers. The third is the anticipated exchange rate depreciation of the currency. Equation (7) is the equation for the real debt service, where the first term is deterministic and the second term is stochastic. Each component varies and produces a variance of $(\sigma_r L_t)^2$ on the real debt service.

$$r_t L_t dt=rL_t dt+\sigma_t L_t dw_r \qquad (7)$$

Each source of uncertainty is modeled as a Brownian Motion. Each expectation of dw_y and dw_r is equal to zero, but they are correlated. During the Asian crisis period, the growth of GDP and real interest rate were negatively correlated and that can be explained briefly as follows.

A decline in GDP may occur because of a decline in the terms of trade and/or the anticipated return on investment turns out to be an illusion and the asset bubble collapses, $dw_y < 0$. Since firms borrow primarily from the banks to finance real investment and the banks in turn primarily finance their loans by borrowing US dollars in the international capital market, a domino effect is created in the event of a financial panic. When debtors are unable to repay their loans to the banks, the banks in turn become unable to repay their loans to international creditors. Financial panic leads to a short term capital flight. The government may try to help out by using the dollar reserves, but that is only a stopgap measure. Sooner or later the monetary authorities will raise interest rates and, when that fails to stem the outflow, the currency will suffer a devaluation/depreciation. The depreciation of the currency implies that the real rate of interest, measured in terms of the prices of goods produced, rises ($dw_r > 0$). The situation is exacerbated when banks denominate their loans to the domestic firms in US dollars. Firms would find it very difficult to service debts denominated in foreign currency because they are faced with both a rising rate of interest and a depreciating currency.

Faced with these sources of uncertainty, how then should a country select its optimal debt and level of consumption to maximize the expectation of the discounted value of the utility of consumption over an infinite or finite horizon? The intertemporal nature of the process is seen in equations (4) and (5). A rise in the debt at one time will affect consumption at a later date. The standard approach in the economics literature is to maximize the expectation of the discounted value of the utility of consumption subject to an "Intertemporal Budget Constraint" IBC. The IBC requires that the expectation of the discounted value of consumption be equal to the expectation of the discounted value of GDP.

Given the uncertainty concerning the growth rate (equation 6) and real interest rate (equation 7), the future is unpredictable. *The IBC is unknowable and unenforceable.* How can anyone know if any country is, or is not, violating the constraint? *The IBC is a non-operational concept.* This profound deficiency of the IBC approach led Fleming and Stein to use the dynamic programming (DP) approach.[15] The controls are the debt and consumption. The optimal controls are functions of the state of the system, which are observable/measurable variables.

As shown in Fleming and Stein (2004) and Stein (2004), the solution for the optimal ratio of debt/net worth is equation (8). Only an intuitive explanation is presented here. Using Stochastic Optimal Control/Dynamic Programming we derive the optimal ratio f^* of debt/net worth.[16] The derived optimal debt in equation (8) is a benchmark measure of performance.

$$f^* = (b-r)/(1-\gamma)\sigma^2 + f(0), \quad \sigma^2 = var\,(dY_t/Y_t - r_t) \tag{8}$$

where b is the *mean* return to investment (in equation 6), r is *mean* real interest rate (in equation 7), quantity $(1-\gamma)$ is a measure of risk aversion and σ^2 is the variance of the quantity $(dY_t/Y_t - r_t)$, the current growth rate less the current interest rate, so that it also contains a covariance term. Equation (8) is graphed in Figure 2.2 as line *US*.

The optimum ratio of debt/net worth, f^* is positively related to the *mean* rate of return on investment less the *mean* real rate of interest $(b\text{-}r)$. The slope is the reciprocal of the product of risk aversion and risk. The intercept $f(0)$ is the optimal ratio of debt/net worth, when the expected net return $(b\text{-}r)=0$. When the correlation coefficient between the growth rate and interest rate is less than $\sigma_y\sigma_r$, the intercept is $f(0)<0$. Any nonpositive correlation implies $f(0)<0$ as drawn in Figure 2.2. The country should be a debtor only when the net return $(b-r)>A>0$, where A is the risk premium implied by equation (8).

Curve *US* is the optimal ratio, if there were no transactions or liquidation costs in selling capital to repay debt. When there are transactions/liquidation costs of selling capital to repay debt, there is another line *U'S'* above *US*. The optimal control is as follows: (i) if the debt/net worth is above *U'S'*, lower it immediately to this line; (ii) if the debt/net worth is below *US*, raise it immediately to this line; (iii) if the debt/net worth is between the two lines, do nothing. Most of the time, the optimal debt ratio will lie in the region between the curves. The proof of these statements is difficult[17], but the intuition can be conveyed. As the net worth changes drastically and very frequently due to the Brownian motion, given the same mean net return $(b-r)$, the capital should be bought and sold to keep the debt ratio constant given by line *US*. The sales of the capital to repay the debt would have to occur at "fire sale" prices. Then, as net worth rises again due to the Brownian motion, the capital would have to be repurchased

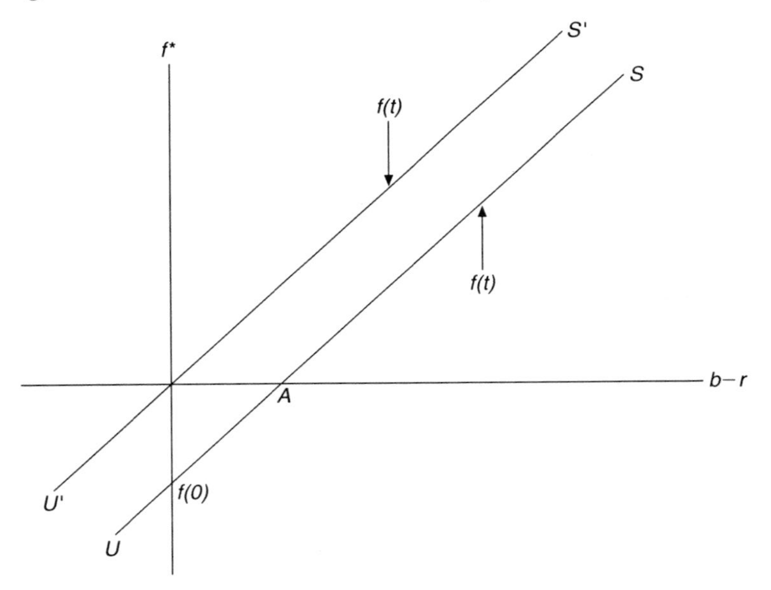

Figure 2.2 Optimal ratio debt/net worth f^* curve *US*, when there are no liquidation costs and curve *U'S'* with liquidation costs.

with new debt. All of these sell–buy transactions involve significant costs. Such a process would quickly dissipate the net worth. The optimum control is not to vary the capital or debt unless the ratio is sufficiently far from the optimal to justify the huge liquidation costs. In the graph, we assumed that there were only "liquidation costs" and not costs of acquisition. Therefore, only if the debt ratio is above *U'S'* should the ratio be reduced. Even then, it should only be reduced to U'S' and not to US. The difference between these curves is a complicated function of the liquidation costs.

The optimum debt ratio, our benchmark of performance, has several important characteristics. It is the value where: (i) The expected present value of the utility of consumption is maximized, (ii) the expected growth rate – of consumption, net worth and GDP – is maximized.[18] The major implications of the analysis are as follows.

- As the debt ratio rises above the optimum f^*, the expected growth rate declines, and the risk – the variance of the growth rate – increases.
- Since optimal consumption is proportional to net worth, as the debt ratio rises above the optimum, the expected growth of consumption declines and its variance rises. The probability of a decline in consumption increases and the probability of a debt crisis increases.
- Insofar as there are liquidation costs in selling capital to repay debt, the optimal ratio should lie between lines *US* and *U'S'* in Figure 2, where the difference is a function of liquidation costs.

In summary, when the net return *(b–r)* is falling and the debt/GDP ratio is rising, it is more probable that the debt ratio is in the region above the curve *U'S'*. Hence divergent movements of the net return *(b–r)* and the debt/GDP ratio can serve as an operational warning signal that foreign debt is becoming "excessive"[19] and that the economy is becoming susceptible to default. In the fourth section, we examine the time-paths of actual debt/GDP ratios relative to the time-paths of their *(b–r)* values to explain the pattern of debt defaults during the period of the Asian financial crisis.

Empirical analysis

The next sub-section discusses whether the Asian currencies were overvalued, and the second sub-section below discusses whether they had excessive debt. Table 2.6 below summarizes the results. In the final concluding section, we explain the interaction of these two sources of crisis. The reader may want to look at this table while reading these two parts.

Were the Asian currencies overvalued?

In this section, we examine the proposition that the nominal exchange rate depreciated in 1997, because the real exchange rate R_t was overvalued relative to the equilibrium rate suggested by NATREX. The real exchange rate R_t is defined as $R_t = N_t(P_t/P^*_t)$ where the nominal rate N is defined as the number of *US$* per domestic currency (a rise is an appreciation), and P (P^*) is the domestic (foreign) price index. The currencies of Thailand, Malaysia, Philippines and Indonesia were linked to the US dollar, which appreciated from 1995–98 relative to both the Japanese Yen and to a trade weighted index. Misalignment would occur if the actual real exchange rate deviated significantly from the NATREX suggested rate.

Following the discussion above, we estimate the deviation of the actual rate from the NATREX equilibrium rate as our measure of the degree of over and under valuation, i.e. "misalignment". To compute our empirical measure of misalignment, first recognize that misalignment $\Phi_t = R_t - R^*_t$ can be rewritten as $\Phi_t = (R_t - R_{t-1}) - (R^*_t - R_{t-1})$. The first term is the actual change in the exchange rate. The second term can be written as: $(R^*_t - R_{t-1}) = (R^*_t - R^*_{t-1}) + (R^*_{t-1} - R_{t-1})$. Term $(R^*_t - R^*_{t-1}) = \alpha\Delta Z_t$ is the change in the NATREX based upon changes in the fundamentals in vector Z, and term $(R^*_{t-1} - R_{t-1}) = \epsilon_t$. Thus term $(R^*_t - R_{t-1}) = \alpha\Delta Z_t = \epsilon_t$. Then use *recursive least squares* to estimate the coefficient α in the regression equation $\Delta R_t = \alpha_t \Delta Z_t + \epsilon_t$ Finally compute misalignment $\Phi_t = R_t - R^*_t$ as:

$$\Phi_t = \Delta R_t - \hat{\alpha}_{t-1}\Delta Z_t \tag{9}$$

Vector Z contains three fundamental variables:[20] productivity (θ), time-preference[21] (ρ) measured as the ratio consumption/GDP – which is negative thrift, and the differential of long-term real net return (b–r). *The b is the domestic real return and r reflects the cost of capital.* Our method of estimation avoids the problems associated with non-stationary time-series data and more importantly, the coefficients contained in the vector $\hat{\alpha}_{t-1}$ are estimated by recursive least squares and hence are based only on information up to time t. *Post-crisis information is not used before the event to predict the event.* As presented above, Φ_t may be interpreted as the deviation of the actual change in the real exchange rates from the change that should prevail at time t, given changes in the explanatory variables, ΔZ_t suggested by NATREX.[22] Note however that Φ_t is an estimate of the difference between the level of actual R_t and the NATREX estimated R^*_t.

Productivity (θ) is measured as real GDP per capita and time preference (ρ) is the ratio of household and government consumption expenditure per GDP. The real return to investment expenditure (b) is computed as the (growth rate of GDP)/(investment/GDP). The long term real return r is the ten-year US bond rate less US inflation.[23] These variables are all readily available from the IMF, International Financial Statistics.

Charts 2.1–2.5 present our analysis for the ASEAN 4 countries (Indonesia, Malaysia, Philippines, Thailand) plus Korea. The *pre-crisis period 1994–96 is shaded*.

Each chart shows a plot of the deviations of the level of the actual rate from the NATREX rate (expressed in standardised units, that is in the form:

$[\Phi_t - mean(\Phi_t)]/std(\Phi_t))$ as well as information about the explanatory variables, $\Delta\theta$, $\Delta\rho$ and $(b\text{–}r)$ pre, during and post crisis. Recall that the NATREX is a positive concept – the real exchange rate satisfying conditions (C1)–(C4) above – and not a normative concept such as Williamson's FEER.

The crisis started in *Thailand*, whose currency was linked to the US$ which was appreciating relative to the Yen and other major currencies. As shown in the charts, Thailand is the country with the prolonged pre-crisis period of misalignment from about 1990 to 1995/96. The decline in productivity, increase in the propensity to consume, plus decline in relative return – all signaled that a depreciation of the nominal exchange rate (given sticky prices) was necessary to realign the real exchange rate. Deviation Φ_t is a warning signal of misalignment.[24]

The signals for Korea were the same as for Thailand, but in this case the exchange rate was not seriously misaligned. A crucial variable that is common to both the misalignment and excess debt is the net rate of return on investment. In both Thailand and Korea, the net return $(b\text{–}r)$ declined drastically from 1995 to 1997. This means that the medium run equilibrium exchange rate should be falling from R_t towards R^* in Figure 2.1. Thereby we have warning signals of exchange rate misalignment for Thailand and Korea.

In contrast, over the period 1981–96 the Indonesia rupiah was aligned with the NATREX rate and there were no signals, based upon trends of productivity, time-preference or returns, that the currency was misaligned. Malaysia and the Philippines show no prolonged periods of misalignment. In fact the pre-crisis signals, such as a decrease in the propensity to consume, supported the appreciation then underway.

Were the Asian foreign debts unsustainable?

Following the discussion in the earlier section, our strategy is to compare the evolution of the actual debt/GDP ratios h with the evolution of the relative returns $(b\text{–}r)$ on investment in the Asian countries. If the relative return is declining significantly but the debt ratio is rising significantly or not declining, then the debt ratio is moving into the region above the line $U'S'$ and the probability of default increases for the following reason. Growth is expected to decline and the variance/risk to rise. For any consumption ratio, a decline in expected growth and a rise in its variance will augur a decline in consumption and hence a debt crisis. *A sufficient condition for a crisis is a strong decline in the relative net return and a rise or at least not a decline in the debt ratio.*

We know with hindsight that the Asian countries that defaulted were Indonesia (1998), Korea (1998) and the Philippines (1984–96) and the countries that did not default were Malaysia and Thailand. We now explore whether our suggested warning signal variables h and $(b\text{–}r)$ for *Korea* would have indicated the likelihood of default whereas the signals for *Malaysia* would have indicated no financial vulnerability.

For each country, h_t is the actual debt/GDP ratio based on data published by the Economic Intelligence Unit. The debt is total external debt stock "comprising public and publicly guaranteed long term debt, private non-guaranteed debt, use of IMF credit and short term debt, end of period". The net return *(b–r)* is as defined above. Again, these are publicly available data and subjected to no manipulations. The plots of h_t and $(b-r)$ are shown in Charts 2.1–2.5. The *pre-crisis period 1994–96 is shaded.*

The return b_t varied significantly, but the interest rate spread and credit ratings were practically constant until the crises, as noted above. Therefore, any anticipated exchange rate depreciation was not reflected in the cost of capital. Variations in (b_t-r_t) are almost exclusively due to variations in the return on investment b_t. We do not arbitrarily select a comparison period, rather we use the information contained in the two time series. When they diverge in the manner described above, we anticipate a crisis. The data are annual, which irons out random fluctuations.

Korea and *Thailand* both gave warning signals that they were incurring excess debt. In both cases, prior to the crisis, there was a clear upswing in the debt/GDP ratio and a clear downswing in relative returns. Industrial policy in *Korea* involving the government, the banks and the "chaebols" aimed for rapid growth with little concern for the rate of return *b* on investment. The banks were used as the means to finance the growth. The banks were not concerned about the risk, because there was an implicit government guarantee. That is why the total external debt ratio rose, even though the net returns were declining. In *Thailand*, the net return declined from 12 percent p.a. in 1994 to 4.77 percent p.a. in 1996 (see Chart 2.5), but the external debt rose by 40 percent during that period. Rajan *et al.* (2002) show that half of the debt was short term, 45 percent was denominated in Yen and Japanese banks were the major creditors.

Warning signals for Korea and Thailand mean that the expected growth of consumption was low and its variance was high. Any random event could lead to a debt crisis, where the economy could not service its debt without reducing consumption. Such random events were the bankruptcies of major Korean concerns in 1997 before the crisis, and the collapse of the bubble in the construction sector in Thailand that led to bank failures.[25]

Whereas Korea and Thailand both showed warning signals of an excess debt, in Malaysia, Indonesia and the Philippines there was no evidence that the debt ratio was "excessive" in the pre-crisis period 1994–96. However for the Philippines, there were clear warning signals of the debt crises period 1984–94.

Conclusions: interactions of types of crisis

Much has been written, with hindsight, about the causes of the Asian financial crisis. The crises were unexpected by the market and many countries in the region experienced it at about the same time. The traditional warning signals in use then[26] were inadequate. To this end, we analyzed the Asian financial crisis from two related perspectives – whether the crisis was precipitated by a failure of the real exchange rate to be aligned with its fundamental determinants, and/or whether the crisis was precipitated by a divergence of the foreign debt from its optimal path. Our models produced a set of objective, theoretically based warning signals and our empirical analysis allowed us to assess whether there were signs of financial distress before the crisis.

Table 2.6 presents a summary of the warning signals, based upon Charts 2.1–2.5. *Our warning signals and measures of misalignment are based upon available information before the crisis.* In all of these countries during the crisis, the exchange rate depreciated and the GDP declined significantly, as shown in Table 2.1.

The two types of crises are inter-related. In both cases, *the level of either the real exchange rate or the debt is irrelevant.* The relevant variables are: (a) the *misalignment* $\Phi(t)$ of the real exchange rate from the NATREX in Figure 2.1, and (b) the *deviation* of the debt ratio from its optimal level – if the debt ratio has risen above curve *U'S'* in Figure 2.2.

A currency crisis may lead to a debt crisis in the following way. In Figure 2.1, the exchange rate R_t is overvalued relative to the longer run NATREX R^*, because a speculative/unsustainable bubble led to a differential anticipated rate of return on assets. Capital inflows raise the debt. Initially the inflow is 0B per unit of time. When the anticipated return turns out to be an illusion, such as in Korea and Thailand, the capital inflows will not continue at the same level and the real exchange rate will fall drastically to a lower NATREX. If the nominal exchange rate is free, there will be exchange rate depreciation and the real interest rate – measured in terms of the GDP deflator – on the foreign debt will rise. If the nominal exchange rate is pegged, reserves will decline. The monetary authorities may raise interest rates. Eventually, the currency will be depreciated. In either case, real interest rates rise. If the debt is sufficiently high, then term r_sL_s in equation (5) will rise drastically and tend to reduce consumption C_s in equation (5). Moreover when the exchange rate depreciates, there may also be a capital outflow – term dL_t falls.

Once the exchange rate collapses, it is easy to understand why defaults may occur. The collapse of the exchange rate raises the cost of servicing the foreign debt, which leads to bankruptcies and financial market stringency. As a result, the country is thrown into a recession when the GDP falls. Even though the level of the debt has been relatively stable, the decline in the GDP raises the debt/GDP ratio. The attempt to service the debt would reduce consumption below a tolerable level and the country will default. In this way, a currency crisis may lead to a debt crisis. If the value of r_sL_s is not too high, then misalignment $\Phi(t)$ will only generate a currency crisis.

A *debt crisis* occurs with positive probability when the debt ratio has risen above the *U'S'* curve. A rise in the debt ratio occurs if there have been sustained capital inflows, current account deficits. If the debt ratio rises along curve *US* because of rises in $(b–r)$, the rise in the debt ratio is optimal. Therefore current account deficits or rises in the debt *per se* do not imply that there will be a crisis. Table 2.5 shows that the debt service/exports did not rise in the Asian countries before the crisis. However, there cannot be a debt crisis without a prior rise in the debt. It is not revealing to state that current account deficits lead to a debt crisis.

However, if the debt ratio tends to rise above curve *U'S'* in Figure 2.2, then the situation is unstable. Any random event – decline in Y_t or a rise in r_t – can generate a debt crisis. Once the country is unable to service the debt, then there will be a capital outflow, particularly short term capital. See net private capital flows: bank loans and investments from 1995–98 in Table 2.3. As a result of these outflows, the exchange rate collapses. In this way a debt crisis leads to a currency crisis.

Our analysis focuses upon two countries: Thailand and Korea. Table 2.6 suggests that *Thailand* was primed for a collapse of the currency. Its exchange rate was severely misaligned and its foreign debt was sub-optimal. The warning signs for *Korea* were the same as for *Thailand* – consumption was increasing at a time of falling productivity and relative returns. The Korean exchange rate was not severely misaligned, but there were clear warning signals and the financial crisis took the form of a debt crisis.

Our analysis did not find objective warning signals of the 1997–98 crises for Indonesia, Malaysia and Philippines. There were no declines in productivity or in the differential returns prior to the crisis. The situation for *Indonesia*, *Malaysia* and the *Philippines* may be symptomatic of a "contagious effect". When the crises occurred in Thailand and Korea, because the situations were not sustainable in terms of our objective criteria, the Japanese commercial banks – which were the common lender – raised risk premia for loans to the other countries in the region. The Japanese banks tried to reduce their risk exposure to the other borrowers. Short term capital flowed out of the other Asian countries and their exchange rates depreciated.

Table 2.6 Summary of warning signals analysis for 1997–98 crises

Country	*Actual changes*	*Analysis of misalignments pre-crisis*	*Warning signals of excessive debt during pre-crisis period*
Indonesia	Rupiah depreciated and debt defaulted 1998	No evidence of significant misalignment	No warning signals
Korea	Won depreciated and debt defaulted 1998	No evidence of significant misalignment	Evidence of growing debt/GDP ratio despite falling excess returns
Malaysia	Ringgit depreciated but there was no debt default	Evidence of misalignment, but not prolonged	No warning signals
The Philippines	Peso depreciated and debt defaulted 1984, 1986, 1987, 1990, 1991,1992, 1994	Evidence of misalignment, but not prolonged	No warning signals (warning signals for 1984 default)
Thailand	Baht depreciated but there was no debt default	Evidence of prolonged, persistent misalignment	Growing debt/GDP ratio despite falling net returns

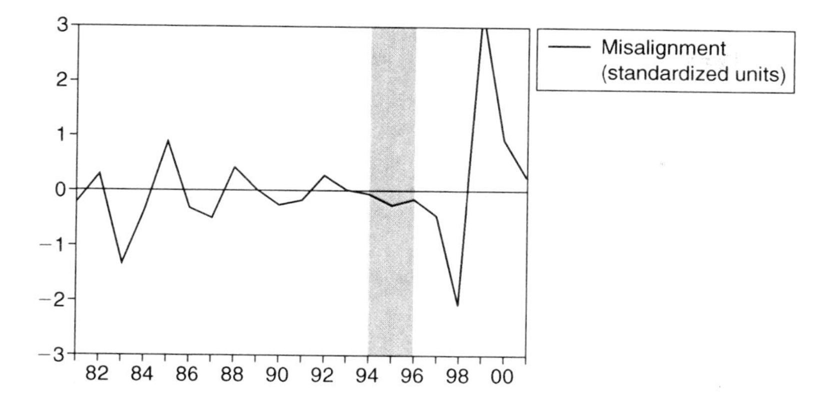

Warning signal variables: pre-, during and post-crisis (Indonesia)			
	Δv (%)	*$\Delta \rho$ (%)*	*(b–r) (%)*
1994	5.72	0.39	13.68
1995	6.39	2.35	14.96
1996	6.06	0.74	14.21
1997	3.16	–2.04	5.67
1998	–15.47	6.99	–104.57
1999	–0.58	9.19	–18.06
2000	3.44	–7.42	15.69
2001	1.95	–0.44	2.07

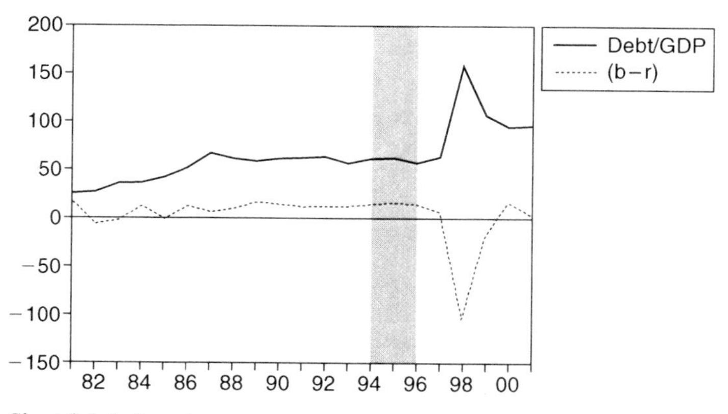

Chart 2.1 Indonesia.

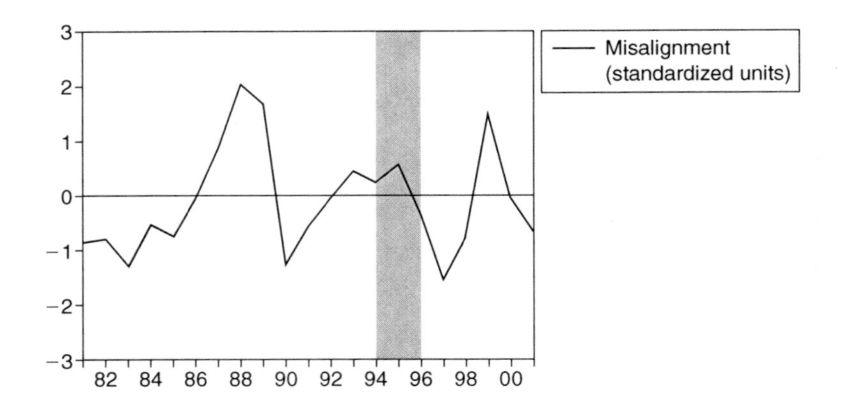

Warning signal variables: pre-, during and post-crisis (Korea)

	Δv (%)	$\Delta \rho$ (%)	(b–r) (%)
1994	6.94	0.93	11.50
1995	7.61	–0.34	15.13
1996	5.65	2.50	9.34
1997	4.06	0.52	5.58
1998	–7.70	–1.06	–34.24
1999	9.60	1.39	32.91
2000	8.22	1.22	26.47
2001	2.40	3.14	5.12

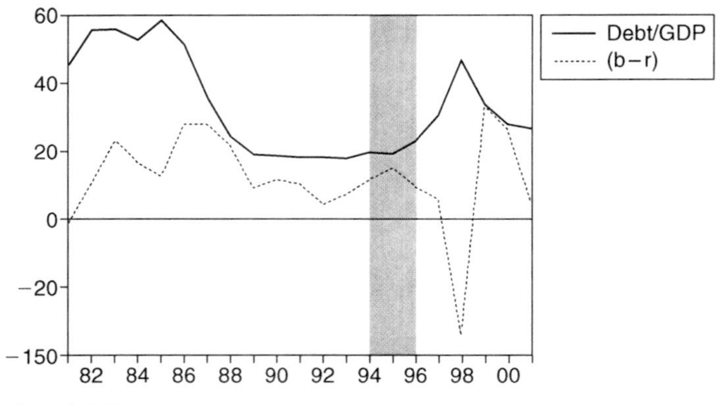

Chart 2.2 Korea.

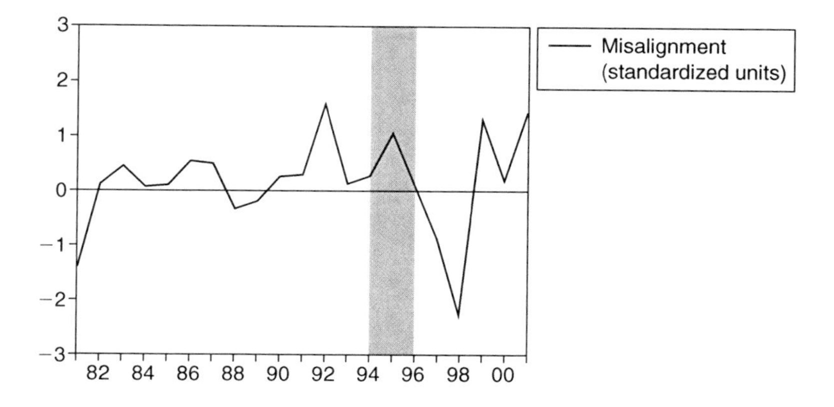

Warning signal variables: pre-, during and post-crisis (Malaysia)

	Δv (%)	$\Delta \rho$ (%)	(b–r) (%)
1994	6.17	–0.84	13.73
1995	6.77	–0.18	14.30
1996	6.96	–5.38	15.45
1997	4.53	–1.81	9.72
1998	–10.11	–8.91	–37.35
1999	3.59	2.38	21.03
2000	5.76	0.52	27.02
2001	–1.66	8.72	–1.84

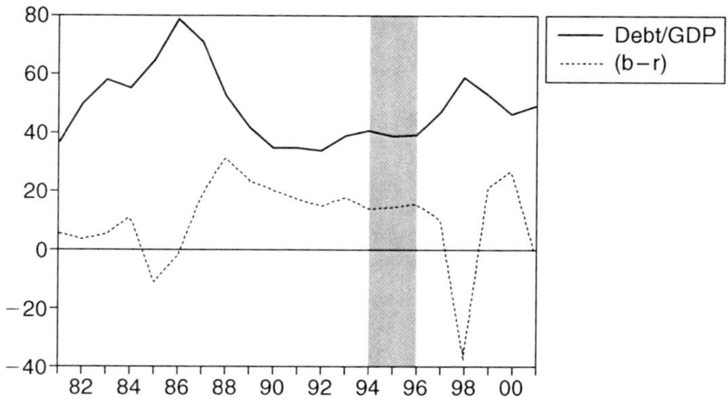

Chart 2.3 Malaysia.

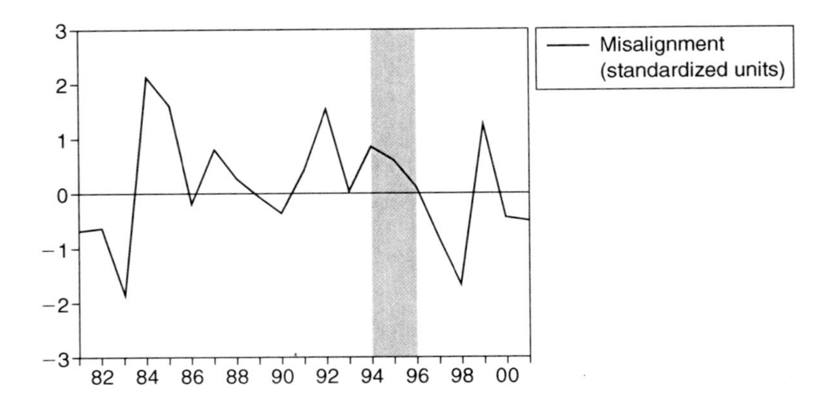

Warning signal variables: pre-, during and post-crisis (Philippines)

	Δv (%)	$\Delta \rho$ (%)	(b–r) (%)
1994	2.07	–1.27	5.63
1995	2.39	0.37	9.08
1996	3.55	–0.07	12.06
1997	2.97	0.45	10.97
1998	–2.61	2.08	–15.73
1999	1.36	–2.20	7.53
2000	1.99	–3.55	11.58
2001	1.46	–0.94	8.89

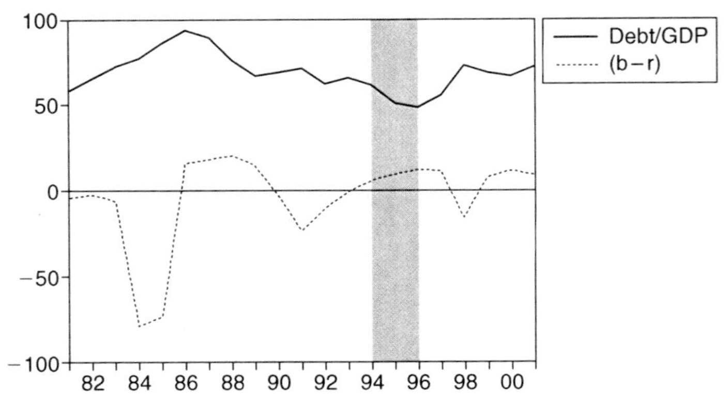

Chart 2.4 The Philippines.

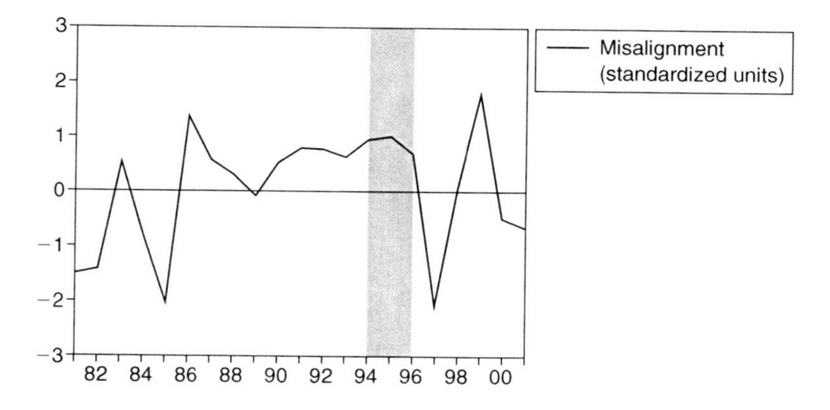

Warning signal variables: pre-, during and post-crisis (Thailand)

	$\Delta \upsilon$ (%)	$\Delta \rho$ (%)	$(b–r)$ (%)
1994	7.42	−1.44	12.11
1995	7.69	−1.05	12.06
1996	4.64	1.41	4.77
1997	−0.02	1.20	−13.59
1998	−0.12	0.73	−61.10
1999	0.03	3.39	17.03
2000	0.03	−0.19	16.39
2001	0.01	1.63	3.87

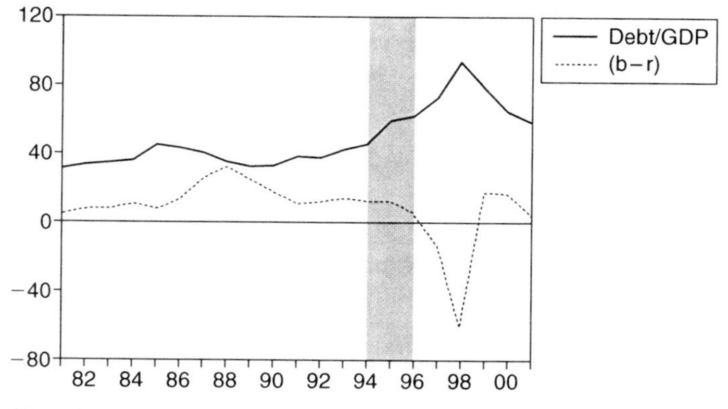

Chart 2.5 Thailand.

The "contagion" argument is a description rather than a precise analytical concept[27]. Rajan and Siregar (2002) compared the experiences of Hong Kong with those of Singapore. They are similar economies, subject to similar shocks. The main difference between them is the flexibility of the exchange rate to real shocks – our fundamentals discussed in the fourth section. The Hong Kong currency was linked to the US$ via a currency board. The Singapore currency was much more flexible. Rajan and Siregar estimated the NATREX for each economy and then examined ex-post, the degree of misalignment. They found that, in the period leading up to the crisis, the Hong Kong currency was misaligned, whereas the Singapore dollar was not. When the Asian crises occurred, the Hong Kong growth rate fell severely from 5.15 percent p.a. in 1997 to –5 percent p.a. in 1998. In Singapore the growth rate declined from 8.8 percent to 0.5 percent, a significantly better performance than in Hong Kong. A message here seems to be that "contagion" can be mitigated by avoiding exchange rate misalignment and by adopting a more flexible exchange rate system.

Notes

1 We thank Palle Andersen and John Williamson for comments on an earlier draft.
2 Dean (2001) contains the basic references on this subject, and the reader is referred to his article for the extensive bibliography. Flouzat (1999) and recent International Monetary Fund WEO reports describe the consensus view country by country.
3 Available measures of expectations by market participants display a poor record in anticipating crises. The secondary market yield spreads on US dollar denominated Eurobonds did not vary much before the Asian crisis, see IMF, WEO December 1997, figure 14; International Capital Markets, September 1999: 107–12. See also Berg and Pattillo (1999).
4 Some economists have argued that the way to avoid currency crises is to adopt a currency board or to replace the domestic currency with a foreign currency.
5 Both domestic and foreign investors held domestic debt. Since part of the domestic debt was sometimes denominated in foreign currency or linked to the exchange rate, the distinction between domestic and foreign debt becomes blurred (see Berg and Pattillo, 1999).
6 See IMF, WEO, May 1998: p. 85.
7 See IMF, WEO, May 1998: 86–7; October 2003, ch. III.
8 Source: International Monetary Fund, WEO, Crisis in Asia, December 1997, table B7.
9 For example, "In Korea, despite the growing awareness of financial sector vulnerabilities following the collapse of Hanbo Steel in January 1997, there were no actions by the rating agencies until Moody's placed it on negative outlook in June 1997. The downgrade on October 24 by S&P's (from AA– to A+) was accompanied by a sharp rise in yield spreads." In Thailand, "S&P made no rating changes in the period between 1994 and July 1997. No further rating changes occurred during the severe speculative attacks on the baht in May and the subsequent floating of the baht in July 1997. Interest rate spreads began to rise in the third week of August prior to the downgrade of Thailand's rating by S&P's (to A– on September 3)..." (p. 187).
10 The NATREX was originally presented in Stein and Allen (1997). Our exposition here is intuitive and the reader is referred to the basic articles for the formal derivations and analyses. The NATREX model has been shown to have significant explanatory power for the US dollar, the euro, the D-Mark, the Italian Lira, Australian dollar

Asian currencies. The special issue: "Exchange Rates in Europe and Australasia", Australian Economic Papers, 41 (4) December 2002 contains the basic articles referred to above. The Introduction by Stein and Lim (2002) and Stein (2002) put the articles into perspective

11 This occurs more strongly in the industrial countries than in the emerging market countries; see IMF (WEO9–2003, p. 128) for observed relations between these two variables.

12 This rate of return could be on fixed income instruments, equity or real property.

13 The analysis is based upon Fleming and Stein (2004), Stein (2004) and Fleming (2004). The reader is referred to these papers for the technical details and proofs. This analysis was used by Stein (2004) to explain the US farm debt crisis of the 1980s.

14 In Korea, the investment/GDP ratio fell from 35 percent in 1997 to 21 percent in 1998. In Thailand the investment ratio fell from 41 percent in 1996 to 22 percent in 1998.

15 The DP approach is used in mathematical finance, starting from the work of Robert Merton.

16 Net worth is "capital" less debt. Capital is the Frank Knight concept, the discounted value of current income, Y_t/b, where Y_t is current GDP and b is the mean return on investment in equation (6). This is a measurable and logical concept. The ratio of $h_t=$ debt/GDP is positively related to the ratio of $f_t=$debt/net worth. Therefore, we can speak about either ratio f or h interchangeably. The optimum ratio of consumption/net worth is constant, $c^*=C_t/X_t$. Therefore consumption, net worth and GDP grow at the same rate.

17 The references to the proofs in the mathematical literature, especially by Davis and Norman, Fleming and Soner, is in Stein (2004).

18 This is true in the case of the logarithmic utility function.

19 The stochastic optimal control approach to deriving a benchmark for the optimal debt is conditional upon the model and the stochastic processes. In the model above, we assumed that the debt was long term at a variable interest rate. Thus there were two shocks, which were correlated. On the other hand in Stein and Paladino (2001), based upon Fleming and Stein (2001), the model assumed that debt was short term foreign currency debt that must be repaid at the end of the period, such as the category "Bank loans, investments" in Table 2.3 above. The stochastic variable was the return on investment, variable b_t. The "bad" state of nature is a value of the return below the interest rate. We calculated both an optimal debt/GDP ratio and a maximal ratio of debt/GDP called *debt-max*. If the debt exceeded the *debt-max* then – if the "bad" state of nature occurs – consumption would have to be reduced below a tolerable level and the country would default. In the empirical work, the debt was the total sovereign debt to both sovereign and private creditors, denominated in US dollars. We used as our Warning Signal the difference DEF=[(debt/GDP)–(debt-max)]. Stein and Paladino showed that the actual debt ratio was not able to explain default. On the other hand, a *sufficient condition* for rescheduling/default was that DEF>0, the debt ratio exceed (debt-max). A second warning signal of an excessive debt is that DEF>0 and/or rising significantly.

20 We also tested a terms of trade variable, but they were not always significant.

21 From SOC/DP analysis the optimal ratio of consumption/net worth is the discount rate, when a logarithmic utility function is used; see Fleming and Stein (2004).

22 Note that this approach avoids a problem associated with estimation over the whole sample period and then defining the residuals of a regression model as a measure of misalignment. Here post-crisis information is not used before the event to predict the event.

23 The real interest rate should take into account the anticipated depreciation of the currency. Since the exchange rates were linked to the US$, the market did not take the likelihood of depreciation into account.

24 Rajan, Sen and Siregar (2002) conducted an ex-post study of the Baht's misalignment with respect to the Japanese Yen since Thailand's main trading partner was Japan, which was also the major creditor. They concluded that it was relatively larger than that for the US$ and that the misalignment with respect to the Yen is consistent with a widening of the Thai trade deficits before the crisis.
25 See Flouzat (1999, Chapter 2) and Rajan *et al.* (2002) for stimulating discussions of the developments in the Asian countries.
26 These signals were the budget deficit, inflation and current account deficit. Table 2.2 shows that they were inadequate.
27 There is a large literature on "contagion"; see Kaminsky *et al.* (2003).

References

Arteta, Carlos (2003), "Are Financially Dollarized Countries More Prone to Costly Crises?", *International Finance Discussion Papers*, 763, Board of Governors Federal Reserve System, March.

Berg, Andrew and C. Pattillo (1999), "Are Currency Crises Predictable?", *International Monetary Fund, Staff Papers*, June.

Dean, James (2001), "East Asia Through a Glass Darkly", in Geoffrey Harcourt *et al.* (eds), *Essays in Honour of Mark Perlman*, London: Routledge.

Fleming, Wendell H. (2004), "Some Optimal Investment, Production and Consumption Models", in Yin, George and Q. Zhang, *Mathematics of Finance*, Providence, RI: American Mathematical Society.

Fleming, Wendell H. and J.L. Stein (2001), "Stochastic Inter-temporal Optimization in Discrete Time", in Negishi, Takashi, R. Ramachandran and K. Mino (eds), *Economic Theory, Dynamics and Markets: Essays in Honor of Ryuzo Sato*, Boston: Kluwer.

Fleming, Wendell H. and J.L. Stein, (2004), "Stochastic Optimal Control, International Finance and Debt", *Journal of Banking and Finance*, 28(5), 979–6.

Flouzat, Denise (1999), *La nouvelle emergence de l'Asie, l'évolution économique des pays asiatiques depuis la crise de 1997*, Paris: Presses Universitaires de France.

International Monetary Fund (1998), *World Economic Outlook (WEO), Financial Crises*, May 1998, Washington DC.

International Monetary Fund (1999a), *World Economic and Financial Survey, International Capital Markets*, September 1999, Washington DC.

International Monetary Fund (1999b), *World Economic Outlook (WEO), Financial Turbulence in the World Economy*, October 1998, Washington DC.

International Monetary Fund (2003), *World Economic Outlook (WEO), Public Debt in Emerging Markets*, September 2003, Washington DC.

Kaminsky, Graciela, C.M. Reinhart and C.A. Vegh (2003), "The Unholy Trinity of Financial Contagion", *Journal of Economic Perspectives*, 17(4), 51–74.

Rajan, Ramkishen and R. Siregar (2002), "Choice of Exchange Rate Regime: Currency Board (Hong Kong) or Monitoring Band (Singapore)", *Australian Economic Papers*, 41(4), 538–56.

Rajan, Ramkishen, R. Sen and R. Siregar (2002), "Misalignment of the Baht, Trade Imbalances and the Crisis in Thailand", School of Economics Working Paper, University of Adelaide, Australia.

Stein, Jerome L. (2002), "The Equilibrium Real Exchange Rate of the Euro: An Evaluation of Research", *ifo Studien*, 48(3), 349–81.

Stein, Jerome L. (2004), "Stochastic Optimal Control Modeling of Debt Crises", in Yin,

George and Q. Zhang, *Mathematics of Finance*, Providence, RI: American Mathematical Society

Stein, Jerome L. and P.R. Allen (1995, 1998), *Fundamental Determinants of Exchange Rates*, Oxford: Oxford University Press.

Stein, Jerome L. and G.C. Lim (2002), "Introduction to Exchange Rates in Europe and Australasia: Fundamental Determinants, Adjustments and Policy Implications", *Australian Economic Papers*, 41(4), 329–41.

Stein, Jerome L. and G. Paladino (2001), "Country Default Risk: An Empirical Assessment", *Australian Economic Papers*, 40(4), 417–36.

3 The development of futures markets in China

Evidence of some unique trading characteristics[1]

Anne E. Peck

Abstract

Beginning in 1993, China authorized the opening of commodity futures exchanges on an experimental basis as one of many initiatives to encourage the development of markets in a wide variety of products. Although most of the early exchanges and contracts were closed by 1998, trading on three exchanges in a very limited number of products has proved to be quite successful. Indeed, Chinese authorities in 2004 have allowed the existing exchanges to develop contracts in additional commodities.

The chapter provides evidence of several unique patterns of trading that have developed on China's three exchanges. Most pronounced, trading in each contract on each market reaches a peak some five to six months before the contract's expiration. Thus, the most-traded contracts on China's exchanges are typically those some months away from delivery, not those closest to delivery as is typical on many other exchanges. In addition, trading in both the wheat and the soybean futures markets in China does not evidence the sort of seasonal variation typical of trading associated with agricultural futures markets elsewhere, suggesting that commercial firms in China have different market needs. Of course, the products traded on China's exchanges – wheat, soybeans, aluminum, and copper – are traded on other international exchanges as well, and although trading patterns are unique, the chapter's summary of several studies that have examined linkages among prices on different exchanges shows that prices are surprisingly well connected.

Introduction

Less than five years ago, China's experiment with futures markets appeared to many observers to be all but over, a victim of changing national priorities towards the development of markets as well as of an especially zealous regulatory regime. From the brink of apparent closure, however, China's three futures exchanges have staged a remarkable recovery and trading in wheat, soybean, and to a lesser extent copper and aluminum futures contracts reaches new highs each year. By 2004, the Dalian Commodity Exchange for example was the second largest soybean futures market in the world, and the largest trading a non-GMO soybean contract. Moreover, in 2004, each exchange received long-hoped-for permission to offer contracts in new commodities – cotton at the Zhengzhou Commodity Exchange, fuel oil at the Shanghai Futures Exchange, and corn at Dalian – and these contracts are already trading. With the future of futures exchanges in China evidently secure, it seemed especially appropriate to pause a moment to review the history of their development, to identify some of what are surely many distinctive patterns in trading, and to assess their links with other markets both in China and internationally.

Background

Beginning in 1993, China authorized the opening of commodity futures exchanges on an experimental basis as one of many initiatives to encourage the development of markets in a wide variety of products. As was true in many transition economies in Eastern Europe and the former Soviet Union, there had been a long tradition in China of trading in commodities (and financial assets) before China's leaders centralized planning of all economic activity in the early 1950s. For example, several exchanges evidently developed in the early 1900s in Shanghai, the center of much of the trade in agricultural products.[2] They included markets for rice, soybean meal and oil, and wheat and flour. Some, including the flour market, also permitted trading in forward contracts as well and had well-developed rules for margining by both buyer and seller. Trade on these exchanges continued up until the mid-1930s when they were closed, and some then reopened after the war although trading was sporadic. All were closed permanently with the establishment of direct government management of food supplies in 1953. Not until the late 1970s did these controls begin to change. First, authorities introduced the household responsibility system and began to support a more important role for markets in the agricultural economy. By the late 1980s, it was a logical step to reintroduce more organized markets and to allow individual traders and trading companies to participate in the marketing, distribution, and processing of agricultural commodities. Thus, by 1993, there were both wholesale markets and independent trading firms – developments that underpinned the opening of futures markets in 1993.

This chapter describes the development of futures markets in China with particular emphasis on agricultural markets since the two most successful futures markets in China are those for soybeans and wheat. The initial section of the paper summarizes the many changes underway in the agricultural sector that mostly, but not always, supported the development of markets. The next section describes the early development of futures markets in China, from the virtually uncontrolled environment of the initial years until 1998 and the continued authorization of just three exchanges – the Dalian Commodity Exchange (DCE), the Shanghai Futures Exchange (SHFE), and the Zhengzhou Commodity Exchange (ZCE). The remainder of the paper examines various aspects of market performance, and comparative evidence from the successful copper and aluminum futures markets is included in addition to that for wheat and soybeans. The third section identifies the unique pattern of increase and decrease in amounts of trading in the typical Chinese futures contract over its life. The next section examines trading for evidence of seasonality in either its daily volume or the number of open contracts. The fifth section summarizes the results of the several studies that have examined aspects of pricing efficiency as well as price linkages with other exchanges. Finally, the paper concludes with a discussion of additional research issues.

Ongoing changes in China's grain and oilseeds economy[3]

The development of successful futures markets in the 1990s for soybeans and wheat – both of which contribute importantly to China's national food security – is all the more remarkable given the considerable degree of state control which continued to govern many aspects of their production, distribution, and trade. Throughout the period, China's concern with national food security continued to mean that many policies encouraged self-sufficiency in production of staples and that reliance on imports was discouraged. For example, quota prices for wheat as well as numerous controls on inputs continued to guide production decisions for most of the period. Import and export decisions continued to be made by the state and then implemented by the China National Cereals, Oils, and Foodstuffs Import and Export Corporation (COFCO). In some years, COFCO accounted for as much as 16 percent of the wheat traded throughout the world, and even though there was some reform of COFCO's monopoly, state decisions still governed much of China's trade in grains (Huang and Rozelle, 2003).

Moreover, food security concerns have always meant that reserve stocks of grains and soybeans should be held in very substantial amounts. In the 1990s, the target reserve levels were some 90 percent of consumption, and these levels represented an easing of the previous goal of maintaining a full year's consumption in reserve.[4] In addition, because the levels of grain and oilseed stocks were a matter of national security, their amount was considered a state secret. Almost never was quantitative information about their size made public. Some measure of the secrecy with which reserves figures were guarded became apparent in 2001 when USDA (and other world) estimates were increased by some 250 percent because of new information (Hsu and Gale, 2001). Overnight, estimated reserves of wheat, corn, and rice in China went from 65.7 to 229.7 million tons, an amount which, when added to on-farm stocks, meant that about 500 million tons of grain (or more than a year's consumption) was on hand. Virtually all yearend stocks of grains in China were either in state reserves or were still on farms. Under similar conditions in the US when commodity price support programs in the 1960s resulted in government ownership of most grain stocks, the grain markets at the Chicago Board of Trade (CBOT) virtually closed. For these reasons alone, the development of markets, not to mention more formalized futures exchanges, in China under these conditions is all the more remarkable.

One reason exchanges for soybeans and wheat developed in the 1990s was that China's leaders also adopted many policies that encouraged an increased reliance on markets and market institutions for production, marketing, and processing decisions, even if storage decisions remained the basic responsibility of the state. To be sure, food-security concerns also led authorities to attempt to re-establish greater control of production or marketing from time to time, but more often than not encouragement was given to develop a marketing system with significant breadth and depth.

Among the important policies encouraging greater reliance on markets was the decision to reform the food ration system. By the late 1980s, the costs of maintaining comparatively high producer prices while subsidizing urban consumption through the vast network of urban ration shops had grown to absorb more than 20 percent of the national government revenues (Crook, 1997). China's leaders decided to end the ration system and by the end of 1993 urban ration networks in 28 of 31 provinces had begun to be phased out. Policies were also adopted to encourage the commercialization of the provincial grain bureaus, providing incentives for market participation and to reduce budgetary obligations.[5] Many provinces also established wholesale markets, beginning in 1990 with the Zhengzhou Grain Warehouse Market (ZGWM) in Henan province. In total, 13 wholesale markets were built between 1990 and 1993 by provincial authorities (Wu, 2002). The value of trading at rural markets grew rapidly – from about 200 million yuan per market in 1990 to more than 850 million in 1995. By 1995, more than three-quarters of agricultural goods were sold through markets (Lardy, 2001). To be sure, the state remained an important buyer of grains from producers, both through quota and open-market purchases in order to meet their supply obligations as well as to maintain significant stocks. Rozelle *et al.* (2000) estimated that by 1995 some 23 percent of the wheat crop was marketed through private traders, an amount which was nearly double the 12 percent privately traded just seven years earlier.

By the mid-1990s, both the state and individual traders had made substantial investments in market infrastructure. From just 1992–94, for example, investment totaled over ten billion yuan (Rozelle *et al.*, 2000).[6] All physical measures of the transport system in China show remarkable growth during the 1990s. New highway construction increased mileage 36 percent, and new railways increased mileage 19 percent (Gilmour and Gale, 2002). Freight traffic on highways increased 43.5 percent, that on railways increased 15.8 percent, and that on waterways 52.8 percent. The communication infrastructure expanded greatly as well.[7] Not surprisingly, studies of regional price interrelations in China consistently reported that market prices for most grains and soybeans in most locations were substantially better integrated than had been the case in the prior decade.[8] In addition, Park *et al.* (2002) estimated that the rate of arbitrage between markets for rice and for corn also had substantially increased.

All the while markets and traders were gradually becoming more important, there were also periods of retrenchment when China's leaders tried to re-establish greater control. The most important retrenchment was caused by the

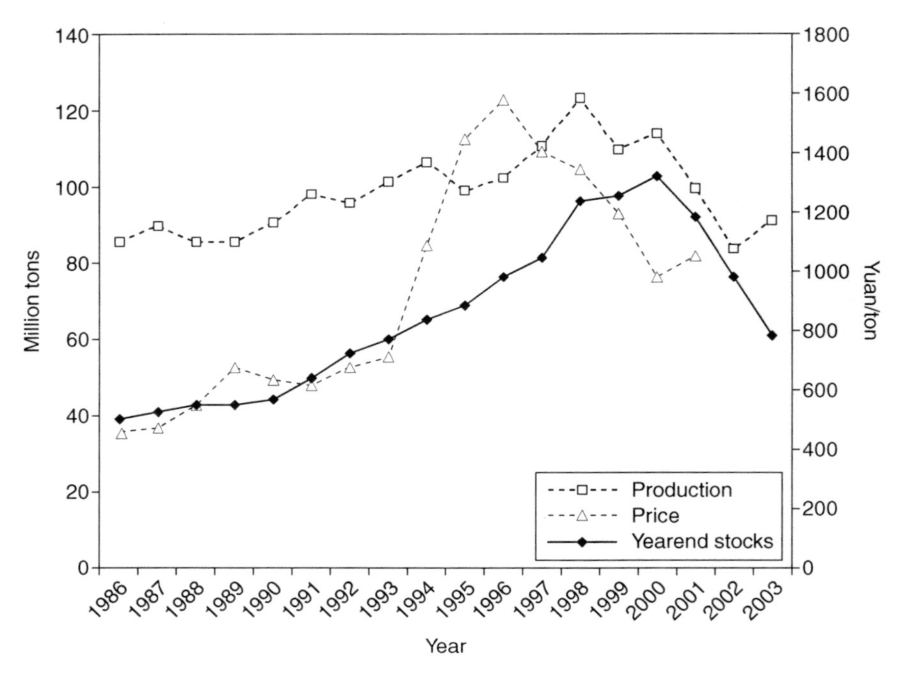

Figure 3.1 Production, price, and year-end stocks of wheat in China 1986–2003.

sudden and unexplained increases in prices for most food grains in 1993 and 1994. Prices in the wheat market are illustrative and are shown in Figure 3.1, along with data on annual production and year-end stocks. As evident, throughout the late 1980s and early 1990s, production of wheat increased gradually with increases in producer prices. Domestic supplies were supplemented each year by substantial imports, ranging between 6.6 and 15.9 million tons, in part because authorities also wanted to increase year-end stocks. By 1994, stocks totaled some 65 million tons, an amount that exceeded 50 percent of annual consumption. Despite the seeming surplus, wheat (and especially rice) prices increased sharply in 1993 and 1994, increases which caused China's policy-makers to become concerned once again about longer-term food security.[9]

The new policies – collectively called the Governors' Grain Bag Policy – emphasized provincial responsibility for almost all aspects of local grain security, including stabilizing areas devoted to grains production, guaranteeing inputs, holding reserves, transporting grain from surplus to deficit regions within provinces, stabilizing prices in urban areas, and controlling 70–80 percent of commercial grain sales as well as imports to or exports from the region (Crook, 1997). The central government was to facilitate coordination among the provinces, assisting in securing grain for deficit provinces from surplus ones, as well as retaining control of imports and exports. The new policy was in many regards too successful, whether by design or by an especially fortuitous series of growing seasons.[10] By 1998, wheat production had increased to 123 million tons, an amount which itself exceeded annual consumption requirements. If the goal was self-sufficiency, it was more than met. Not surprisingly, imports of wheat declined rapidly to just 2.7 million tons in 1997 and have remained very low ever since. Indeed, in 2000/01 China was a net exporter of wheat for the first time and in 2002/03 exported over one million tons net.

The surplus of production over consumption requirements accumulated mostly in year-end (provincial) stocks (see Figure 3.1), and the large accumulations clearly put great pressure on average prices. Quota prices for wheat were reduced in 1997 and again in 1998; market prices were substantially lower until at least 1999 when quota prices were lowered to market price levels. With market prices below quota prices and quota prices declining over time, quota wheat could be sold back onto the market only at substantial loss and provincial budgets were increasingly burdened. Losses by state-owned grain enterprises were 19.7 billion yuan in 1995/96, 40 billion in 1996/97, and 100 billion in 1997/98 (Crook, 1998). In 1999, the government budgeted 50 billion yuan for storage and interest costs alone, while an estimated 200 billion yuan was tied up in debts from prior years' grain purchases (Crook, 2000). Worse, much of the wheat that accumulated in regional grain reserves was of low quality, there was significant deterioration in storage, and much would eventually have to be sold for feed use at even greater losses.

All the while increasing control of the production of grains in the mid-1990s, China's leaders continued to permit greater independence in the soybean sector.[11] Figure 3.2 shows soybean production, imports, and prices from 1986–2003. Like wheat, soybean prices generally increased through the late 1980s and early 1990s. Production was slow to respond, but in 1993 and again in 1994 it exceeded 15 million tons. Despite the record production, prices rose sharply both years. However, unlike the price increases for wheat and rice, the increases in soybean prices did not induce authorities to re-establish controls. By the mid-1990s, many provinces no longer supported soybean production directly, and by 2000 only Heilongjiang (admittedly the most important soybean-producing province) still had a system of government procurement and maintained a procurement price. In 2001, even Heilongjiang eliminated procurement prices. By the end of 1998, only three provinces – Heilongjiang, Jilin, and Inner Mongolia – still held official reserves of soybeans (Hsu, 2000).

Also, as provincial authorities raised quota prices for grains under the Grain Bag Policy, the comparative incentive to produce soybeans declined and soybean production contracted substantially in many areas. China's leaders turned to world markets and allowed very substantial increases in imports to meet domestic demand (see Figure 3.2).[12] Soybean imports (and China's domestic crushing industry) received another boost in 1999 when authorities imposed a 13 percent value-added tax on soybean meal imports. In 1998, production once again exceeded 15 million tons and has been consistently above that since 2000. However, growth in demand has been such that imports now

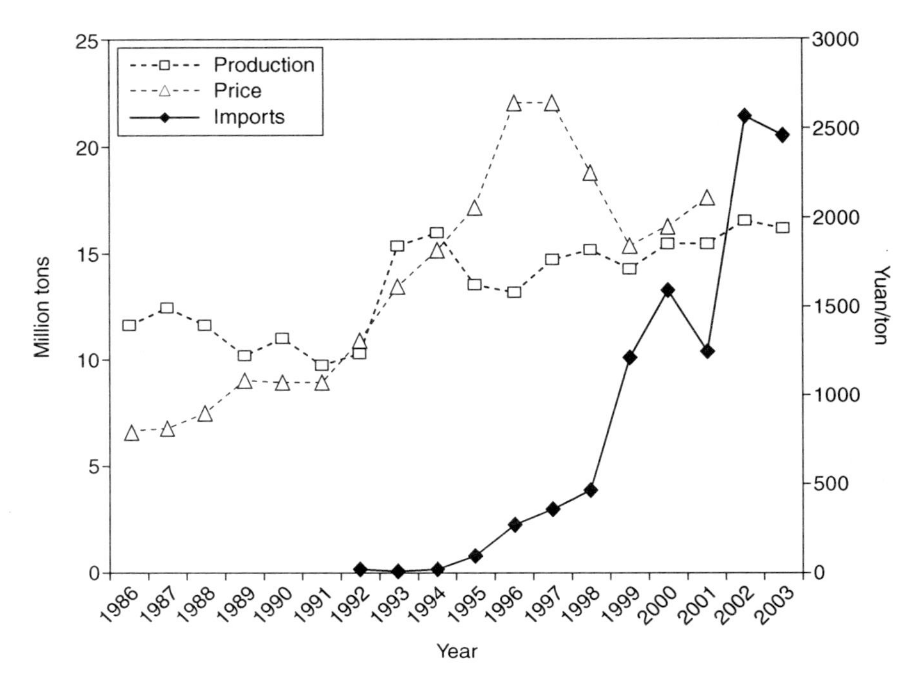

Figure 3.2 Production, price, and imports of soybeans in China 1986–2003.

exceed production, which occurred for the first time in 2002 when they reached 21 million tons.

In addition to specific grain and oilseed policies, the strong growth in incomes in China over the last decade has also had important consequences for the development of grain and oilseed markets. For grains, income growth has meant that China's consumers could afford better qualities of many grains and could substitute other foods for grains. In particular, the demand for wheat for food peaked at 104.2 million tons in 1996/97 and has declined each year since, thereby both hastening and exacerbating the accumulation of surpluses. Also, as more consumers were able to afford higher quality varieties of both wheat and rice, the marketing system had to find effective ways to differentiate quality and to provide incentives for producers. New national standards for both wheat and rice were adopted in 2000, and they identified for the first time so-called 'quality' grades. For wheat, the new standards identified two grades of high-gluten quality wheat (where the two would be differentiated on the basis of protein content) and one of low-gluten quality wheat alongside five grades of standard wheat classified according to weight, imperfect grains, and foreign materials.[13] For soybeans, income growth has meant increasing demand – for direct consumption, for vegetable oil, and for meal as a feed ingredient.

Another important factor strengthening the development of markets in China was its decision to seek admittance to the World Trade Organization.[14] As an initial step, China and the US concluded a bilateral trade agreement in November 1999 which specified many terms governing agricultural trade relations that would be adopted in the WTO negotiations. Among the terms, China's leaders committed to gradual reductions in tariffs and to the elimination of non-tariff barriers for agricultural trade, and they committed to increasing the role of private traders in import and export transactions. The tariff-rate quotas for wheat, corn, rice, soybean oil, and cotton were agreed which not only reduced tariff levels but specified the percent of the within-quota trade which would be allocated to non-state traders. In wheat, where imports had been the exclusive responsibility of COFCO, the state trading company, 10 percent of the import quota (itself gradually increasing) was to be allocated to private traders from 2000 to 2004; in corn, the percent would increase from 25 percent in 2000 to 40 percent in 2004; and in rice, the quota amounts and rates differed for long-grain and other varieties, but non-state traders were to be allowed as much as 50 percent of traded amounts. For soybeans, tariff rates were bound at just 3 percent through 2004. Quotas for soybeans, which had been discussed many times, were not adopted in the WTO negotiations.[15] Moreover, licenses to import soybeans were generally more readily available, and competition among importing agents increased.

These and many other factors have contributed to a growing reliance on markets in China in recent years. The number of markets continued to increase, the number of traders and their investment in trucks increased, investments in market communication and other infrastructure increased, and transport linkages improved. By the mid-1990s there already were numerous signs of a significantly increased degree of integration among market prices. By 2000, most markets throughout China were linked, and prices in one were tied to prices in all the others. For example, whereas soybean prices in 28 percent of markets sampled in 1989–95 were found to be integrated, from 1996–2000 some 68 percent of the markets were integrated (Huang and Rozelle, 2002). For corn, the increase in integration was even greater, from 28 percent of markets to 89 percent. For rice the increase was from 25 percent to 60 (48) percent for rice in the Yellow River Valley (Yangtze Valley and South China). Wheat markets were not included in the study, but the increased integration among rice markets in the Yellow River Valley, which is the major wheat producing region as well, suggests similar results would obtain for wheat. Moreover, as will be described below, most of China's markets have become significantly more connected to international markets as trade barriers have been reduced and the number of agents have been allowed to increase. It is against this background that the decision was taken to permit experimentation with futures markets.

The opening of futures markets in China

China's leaders authorized the trading of futures contracts for the first time in modern China with the opening of the Zhengzhou Commodity Exchange (ZCE) by the Zhengzhou Grain Warehouse Market on 28 May 1993. Officials at

ZGWM, itself opened only in 1990, had been working for more than three years to develop the experimental futures market, establishing first a wholesale market for grains, studying successful markets elsewhere, and developing necessary futures market infrastructure like trading systems, detailed contract specifications, brokerage arrangements, contract settlement and clearing systems, and so on. Perhaps predictably, once futures markets were authorized – even if only on an experimental basis – groups in many cities throughout China quickly acted to open their own exchanges. The Dalian Commodity Exchange (DCE) opened in February 1993 and trading of futures contracts began in November (Zhao, 2002). Three futures exchanges opened in Shanghai; in addition, treasury futures were traded on the Shanghai Securities Exchange. In total, more than 40 organizations in various localities began calling themselves futures exchanges at the end of 1993, and there was actual trading at 33 such exchanges with an estimated volume of nearly 27 million contracts worth more than CNY715 billion (about US$90 billion).[16]

Brokerage firms were required to register with state authorities, but there was no national regulatory scheme and exchanges were expected to be largely self-regulatory as regards trading standards, customer protections, margin and clearing operations, and the like. Indeed, it was not until November 1993 that overall regulatory responsibility for the fledgling commodity exchanges was given to the China Securities Regulatory Commission (CSRC) – itself only formed in 1992 to regulate securities trading (Yao, 1998). Initially at least, the CSRC exerted little direct control of the new futures exchanges, although even in 1994 officials had to deal with specific concerns about the pricing of various commodities on some exchanges. For instance, when sharply rising rice prices in 1994 prompted regional authorities to impose price ceilings, CSRC restricted rice futures trading on the Shanghai Cereals & Oils Exchange to minimal levels for many months in part because of a perceived inadequacy in the exchange's ability to monitor trading.

For the most part, however, trading on the new futures exchanges grew with little restraint. By the end of 1994, the volume of futures trading had surpassed 120 million contracts (see Figure 3.3). In 1995, it totaled some 667 million contracts. To no-one's surprise, such rapid growth was accompanied by a number of problems as well. Speculative frenzies at some exchanges became so intense that some investors were injured and had to be hospitalized (Yao, 1998). Authorities continued to be especially concerned whenever price increases for individual commodities were too rapid. Trading suspensions were imposed in markets as diverse as steel, sugar, raw silk, and soybean oil (Wu, 1996).

Ironically, the most widely publicized scandal involving futures trading in China occurred not at these fledgling commodities exchanges but at the Shanghai Securities Exchange where the treasury bond market had become the largest futures market in China.[17] One firm, the Shanghai International Securities Co. Ltd. (SISCO), established very large short positions in treasury bond futures in February 1995 in the expectation that prices would decline as the government came to market with a record new issue. In the event, the issue was canceled, prices did not decline, and SISCO tried to force prices down with even larger sales at the very last minute. In total, SISCO's losses were estimated to be more

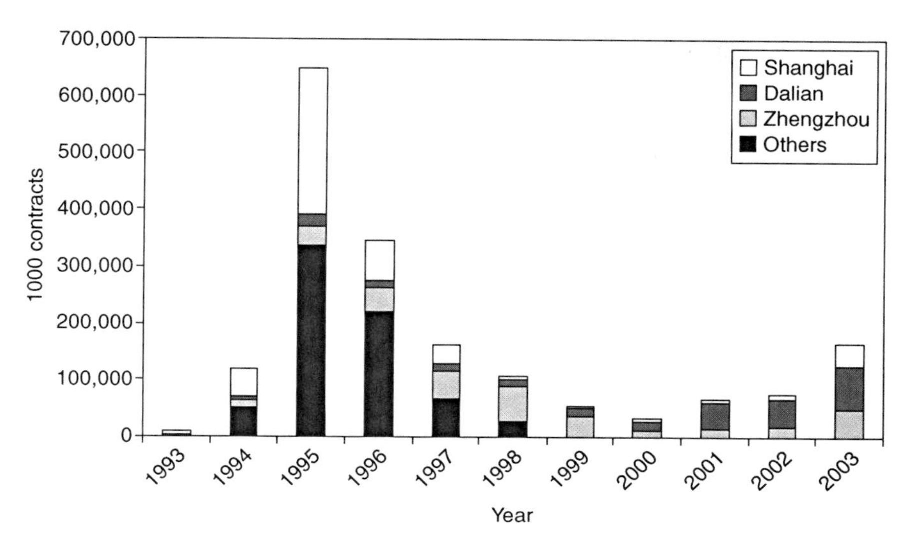

Figure 3.3 Volume of trading on China's futures markets 1993–2003 (source: based on data from Wang and Chang (1997) and the Dalian, Shanghai, and Zhengzhou Futures Exchanges).

than US$120 million. All trading in treasury futures on the Shanghai exchange was suspended for two weeks while positions and accounts were cleared. The market was then allowed to reopen, but when further trading violations occurred, CSRC suspended permanently trading in treasury futures – by then occurring at ten exchanges – and closed the futures market at the Shanghai Securities Exchange.

CSRC also undertook a formal review of all futures markets to determine if they met official standards of membership as well as of breadth and depth of trading activity in order to be allowed to continue as experimental exchanges. Only 14 of the multitude of futures exchanges met the CSRC standards, including those in Dalian, Shanghai, and Zhengzhou; the rest were closed. The period of virtually unfettered growth in futures trading in China came to an end. In 1996, 187 million contracts were traded in aggregate, only 30 million more than in 1994 and well over two-thirds fewer than had been traded in 1995. Futures markets in many individual commodities also had been suspended. Whereas the leading exchanges (in terms of volume of trading) in 1994 were the Beijing Commodity Exchange and the Shanghai Cereal and Oils Exchange, in 1996 the leading exchanges were the Suzhou Commodity Exchange and Shanghai Commodity Exchange (Wang and Chang, 1997). The leading commodities traded on the exchanges in 1996 were a comparatively odd assortment of mostly minor commodities including mungbeans, plywood, rubber, coffee, soybeans, and red beans. Even with just 14 exchanges, however, there were still many duplicative contracts among exchanges. The degree of self-regulation also varied a great deal among exchanges and there was still no comprehensive national law governing operations on futures exchanges and by members and participants, although by this time many specific practices had been expressly prohibited. Some exchanges, like the Zhengzhou Commodity Exchange, had developed detailed trading rules and member regulations, and the rules had been reviewed and approved formally by provincial officials.[18] Many other of the 14 exchanges did not adopt formal rules.

Officials at CSRC also remained very concerned about the ability of some exchanges to manage episodic flurries of excessive speculation as well as specific instances of market manipulation. In 1997, for example, there was a major manipulation in rubber futures at the Hainan China Commodity Futures Exchange (Hoo, 2000). In 1998, CSRC again tightened control of the futures industry, merging the three remaining exchanges in Shanghai into the Shanghai Futures Exchange (SHFE) and closing all other exchanges except those at Zhengzhou and the Dalian. Moreover, only 12 commodities were officially designated for trading and there were to be no duplications of products between exchanges. SHFE was permitted to trade copper, aluminum, and rubber and it was to develop futures markets in rice and plywood. ZCE could continue to trade mungbeans, red beans, corn, wheat, and peanuts – of which only mungbeans was actively trading in 1998 – but was given clear direction to redouble efforts to develop wheat futures as its principal contract. ZCE also could explore developing futures markets for cotton and sugar. DCE was permitted to continue trading its soybean and malting barley contracts, and began developing soybean oil and soybean meal contracts.

With the major consolidation and restructuring of exchanges accomplished by CSRC in 1998, one might have anticipated that growth would resume. As evident in Figure 3.3, however, the overall decline in volume of trading on China's futures markets did not end, but continued for two more years. The reason was that trading in ZCE's mungbean contract, by far the highest volume contract at the time, experienced significant problems in both 1999 and 2000.[19] In January 1999, ZCE officials were forced to restrict trading to liquidation-only when confronted with a serious manipulation attempt; full trading was not resumed until 22 March. Then in late November, when exchange officials again sensed the mungbean market might be threatened by an attempted manipulation, they first responded by increasing margins in order to discourage speculation. Several additional margin increases were not sufficient, however, to bring the market under control. CSRC and ZCE officials remained concerned about excessive price volatility, and in January 2000 trading in mungbeans was suspended again. Although the market reopened three months later, margins and capital requirements were at such high levels that very little trading resumed. The severity of the problems on the mungbean market caused a precipitous drop in the volume of trading at ZCE in both 1999 and 2000 – it was down by nearly one-third in 1999, to 40 million contracts, and then to just 11 million in 2000.

The decline in trading at ZCE, totaling nearly 47 million contracts over two years, was larger than the level of trading on the other two exchanges combined, so that even though trading was in fact increasing at both the Dalian and Shanghai exchanges by 2000, the total volume of futures trading in China continued what seemed to be an inexorable decline. Many observers declared the futures market experiment was over in China. Headlines like "In Beijing, the Futures Look a Bit Grim – Commodities 'Experiment' Now is a Thing of the Past" summed many observers' views. In fact, the slow and steady growth in trading of soybean futures at Dalian, of copper and (more recently) aluminum futures at Shanghai, and of wheat at Zhengzhou (beginning in 2000) were the true harbingers of the future of futures markets in China.[20] Figure 3.4 shows the growth of trading in each of these contracts since 1998.[21] Until very recently, trading in soybean futures at the Dalian exchange has dominated trading at all others. Trading in copper futures on the Shanghai exchange has grown, albeit slowly, until mid-2003 when it increased markedly. Aluminum futures at SHFE have only been active since mid-2001. Finally, after a very erratic start, trading in wheat futures at the Zhengzhou exchange has increased steadily since 2000, and in 2003 it became the most actively traded contract. These trends clearly mirror changes in agricultural policies more generally and the growing role of markets in China's economy.

In sum, what began as an experiment in which it seemed as though many exchanges trading relatively minor commodities were to dominate has been transformed into an important component of the development of markets in China with three major exchanges where important agricultural and industrial commodities are traded. CSRC has established a strong regulatory presence and reports of excessive speculation or alleged manipulation are much less frequent.[22] Trading on the three exchanges was linked through a unified computer network in May 2001 so that traders at any one exchange could easily trade on either of the other two (*Financial Times*, 1 May 2001, p. 27). The exchanges also have plans for significant expansion. The Zhengzhou exchange added a second wheat contract in 2003, calling for

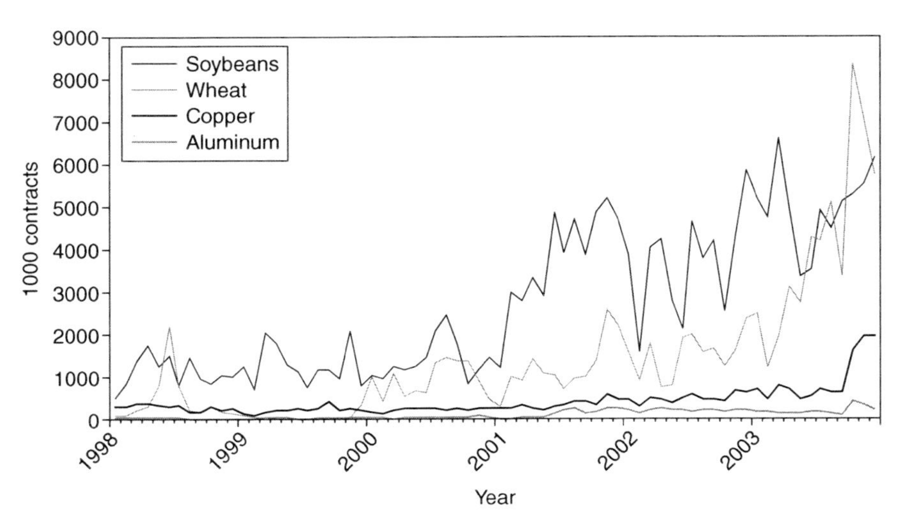

Figure 3.4 Volume of trading in China's soybean, wheat, aluminum, and copper futures markets 1998–2003 (source: based on data from CSRC and the Dalian, Shanghai, and Zhengzhou Futures Exchanges).

delivery of high-quality strong-gluten wheat and both its wheat contracts are trading well. Pending regulatory approvals, all three exchanges anticipate offering several new contracts in 2004 – in cotton[23] and sugar at Zhengzhou, in corn at Dalian, and in fuel oil at Shanghai (Sun, 2004).

Trading in the middle: the unique pattern of trading in China's futures contracts

Perhaps the most pervasive characteristic of trading on Chinese futures exchanges is that activity is concentrated in contracts that are still some months from maturity. In a pattern that was first documented in soybean futures at DCE, Guo and Li (2003) observed that trading tended to peak some five to six months before expiration. In contrast, trading in the typical CBOT soybean futures peaks just one or two months before expiration while that in the Tokyo Grain Exchange soybean futures peaks as much as a year before expiration. Guo and Li argued that the pattern observed in the volume of trading on DCE contracts, which they named "trading in the middle," was due to the rules on Chinese exchanges which increase margins and lower position limits in the month preceding delivery and thus encourage traders to trade out of positions comparatively early, well before a contract approaches delivery. The specific margin and position limit rules apply to all exchanges in China, and they were adopted universally in May 2000 (although some exchanges had adopted similar rules earlier).

The patterns shown in Figures 3.5–3.8 confirm that trading-in-the-middle is a characteristic common to futures contracts on all three exchanges in China and applies equally to the volume of trading and the open interest in each contract. Both the volume and open interest increase more or less regularly until four to six months before contract expiration and then decline. The pattern in DCE soybean futures, based on data from 1998–2003 (i.e. contracts expiring from January 1999 through November 2003) is shown in Figure 3.5.[24] Over most of the period, trading in each contract began one year in advance of the expiration date (e.g. in January 1998 for the January 1999 delivery), although beginning with the May 2003 contract trading in each contract has started earlier.[25] The levels of both the volume of trading and open interest increase for the first six months, reaching an amount equal to about 200 percent of the contract average, and then decline quite smoothly as contract expiration approaches. Put differently, the most actively traded soybean future is generally some five to seven months from expiration. The November future is most actively traded the preceding April through June, the January future from June to August, the March future from August to October, and so on.

Figures 3.6–3.8 show the average trading-in-the-middle patterns for wheat futures at ZCE and for copper and aluminum futures at SHFE. For wheat, the averages are based on data from 2002–03, and thus include only eight complete contracts since trading on each begins some 18 months prior to expiration. The growth in trading and in the number of open contracts in each wheat contract on ZCE (Figure 3.6) is rather more gradual than was typical with the DCE soybean futures and they peak a month later, just five months prior to delivery. In amount,

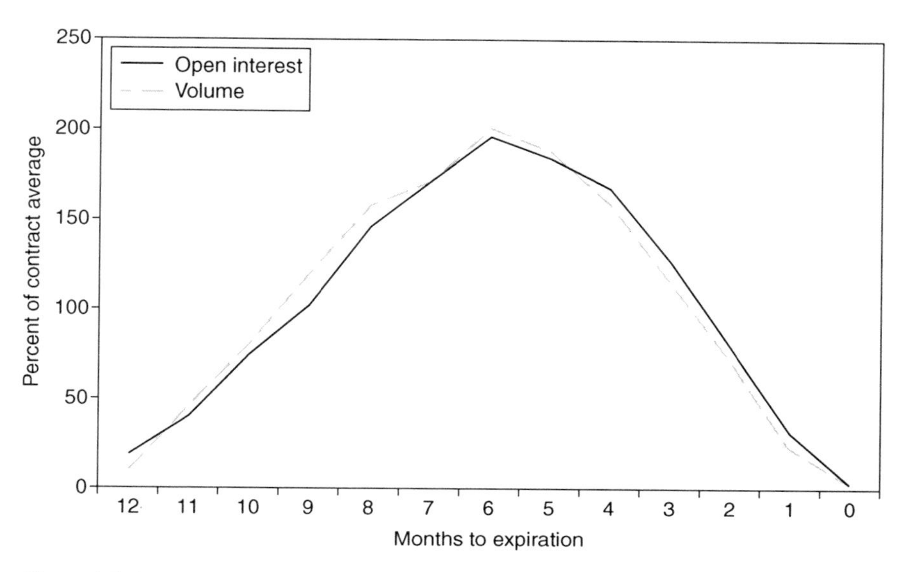

Figure 3.5 Average pattern of trading in soybean futures at DCE 1998–2003 (source: based on data from the Dalian Commodity Exchange).

however, the maximums are quite similar to those for soybeans, roughly twice the average for the contract. The patterns in volume and open interest in copper (Figure 3.7) and aluminum futures (Figure 3.8) at SHFE are also similar. Because trading in each of these futures did not begin until seven months prior to expiration for most of the period (1999–2003), the increases and decreases in trading activity were rather more rapid. In copper, both measures of trading activity peaked five months before the typical contract's expiration at levels between 250 and 300 percent of the contract average. For the less active aluminum futures, trading peaked three to four months prior to expiration at levels between 170 and 180 percent of average. In both copper and aluminum, a significant percentage of contracts in each maturity were settled in actual deliveries since there were regular reports of substantial numbers of open contracts at the end of the delivery month.

The patterns in trading activity typical of futures contracts on China's exchanges displayed in Figures 3.5–3.8 have important consequences for both market users and researchers. In general, more traders will be following the relationship in prices between contract maturities on China's exchanges much earlier than is common in US markets. Whether trading-in-the-middle also means that convergence between cash and futures prices in the delivery month is different from that observed in markets on US exchanges is a question that requires further research. Similarly, while analysts of US futures markets typically rely on prices from the nearby future as the most reliable indicator of commodity value because it is usually the most actively traded contract, should analysts of China's markets make the same choice? Perhaps prices from a more distant future are more representative because they are more closely observed and actively traded.

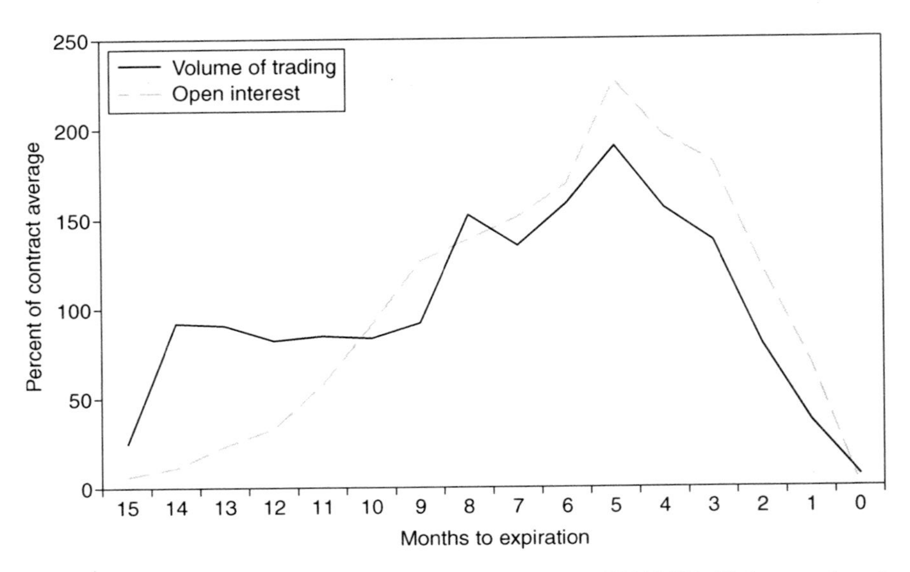

Figure 3.6 Average pattern of trading of wheat futures at ZCE 2002–03 (source: based on data from the Zhengzhou Futures Exchange).

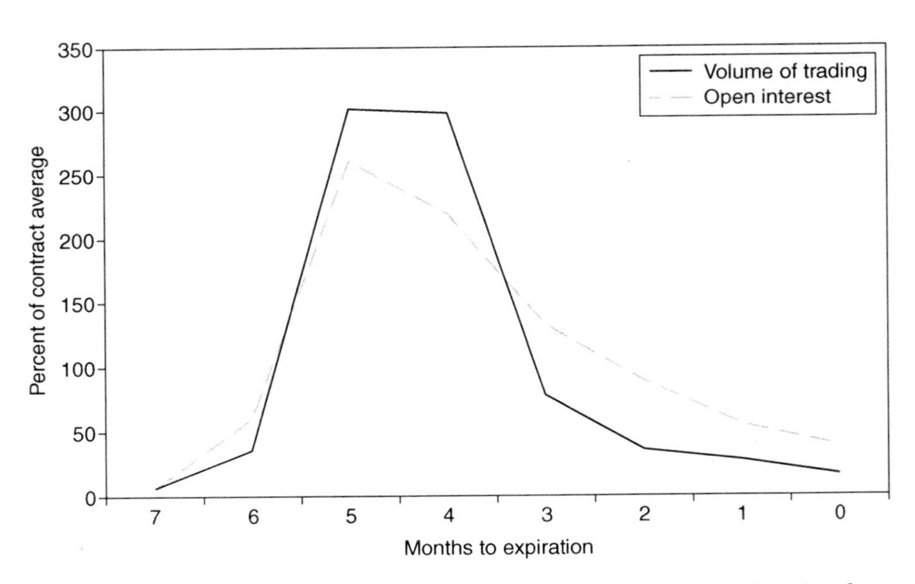

Figure 3.7 Average pattern of trading of copper futures 1999–2003 (based on data from the Shanghai Futures Exchange).

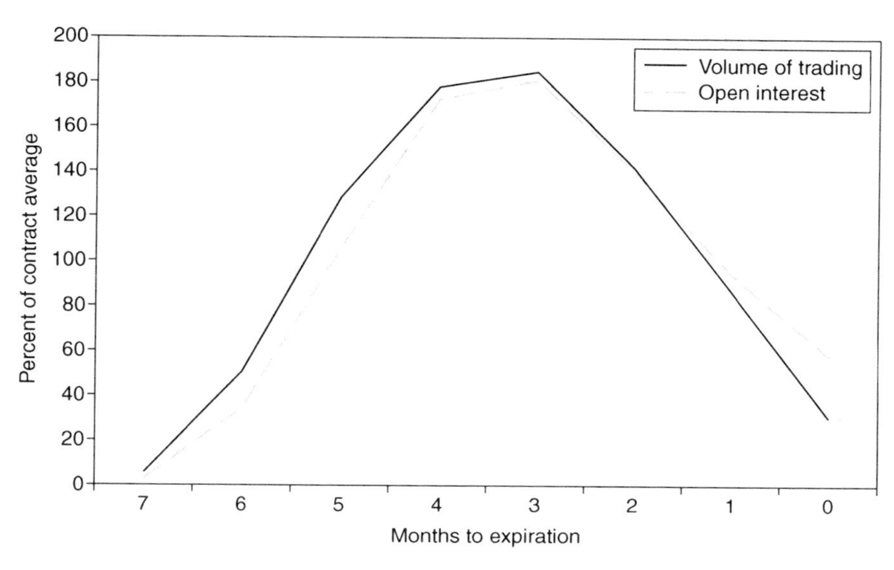

Figure 3.8 Average pattern of trading of aluminum futures 1999–2003 (based on data from the Shanghai Futures Exchange).

Evidence of seasonality in the amount of trading on each exchange

Some seasonal regularities in trading on China's futures exchanges can also be deduced from the data on volume of trading and open interest for each market. The upper half of Table 3.1 summarizes the results of simple regressions of the monthly volume of trading in each market, expressed as a percentage of the annual average volume in that market, on a set of monthly zero-one variables; the lower half summarizes similar results using data on the open interest. Looking first at the results for the volume of trading, trading in all four futures contracts share some seasonal tendencies. The amount of trading in January and February tends to be below average in all markets, a clear reflection of the fact that markets in China are closed for nearly two weeks over the New Year holidays. The level of the open interest also tends to be below average in these months, although the amount is not significant in the ZCE wheat or SHFE aluminum markets. Trading on all four markets tends to be most active in November and December and the level of open interest tends to be above average in these months too (with the exception of soybeans in December). Somewhat surprisingly, trading in copper futures at SHFE showed substantially more evidence of seasonality than did trading in either of the agricultural futures. Both the monthly volume of trading and the month-end open interest tend to be below average in the first half of the year and above average in the last half, a pattern that is more pronounced for the open interest than for the volume.

Table 3.1 Seasonal variations in trading on Chinese futures exchanges

Volume of trading (as percentage of annual average)

Exchange/ commodity	*SHFE copper*	*SHFE aluminum*	*ZCE mungbeans*	*ZCE wheat*	*DCE soybeans*
Period	2000–03	2000–03	1995–99	1996–2003	1997–2003
January	80*	79	69*	67*	82*
February	62**	76*	39**	38**	65**
March	98	109	102	89	117*
April	98	95	118*	92	113*
May	86*	85	93	107	89
June	98	104	113	151*	98
July	105	101	110	109	107
August	91	93	105	104	116*
September	105	85	93	79	112*
October	109	109	108	104	85*
November	138**	132*	126*	112	112*
December	130**	132*	113	147*	105

Open interest (as percentage of annual average)

Exchange/ commodity	*SHFE copper*	*SHFE aluminum*	*ZCE mungbeans*	*ZCE wheat*	*DCE soybeans*
Period	2000–03	2000–03	1995–99	1996–2003	1997–2003
January	91*	96	59**	84	82**
February	78**	97	82*	76	90*
March	86**	111*	102	75	107
April	88**	102	103	68*	102
May	99	95	104	86	94
June	105	84*	102	99	100
July	118**	94	119*	98	107
August	114**	94	101	90	109*
September	102	94	92	88	105
October	101	103	113*	124	107
November	107*	101	128*	136*	107
December	105	129**	94	176**	88*

Notes
* indicates reported percentage differs from the annual average by more than one standard error.
** indicates the percentage is more than two standard errors from average.

The absence of strong seasonality in trading in the wheat and soybean markets distinguishes China's markets from those in the US where trading in both wheat and soybeans futures is very seasonal. There, both the volume and open interest are seasonally high in the months immediately after harvest when stocks of the commodity are highest and seasonally low in the months just before harvest when stocks are lowest.[26] Moreover, the seasonal patterns in US markets mirror the similarly regular increase and then decrease in commercial firms' positions in the markets as they hedge changing levels of stocks. Although not seasonal, trading in wheat and soybean futures in China may well reflect the market needs of typical commercial users. Whereas US grain and oilseed merchants store substantial amounts of the annual crop surpluses, for example, in China most stocks are held either on farm or by the regional grain bureaus, and merchant storage appears to be minimal.[27] In addition, for soybeans, the flow of imports is the biggest source of supply in recent years (see Figure 3.2) and market use may well be much more related to the needs of importers. Before conclusions can by drawn, much more research needs to be done to learn more about typical uses of China's futures markets by enterprises involved in the production, importing, storage, and marketing of each commodity.

The data on volume and open interest can also be used to identify the most active contract maturities in each market. For DCE soybeans, there are six contracts each year, one delivery every other month – January, March, May, July, September, and November. Of these, the aggregate amount of trading in the March delivery is lowest on average and trading in the September delivery is greatest.[28] Trading in the May future was also consistently above average, although the amount was not significant. These results suggest that one alternative method to create a series of representative prices of the most active contract in the soybean market would be to link prices from just two contracts, the May and September deliveries, when each is between nine and three months to maturity. Whether such a series is more or less representative of soybean values is another issue for future research. For copper and aluminum, there are contracts maturing in every month and only a few traded in amounts which differed significantly from the others. In copper, the volume of trading in the February contract was the only contract in which trading was significantly below average and none were above. In aluminum, the volume in all contracts was similar. The open interest in copper was significantly above average in the July and August contracts; none were significantly below average. In aluminum, variations in the open interest in each contract were not significant.

Price efficiency on China's futures markets

Finally, there have been a number of studies of various aspects of the informational efficiency of prices on China's futures markets. The number is perhaps surprising because almost all of the studies begin by noting how new the markets are and that there have not yet been many studies of their prices, either in relation to other prices (like cash prices or other futures prices) or in relation to other measures of market activity. There have been five such studies, with two more treating not unrelated questions of price volatility. Soybean futures prices at Dalian have been studied most, while no studies have included prices from either the rubber or aluminum futures markets at Shanghai. With such uneven coverage, the results are hardly generalizable. Table 3.2 summarizes the studies.

Table 3.2 Studies of pricing linkages with China's futures markets

Links w/:	*Type of test*	*Author (date)*	*Markets*	*Period*	*Result*
Dalian commodity exchange soybean futures prices					
Domestic markets					
	Cointegration	Zhao (2002)	Heilongjiang	1995–99	Yes
		Wang and Ke (2002)	National average	1998–2002	Yes
			Tianjin wholesale	1998–2002	Yes, plus efficient in short run
			Zhengzhou wholesale	1998–2002	No
International markets					
	Correlation	Durham and Si (1999)	CBOT	1996–99	Yes, with suggested link to imports
		Zhao (2002)	CBOT	1995–99	Yes
		Fung *et al.* (2003)	CBOT	1995–2001	Yes
	Cointegration	Zhao (2002)	CBOT	1995–99	Yes
	AR-GARCH	Fung *et al.* (2003)	CBOT	1995–2001	US to China; China to US only in long run

Links w/:	*Type of test*	*Author (date)*	*Markets*	*Period*	*Result*
Zhengzhou commodity exchange wheat futures prices					
Domestic markets					
	Cointegration	Wang and Ke (2002)	National average	1998–2002	No
			Tianjin wholesale	1998–2002	No
			Zhengzhou wholesale	1998–2002	No
International markets					
	Correlation	Fung *et al.* (2003)	CBOT	1996–2001	No
	AR-GARCH	Fung *et al.* (2003)	CBOT	1996–2001	Yes, but only through volatility

Links w/:	*Type of test*	*Author (date)*	*Markets*	*Period*	*Result*
Shanghai futures exchange copper futures prices					
International markets					
	Correlation	Fung *et al.* (2003)	NYMEX	1995–2001	Yes
	AR-GARCH	Fung *et al.* (2003)	NYMEX	1995–2001	US to China stronger than China to US

In general, prices on China's soybean futures market have been found to be efficient. Using data from January 1998–March 2002, Wang and Ke (2002) found that soybean futures prices were cointegrated with both national average and Tianjin wholesale market cash prices. Over a slightly earlier period, Zhao (2002) found that soybean futures prices were also cointegrated with cash prices from Heilongjiang province from September 1995–December 1999. In addition, Wang and Ke concluded that soybean futures prices were efficient forecasts of subsequent cash prices, although their analysis showed there was a persistent difference between cash and futures prices such as might be expected because of transport costs.

Several studies examined the links between DCE and CBOT soybean futures prices. Although the data periods vary somewhat among the analyses (1995–99, 1996–99, and 1995–2001), all found there to be some relation between soybean futures prices in China and in the US. In perhaps the most detailed analysis, Fung *et al.* (2003) found prices in China were correlated with same day (although later in the day) prices in Chicago and prices in Chicago were correlated with next day prices in China. The relation was stronger for the correlation of the US to China prices, but both were significant, and both relations were also found to be cointegrated. A significantly more detailed model allowed them to test directly the nature of the cross-market relations, including the possibility of day-of-the-week effects, volatility links, and changes in the relations after August 1997. Their analysis concluded that for soybeans, prices on CBOT play a leading role in pricing on DCE both directly and through price volatility. Prices in China do not affect those on CBOT directly, but longer-term information linkages are significant. Additionally, Durham and Si (1999) suggest that the relation between futures prices in the US and China is affected by the flow of soybean imports from the US to China, with a closer relation between prices in the fall and winter months when most imports occur.

As evident in Table 3.2, similar analyses of prices on the Zhengzhou wheat futures market have not found them to be as well-connected to other market prices either internationally or elsewhere in China. In the single analysis of international linkages, Fung *et al.* (2003) found there were no direct cross-market links between CBOT wheat futures prices and those at ZCE using data from October 1996–March 2001, although there was some indirect linkage through volatility. However, the analysis is based on data taken from periods when there was virtually no trading in wheat futures at ZCE (see Figure 3.3), and it is difficult to know exactly how such periods of inactivity may have affected the results. Moreover, as was described above, 1996–2001 was a period of great change in policies in the wheat market as provincial governors were given greater responsibility, production increased significantly, surplus stocks grew to levels well in excess of annual consumption, and China shifted from being an importer to an exporter of wheat. Indeed, Fung *et al.* (2003) suggest that the contrast in results for soybeans and wheat as regards international links is quite likely due to the much greater degree of control authorities maintained over the wheat markets compared to that for soybeans. Also, as discussed more below, the period of their analysis also included a period of change in specifications of the ZCE wheat contract. Combined with long periods of minimal trading in wheat at ZCE, it is hardly surprising that there was little evidence of linkage.

Even if it were not connected to international markets, however, China's wheat futures market could have been well-integrated with major domestic markets, mirroring results that numerous studies have found of increased integration between market prices throughout China. In fact, Wang and Ke (2002) found little evidence of such integration. Again, however, the period of their analysis, 1998–2002, is problematic. As noted, there was virtually no trading in the wheat contract for a significant portion of the period. Second, ZCE made significant changes in the specifications of the futures contract in 2000 to accommodate changes made in China's official national standards. Figure 3.9 displays series of representative cash and futures prices from ZCE where it is quite evident that there was a very significant period from 2000 to 2001 when the exchange's own reported cash and futures prices were not closely linked, precisely the period that the specifications for ZCE's wheat futures contract changed. Given the coincidence of new standards with apparent pricing anomalies, it is highly likely that the marked differences between cash and futures prices observed there were somehow related, as for example would happen if the "representative" cash quotation did not immediately reflect the new quality standards. But, whatever the exact cause of the pricing differences during this period, it is clear they were substantial and that any comparison of ZCE's wheat futures prices with other market prices must take them into account.

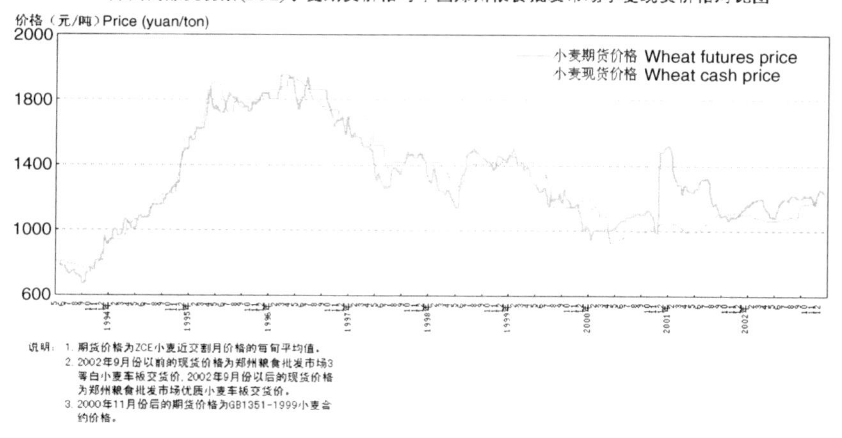

Figure 3.9 Wheat futures prices of ZCE vs. cash prices of China Zhengzhou grain wholesale market (source: ZCE (2002)).

Notes

1 "Futures price" refers to the average price of every ten days in a wheat delivery month.
2 "Cash price before September of 2002" refers to the free on truck price of hard white winter wheat grade 3 on China Zhengzhou Grain Wholesale Market (CZGM), "Cash price after September of 2002" refers to the free on truck price of high quality wheat on CZGM.
3 Futures price after November of 2000 was the same as the price of wheat contract based on National Standard GB1351–1999.

In the single study of pricing on the Shanghai exchange, Fung *et al.* (2003) included copper in the analyses of the relations between prices on US and Chinese exchanges. Copper prices on SHFE, like soybean prices on DCE, were found to be significantly correlated with prices on the US exchange, and the relations were significant in both directions. Prices on the SHFE were correlated with later prices on the New York Mercantile Exchange (NYMEX, formerly the Commodity Exchange), and prices in New York were correlated with later (i.e. next day) prices in Shanghai. Pricing effects were found to be stronger from the US to China, but prices on China's exchange were significant in determining prices in the US. They also found that in copper, like soybeans, price volatility transmitted additional information between markets.

Finally, Chan *et al.* (2004) studied the characteristics of intraday price volatility on China's futures markets and found that they conform very nearly to relations observed on major exchanges elsewhere. With data from 1996–2001 for copper, wheat, and soybeans, the study first identified changes in volatility as levels of trading changed over the period. For wheat and copper, average open interest and volume increased from the first two years (1996–97) to the last four (1998–2001) (see Figure 3.4), and average intraday volatility declined from period to period.[29] Although open interest increased in soybean futures between the two periods, the average volume of trading remained unchanged, as did volatility. More generally, intraday volatility was found to increase when price changes were larger (and there was a greater increase in volatility when the price changes were negative), to decline with higher levels of open interest, to increase when volume was larger, and to increase when there were unanticipated increases in the volume of trading – all comparable to findings from other markets. The authors did not examine whether intraday volatility varied among maturities on each market or whether the choice of the representative contract might affect their measures. In a second study, Liu (2002) examined time-stamped trading records of all participants in the DCE soybean futures market for seven months in 1999–2000, finding that volatility in prices and large trade volumes attracted market-making trading through Dalian's electronic exchange much like that associated open-outcry trading at CBOT. Scalpers' trading comprised some 10 percent of all transactions, but their trading was not sizeable enough to be found to reduce volatility. Only very large volume traders appeared to be informed traders; scalpers and other low volume traders who comprised some 95 percent of the participants were found to be uniformed.

Summary and conclusions

In little more than a decade, trading on China's futures markets has advanced well beyond the frenzied mayhem that characterized early trading on the multitude of exchanges that opened in the first years of the futures experiment. Today, there are three exchanges, and each trades commodities of great importance in China's economy. The Dalian and Zhengzhou exchanges specialize in agricultural products, and the Shanghai exchange in industrial products. The

China Securities and Regulatory Commission has developed comprehensive regulatory capability and each exchange has adopted important trading control mechanisms. The evidence assembled in this paper shows these new markets are assuming increasingly important roles not only supporting the development of markets for the individual commodities in China, but also the linkages between China's markets and others worldwide.

Already, trading on China's exchanges has developed some characteristic patterns. Most activity focuses on contracts when they are several months from maturity – by the time expiration is near both the open interest and volume of trading is very reduced. Trading is also generally at its lowest amount in January and/or February, coincident with the New Year's holidays. Trading in China's agricultural futures also shows no evidence of the sorts of seasonality here-tofore attributed to markets for crops with well-defined production and storage patterns. At the same time, in China imports of both soybeans and wheat have become very important sources of supply. As well, storage of grains and oilseeds has been the responsibility principally of farmers and provincial governments; merchants almost never carry large stocks. Thus, the needs of commercial traders on China's futures markets are likely to be quite different from those typical of large western grain companies.

The distinctive characteristics of trading suggest a host of topics which additional research would clarify in order that the distinctive patterns of trading on China's exchanges are better understood. First, interviews with and studies of the trading of a variety of the typical users of the new exchanges would clarify their importance in China's new market economy. These would also help to explain the aggregate trading data from the exchanges. Second, studies of the convergence of representative cash and futures prices as the futures contract approaches delivery and then as positions close during the delivery month would help assess whether trading-in-the-middle has consequences for traders, for regulators, and for the representativeness of the prices. Third, additional studies might assess the liquidity of contracts when trading is at its greatest and then compare this to liquidity closer to expiration. Finally, it goes without saying that these topics apply equally well to the futures markets for industrial products as they do to agricultural products.

In another sign that the markets are reaching maturity, prices on China's futures exchanges were found to be well integrated with markets both in China and in the rest of the world. In much the same way that a significant body of evidence has accumulated that documents the increased integration of markets throughout China, the results of the several studies cited here document the linkages of futures prices with regional markets and with other international futures markets. Studies of prices on the ZCE wheat futures market were the exception, but the evidence also showed that no study had taken into account ZCE's early difficulties with the contract, significant changes in wheat standards in China, or changing policies in the wheat market more generally. Additional research should clarify these factors.

Additional research needs notwithstanding, the evidence in this paper supports strongly the view that China's futures markets are contributing significantly to the development of markets throughout China. Their success underpins the rapidly spreading impression that such markets can contribute significantly to developing markets for many commodities in China like cotton, maize, sugar, and fuel oil that are now close to approval. Their success is also testament to the persistent hard work of officials at the exchanges and in the regulatory agency to assure all users that the markets themselves functioned properly.

Notes

1 I am grateful to Li Muchun at the Dalian Commodity Exchange and Zhao Wenguang and Lu Xin at the Zhengzhou Commodity Exchange for providing data for this study. Comments or questions are welcome at peck@stanford.edu

2 Drawn from recollections of merchants who participated in the markets. See Chen-Lian-Jia (n.d.), WangLie-Fan (n.d.), and Luo Fen (n.d.).

3 In China, the term "grain" usually included soybeans and various pulses, as well as wheat, rice, and corn. This paper will restrict the use of grain to include wheat, rice and corn, identifying soybeans (or oilseeds) separately.

4 Official concern to maintain significant grain stocks has a very long history in China. *The Book of Rites*, written several centuries BC, recommended reserve stocks should total as much as nine years consumption (Crook, 1997).

5 Rozelle *et al.* (2000) describe the many policies adopted by China's leaders to encourage commercialization of trading by both urban ration shops and provincial grain bureaus. In addition, they include excerpts from many interviews with market participants which provide very useful detail on the effects of the reforms at a very practical level.

6 See Luo and Crook (1997) for a description of the growth in the role of private traders in rice markets throughout southern China. One survey of seven towns in Jiangxi province found there were more than 200 private rice-trading firms in 1996 and a substantially increased number of private rice mills as well.

7 No small irony in the development of futures markets in China is that the early success of markets like ZCE's for mungbeans funded very substantial investments in regional communication infrastructure. See Williams *et al.* (1998) for more detail.

8 See Rozelle *et al.* (2002), Wu (2002), Park *et al.* (2002), and Huang and Rozelle (2002) for a variety of estimates of the degree of integration and its change over time for several commodities.

9 See Crook (1997) for a discussion of the evolution of the new grains policy, the so-called Governors' Grain Bag Policy, as well as an early assessment of its success. Perhaps it was more than coincidence that trading in rice futures was also suspended in 1994 because of dramatic price increases (as noted earlier).

10 See Crook (2000) and Hsu *et al.* (2001) for additional detail.

11 Although soybeans are considered to be a food grain in China, not all food crops were equally important in many policies. In terms of food security, rice, wheat, and corn had highest priority in recent years (Hsu and Crook, 1998).

12 Until 1994, China was a net exporter of soybeans (Crook *et al.*, 1999).

13 Hsu *et al.* (2001) provide more details of the new grading system and argue that the new distinctions of quality wheat might be better identified as "special use" grades. Grade 1 high-gluten wheat, for example, is identified as durum wheat to be used for pasta and spaghetti, grade 2 is hard wheat, for bread and buns, and low-gluten wheat is soft wheat for cakes and biscuits. Grades of regular wheat are intended to distinguish among uses too, from dumplings to instant noodles. The rice standards adopted in 2000 similarly identified several quality categories (Hsu and Liu, 2001).

14 Drawn from Tuan and Hsu (2001) unless otherwise noted.

15 In 1996, for example, China announced tariff-rate quotas would be applied to soybeans, but quotas were never implemented (Diao, 1997).
16 See Wall and Wei (1994) and Fry (1994). Estimated total volume of trading is derived from data in ZCE *Annual Reports*. Estimates of the number of the early exchanges and amount of trading vary considerably. According to Yao (1998) for example, there were more than 60 futures exchanges in China by mid-1994 with seven in Shanghai alone. Also, estimated volume figures often record both the buy and the sell transaction as separate, thereby double counting each transaction, and making comparisons among sources especially difficult.
17 Yao (1998) describes the episode in detail.
18 In addition to approval from Henan Province, ZCE's rules would become the basis for national legislation.
19 Drawn from ZCE *Annual Reports* and Hoo (2000). See Williams *et al.* (1998) for a discussion of various contract development issues as well as trader concerns that ZCE officials dealt with from 1993–98.
20 Soybean meal is also traded at DCE and rubber at SHFE. A mungbean contract is still listed at ZCE but there is no trading.
21 Data here and elsewhere in this paper measure positions (or trades) on one side of the market only.
22 They are not unknown, however. In September 2003, substantial losses by investors trading (illegal) rubber futures at the Hainan Rubber Wholesale Center reportedly led to bomb threats at the Center. The status of the Center's trading in two-month contracts written by its members remains unclear, approved by the provincial government and not under direct supervision of the CSRC (AFX News Limited, AFX-Asia, 26 September 2003). Moreover, there continue to be reports that some brokerage firms are "given to trading on their own account to the disadvantage of clients" (Skorecki, 2004) despite CSRC prohibition of such practices.
23 The Central China National Cotton Exchange, China's first spot market for cotton, opened in Zhengzhou in May 2003, presumably to create a basis for the exchange's development of a cotton futures much as did the establishment of ZGWM in 1990 for the subsequent opening of ZCE (Comtex News Network, Sinocast, 16 May 2003).
24 Data were expressed as percentages of each contract's average volume (or open interest) and averaged by months remaining to expiration.
25 The November 2003 soybean contract, for example, started trading in May 2002.
26 See Peck (1979–80) for a discussion of the seasonality evident in levels of trading of the CBOT wheat, corn, and soybean futures.
27 Luo and Crook (1997) noted that many private trading firms which market much of China's rice crop typically hold very small stocks, operating more like a "just-in-time" auto assembly plant than a large western grain company. They argue that until market risks for traders (especially risks associated with abrupt changes in government policies) are lower, it is unlikely that traders will be willing to store rice in any significant amount.
28 This statement is based on regressions of total volume of trading in each contract maturity (or total month-end open interest) on a trend and a set of contract-specific zero-one variables. ZCE wheat was not included in these tests because there were too few observations.
29 In addition, the results were robust to changes in the comparison periods to 1996–98 and 1999–2001 (Chan *et al.*, 2004).

References

Chan, Kam C., Hung-Gay Fung, and Wai K. Leung (2004), "Intraday Volatility Behavior in Chinese Futures Markets," *Journal of International Financial Markets, Institutions, and Money*, forthcoming, accessed at: www.207.36.165.114/Denver/Papers/Johnny1.pdf.

ChenLian-Jia (no date) "The Flour and Wheat Bran Market in Shanghai and Its Trading Regulation," 8 ms. pages.

China Securities Regulatory Commission (n.d.) "Table 6.1 Trading Volume Summary of Future" and "Table 6.2 Items Distribution of Future Trading Volume I and II," accessed at. www.csrc.gov.cn.

Colby, Hunter, Xinshen Diao, and Agapi Somwaru (2000), *Cross-Commodity Analysis of China's Grain Sector: Sources of Growth and Supply Response*, Market and Trade Economics Division, Economic Research Service, US Department of Agriculture, Technical Bulletin 1884, May.

Crook, Frederick (1997), "Current Agricultural Policies Highlight Concerns About Food Security," in USDA (1997), 19–25.

—— (1998), "Agricultural Policies in 1998: Stability and Change," in USDA (1998a), 8–10.

—— (2000), "China is Awash in Grain," in USDA (2000), 8–12.

Crook, Frederick W. and W. Hunter Colby (1996), *The Future of China's Grain Market*, Economic Research Service, US Department of Agriculture, Agricultural Information Bulleting 730, October.

Crook, Frederick, Suchada Langley, and Francis Tuan (1999), "An Analysis of PRC Government Involvement in Domestic and Foreign Trade of Wheat, Rice, and Soybeans and Soybean Products," draft paper for discussion only, Conference of China's Role in World Food Markets, February, accessed at: www.china.wsu.edu/pubs/pdf-98/crook2–3.pdf

Diao, Xinshen (1997), "China Becoming a Net Importer of Oilseeds, Oil, and Meal," in USDA (1997), 36–40.

Durham, Catharine A. and Wenguang Si (1999), "The Dalian Commodity Exchange's Soybean Futures Contract: China's Integration with World Commodity Markets," accessed at: www.china.wsu.edu/pubs/pdf-99/2-Durham.pdf.

The Economist (1995) "Derivatives Exchanges: The Mung Bean and Its Adventures," 27 May, p. 70.

Fry, J. (1994), "The Regulation of Commodity Exchanges: an International Comparison," *Landell Mills Commodities Studies*, R878, Trowbridge, UK. Manuscript only.

Fung, Hung-Gay, Wai K, Leung, and Xaioqing Eleanor Xu (2003), "Information Flows Between the U.S. and China Commodity Futures Trading," *Review of Quantitative Finance and Accounting*, 21, 267–85.

Gale, Fred (ed.) (2002), *China's Food and Agriculture: Issues for the 21st Century*, Market and Trade Economics Division, Economic Research Service, US Department of Agriculture, Agricultural Information Bulletin 775, April.

Gilmour, Brad and Fred Gale (2002), "Transportation and Distribution: Will Bottlenecks Be Eliminated?" in Gale (2002), 24–26.

Guo Xiaoli and Li Muchun (2003), "Tracking the Forces Behind Volume Patterns," *Futures*, November, 46–50.

Hoo, Stephanie (2000), "China Zhengzhou Commodity Bourse Strives to Lift Volume," *Wall Street Journal*, 20 June.

Hsu, Hsin-Hui (2000) "China Switches from Soymeal to Soybean Imports," in USDA (2000), 13–16.

Hsu, Hsin-Hui and Frederick Crook (1998), "Despite Rise of Market Forces, Continued

Government Intervention in China's Soybean Economy Adds Uncertainty in World Oilseed Markets," in USDA (1998b).

Hsu, Hsin-Hui and Fred Gale (2001), "USDA Revision of China Grain Stock Estimates," in USDA (2001), 53–66.

Hsu, Hsin-Hui and Guicai Liu (2001), "Tradeoffs Between Quantity and Quality of China's Rice," in USDA (2001), 26–29.

Hsu, Hsin-Hui, Bryan Lohmar, and Fred Gale (2001), "Surplus Wheat Production Brings Emphasis on Quality," in USDA (2001), 17–25.

Huang, Jikun and Scott Rozelle (2002), "The Nature of Distortions to Agricultural Incentives in China and Implications of WTO Accession," Working Paper 02–006, Department of Agricultural and Resource Economics, University of California Davis, February.

—— (2003), "China's Maize Economy and Policy," in CIMMYT/IFAD/IFPRI *Synthesis Report of the Collaborative Multi-County Study on Maize Policies in Asia*, draft version.

—— and Francis Tuan (1999), "China's Agriculture, Trade, and Productivity in the 21st Century," in *Proceedings of Chinese Agriculture and the WTO: A Workshop*, 2–3 December, Seattle, Washington, 1–30.

Lardy, Nicholas (2001), "Integrating China in the Global Economy," Brookings Institution, Washington DC.

Legget, Karby (2000), "In Beijing, the Futures Look a Bit Grim – Commodities 'Experiment' Now is a Thing of the Past," *Wall Street Journal*, 28 June, C1.

Li Jingmou (1996), "Development, Problems and Strategies of China's Futures Markets," the Sixth Annual Asia–Pacific Futures Research Symposium. *Research Symposium Proceedings*, Winter 1995, 313–24. Chicago: Chicago Board of Trade.

Liu, Dongquing (2002), "Market-Making Behavior in Futures Markets," unpublished Ph.D. dissertation, University of California at Davis, June.

Luo Fen (No date), "Spots and Forward Business of Rice Market Prior to 1949," ms. 5 pages.

Luo, Xiao-peng and Frederick Crook (1997), "The Emergence of Private Rice Marketing in South China," in USDA (1997) p. 32–35.

Park, Albert, Hehui Jin, Scott Rozelle, and Jikun Huang (2002), "Market Emergence and Transition: Arbitrage, Transaction Costs, and Autarky in China's Grain Markets," *American Journal of Agricultural Economics*, 84(1), February, 67–82.

Peck, Anne, E. (1979–80), "Reflections of Hedging on Futures Markets Activity," *Food Research Institute Studies*, XVII, 3, 327–49.

Rozelle, Scott, Albert Park, Jikun Huang, and Hehui Jin (2000), "Bureaucrat to Entrepreneur: The Changing Role of the State in China's Grain Economy," *Economic Development and Cultural Change*, 48(2) January, 227–52.

Shanghai Futures Exchange (monthly), *Monthly Report*, accessed at: www.shfe.com.cn.

Skorecki, Alex (2004), "China Looks to the Future of Finance: New Rules Will Allow Locals and Foreigners to Trade Financial Derivatives," *Financial Times*, 11 February.

Sun Min (2004), "Brighter Prospects for Chinese Futures Market," *China Daily*, 5 January, accessed at: www.chinadaily.com.

Tarallo, Mark (2002), "The Futures of China's Futures Market," *Futures Industry Magazine*, January/February.

Tuan, Francis and Hsin-Hui Hsu (2001), "U.S.–China Bilateral WTO Agreement and Beyond," in USDA (2001), 5–8.

US Department of Agriculture (1997) *China: Situation and Outlook Series* (Frederick Crook, editor) Economic Research Service WRS-97–3, June.

—— (1998a) *China: Situation and Outlook Series* (Frederick Crook, report coordinator) ERS, International Agriculture and Trade Reports, WRS-98–3, July.

—— (1998b) *Oil Crops Situation and Outlook Yearbook*, Economic Research Service, OCS 1998, October.

—— (2000) *China: Situation and Outlook Series* (Hsin-Hui Hsu and Michael Lopez, report coordinators) Economic Research Service WRS-99–4, March.

—— (2001) *China: Agriculture in Transition* (Hsin-Hui Hsu and Fred Gale, report coordinators) Market and Trade Economics Division, Economic Research Service, US Dept of Agriculture, Agriculture and Trade Report WRS-01–2, November.

Wall, D. and Wei, J. (1994), "Futures Markets in China," University of Sussex, the Chinese Economy Programme.

Wang, Holly H. and Bingfan Ke (2002), "Efficiency Tests of Agricultural Commodity Futures Markets in China," 4 June, accessed under: www.bm.ust.hk (a somewhat edited version dated September 2003 but with the same title was available at www.iaae-agecon.org/conf/durban_papers/papers/045.pdf).

Wang, Xinzheng and Hang Chang (1997), "China Struggles with Derivatives Market Growth," *Futures Industry*, June/July, 19–21.

WangLie-Fan (no date), "The Formation and Development of the Soybean Cake and Oil Market in Shanghai," ms. 5 pages.

Williams, Jeffrey, Anne Peck, Albert Park, and Scott Rozelle (1998), "The Emergence of a Futures Market: Mungbeans on the China Zhengzhou Commodity Exchange," *Journal of Futures Markets*, 18(4), 427–48.

Wu, Laping (2002), "Grain Market Integration and Marketing Margin in China," Technical Report China Economy Papers CE02–3, Asia Pacific School of Economics and Government accessed at: http://eprints.anu.edu.au/archive/00001494.

Wu, S. (1996), "Critical Issues Haunt China's Futures Market," *China Finance*, August, 8–9.

Yao, Chengxi (1998), *Stock and Futures Market in the People's Republic of China*, Hong Kong and New York: Oxford University Press.

Zhao, Jinwen (2002), "Cointegration Analysis of Commodity Futures Prices in Dalian, China and Chicago," *Journal of Emerging Markets*, 7(1).

Zhengzhou Commodity Exchange (annual), *Annual Report*, Zhengzhou China.

4 Issues and research opportunities in agricultural futures markets

Philip Garcia, Raymond M. Leuthold and Thorsten M. Egelkraut

Abstract

This chapter provides a selected review of research literature and contributions to commodity futures markets, focusing primarily on empirical studies. The topics featured include the development of intertemporal price relationships, hedging, price behavior and market efficiency, liquidity costs, and how the trading environment has been affected by fund behavior and the movement to electronic exchanges. Each theme is introduced by assessing the recent contributions. We then identify and motivate future research challenges for agricultural futures markets.

Introduction

Research directions in agricultural futures markets must be based on a vision of the future as well as an understanding of past literature. At the present, agricultural commodity markets are in transition. Producer numbers continue to decline, while producers grow in size, and economic and managerial sophistication. Cash markets are declining in importance, while cash contracting, vertical coordination and insurance programs are expanding. Governments are stepping back from agricultural markets, and global markets with the level of competition they imply are a reality. Demand and supply shocks in these global markets produce a volatile and risky environment in which producers and firms must make daily decisions. Agricultural firms are consolidating and searching for ways to expand their operations to insure their survival. Futures exchanges are also adapting to this new environment, changing their structure and services.

This paper provides a discussion of selected issues and research opportunities in agricultural commodity futures markets. The discussion focuses primarily on the recent empirical literature aimed at resolving the most current issues, and identifies future research challenges in the light of emerging patterns in markets.

Risk management and marketing strategies

Risk management is often identified as the primary rationale for the existence of futures markets. The dominant paradigm used to investigate risk management opportunities in futures markets is the portfolio model where firms select an optimal hedge to maximize expected utility. The conceptual model introduced by Johnson (1960) and Stein (1961) for hedging in a single holding period for a given quantity was extended to include production uncertainty, cross hedging, multiple markets in multiple periods (e.g. McKinnon, 1967; Holthausen, 1979; Anderson and Danthine, 1980, 1983).

Empirical research has concentrated on identifying the optimal hedge and determining its hedging effectiveness, i.e. the percentage reduction in the variability of the unhedged position (Ederington, 1979). Researchers have focused on estimating minimum risk optimal hedges rather than utility maximizing hedges, appealing to a mean-variance framework, market efficiency, and ease of estimation. This focus greatly simplifies analysis, but the simplification comes at a cost.

Empirical findings identify benefits to hedging. The magnitude of the optimal hedges and their effectiveness vary by the situation and market characteristics. However, most optimal hedges are often close to but less than one, indicating the presence of basis risk, and reduce the variability of returns (e.g. Mathews and Holthausen, 1991). Studies provide evidence that production risk reduces hedge ratios and their effectiveness under risk minimization (e.g. Grant, 1989; Lapan and Moschini, 1994). Dynamic hedging models for producers where hedges are revised have been formulated with and without stochastic production (Anderson and Danthine, 1983; Lence *et al.*, 1994). The limited analysis suggests that the gains from the dynamic hedging for producers are small relative to conventional approaches (Martinez and Zering, 1992). Hedging long-term commodity price risk through rollover hedging where the portfolio of contracts is rebalanced has generated a few studies. Gardner (1989) reports that rollover hedging reduces risk for cotton, soybeans, and corn. Veld-Merkoulova and de Roon (2003), using a hedging strategy that minimizes cash and rollover risk, find that the variance of the naïve hedge is reduced by 50 percent for orange juice and lumber. Dynamic models for market participants formulated as time-varying optimal hedges also offer opportunities to improve hedging effectiveness (Baillie and Myers, 1991).

Research on optimal hedging in multiple markets has provided mixed results. Miller (1985) finds modest support for the value of simple and multiple cross-hedges when he examined cross-hedging for products not traded on exchanges. In contrast, Grant and Eaker (1989), who investigated cross-hedging for commodities with and without contracts and with multiple futures, report no evidence of the value of cross-hedging beyond naïve hedging. Other multiproduct studies focused on developing optimal hedges in production-related markets, such as the soybean complex or corn–livestock complex, identify substantial differences between the naïve and optimal hedges (Noussinov and Leuthold, 1999), and report reductions in the variability of returns particularly when dynamic-hedging decisions in markets are made simultaneously rather than independently (Fackler and McNew, 1993; Garcia *et al.*, 1995). Similar results have been reported for multiproduct dynamic hedging in international grain trading where exchange rates, commodity prices, and freight rates are hedged (Haigh and Holt, 2000).

Hedges are often placed selectively to secure basis appreciation or profitable trading opportunities. Kenyon and Clay (1987) find that selective profit-margin hedging for hogs raised average profit and/or reduced its variance. Kenyon and Beckman (1997) identified opportunities for selective hedging in a multiple-year context for corn and soybeans allowing for different marketing triggers. While risky, appropriate strategies can improve producer returns. Combined with forecasts, selective hedging can also reduce the variability in returns (Brandt, 1985; Park *et al.*, 1989).

Recent studies have investigated the effects of government and insurance programs on the use of derivatives. Hanson *et al.* (1999) examined the use of both futures and options when the cash price distribution is truncated due to government programs. Coble *et al.* (2000) and Mahul (2003) investigated the effects of yield and revenue insurance programs on hedging using options or futures markets in the presence of price, yield, and basis risk. These studies suggest that cash price truncation creates an important role for options combined with futures contracts in managing price and quantity risk. Yield insurance programs are complementary to hedging in futures or options while revenue insurance results in lower hedging demand.

Despite findings that identify their value, important challenges have emerged regarding the relevance and usefulness of optimal hedge ratios, particularly when calculated using a minimum risk model. Questions have been spurred by discrepancies between surveys that showed that less than 10 percent of producers use futures contracts despite research indicating that producers should be hedging more. Studies on the activities of commercial firms (Hartzmark, 1988; Peck and Nahmias, 1989) also reported significant inconsistencies between actual and model-derived hedges.

Recent research sheds light on these discrepancies. Lence (1995, 1996), who compares risk-minimizing to utility-maximizing hedge ratios for producers when the assumptions that guarantee their equivalence are relaxed, finds that utility-maximizing optimal hedges deviate substantially from the risk-minimizing hedge and are highly sensitive to borrowing, lending and investing opportunities, transactions costs, and the production stochasticity. In realistic scenarios, he finds the optimal hedge is zero, and demonstrates that the economic value of more precise estimation of risk-minimizing hedge ratios is quite small. Collins (1997) argues that hedging is motivated by avoidance of financial failure rather than by a desire to reduce income variability. Because hedging is costly, producers do not hedge, unless the initial equity of the firm plus expected revenues from the sale of the product is insufficient to meet total financial obligations. Collins' findings are supported by Arias *et al.* (2000), who examined hedging under nonlinear borrowing costs, progressive tax rates, and liquidity constraints. In plausible scenarios, farmers hedge little or not at all.

Pennings and colleagues have examined the determinants of actual hedging behavior. Pennings and Leuthold (2000) find that risk perceptions and attitudes affect hedging along with such factors as debt-to-asset ratios, market orientation, and entrepreneurial behavior but not in a homogenous manner. Pennings and Garcia (2004), using a sample of small and medium-sized enterprises (i.e. hog producers, wholesalers, and processors), also encounter heterogeneity. Risk exposure, size of the firm, financial leverage, risk attitude and risk perceptions, and the level of education all affect hedging, but not in a similar manner. Segments of the industry differ in their decision-making process, organizational structure, and influence of the decision-making unit. The findings confirm that hedging and capital structure decisions are linked and that risk attitudes and perceptions influence hedging.

Research opportunities for hedging are closely linked to developing more general risk management strategies. Researchers have begun to investigate the inconsistency between model-derived hedging recommendations and producer behavior, but further work is needed to explain the gap. It seems critical to develop a better understanding of decision-makers and their environment.

The first issue is to develop a more systematic understanding of their goals, objectives, constraints, and alternatives. What is a realistic objective, and how should risk be measured? Recent research identifies the importance of the linkage between hedging and the investment/capital structure. It seems inappropriate to only consider price risk of a commodity; should we consider also income risk of the farm, or risk of the total firm's equity, which can include land values? The choice of risk measure can have a large impact on whether or not to use futures markets for hedging. Lence (1995, 1996) and Coble *et al.* (2000) also suggest the importance of transaction costs of the relevant marketing alternatives. What are the relevant marketing alternatives? Yield and revenue insurance programs must be considered in more depth. Research is needed to identify the relationships between hedging and insurance programs for other crops, using procedures that jointly determine choices among a portfolio of hedging and insurance alternatives. In addition, as agricultural marketing systems have become more vertically coordinated through integration and contracting, we must expand our ability to identify their effects on producer decisions and derivative use. Hedging can take many forms in practice, and it seems appropriate to consider more comprehensively the effectiveness of selective strategies and their applicability for producers and firms (e.g. Kenyon and Beckman, 1997).

A second issue emerges in investigating producer behavior – the development of good data and their applicability to individual producers. The characterization and estimation of the probability distributions of commodity prices and crop yields remain elusive. Yields are farm-specific. Research is needed to improve measures for understanding of price, basis, and yield risks. Decision makers need information about changes in price distributions as the marketing year progresses in order to make informed decisions. Can we develop a better understanding of the factors influencing basis volatility (e.g. Garcia *et al.*, 1984), and generate more timely basis forecasts (Tomek, 1993; Garcia and Sanders, 1996)? Can we develop useful forecasts of future volatility in prices at nearby and distant horizons (Manfredo *et al.*, 2001)?

Finally, we need more information on producer preferences for risk and other factors that affect actual behavior. Risk preferences can drive choices, but preferences are context-specific so it is important to identify the specific situation, and the conditioning factors such as equity and income that affect choice. For example, Yoon and Brorsen (2002) ask: why do farmers store in the presence of inverted markets that provide a signal to sell? They conclude that anchoring, overconfidence, and regret, concepts from behavioral finance theory, may offer explanations. It is also important to determine if segments of producers exist so that information, strategies, and programs can be developed to address their marketing problems (Pennings and Garcia, 2004).

To this point, we have focused primarily on producers, but many of these issues are relevant for firms. For example, what are firms' risk-management strategies and what role do futures and options play? In a portfolio context, Lence (1996) argues that grain elevators and other firms in related industries should be motivated to hedge to reduce price risks. Hartzmark (1988) reports that commercial firms hedge on a one-to-one basis regardless of price movements, and Peck and Nahmias (1989) find little relationship between optimal hedges and actual behavior. Williams (1987) suggests that reducing transaction costs rather than risk reduction is the primary motivation for firms to use the futures market. Pennings and Garcia (2004) find that firms' hedging behavior is heterogeneous and affected by risk exposure, leverage, size, the influence of the decision making unit, and the owner's risk perceptions and attitudes. Research is needed to integrate and develop a more comprehensive view of firms' futures market use. For firms where the use of futures and options is part of their operations, new procedures to assist them in identifying attractive risk management strategies are needed.[1] Lien and Tse's (2002) review of hedging developments may provide useful ideas.

Price and volatility behavior

Intertemporal price relationships for storables

Working (1948, 1949) formulated a model of cash-futures price relationships where intertemporal price relationships, or spot-futures and nearby-distant price differences, both positive and negative, are viewed as prices of storage. These price spreads provide incentives or disincentives to store and hedge commodities.

Intertemporal price relationships are determined by the net cost of carrying stocks. The futures price for any delivery month is equal to the current spot price plus the cost of storage, which includes physical outlay costs, interest charges, and possibly a risk premium. When stock levels are low, the return for storage can be negative, and an inverse (negative) carrying charge is said to exist as physical costs are dominated by a negative cost, the convenience yield. Marginal convenience yield decreases as aggregate inventory increases, approaching zero at high inventory levels. This yield implies stockholding firms involved in merchandising and processing may retain inventory or working stocks to accommodate these services, despite holding stocks at a loss. The grain industry refers to this inverse carrying charge as backwardation, meaning a price premium exists for early delivery.[2] Williams (1987, p. 1001) points out that prices for more distant delivery months are nearly always less than prices for earlier delivery, including immediate delivery, after allowance for the full costs of carry. Often these spreads are so far below full carry costs that they are negative. Why does backwardation exist?

To date, the cause of backwardation remains an open issue. Early work offered support for the supply-of-storage concept and convenience yield.[3] However, Wright and Williams (1989) suggest that the appearance of convenience yield may be due to aggregation of data or mismeasurement. Brennan *et al.* (1997) apply a mathematical programming model to the wheat marketing system of Western Australia and find that if intertemporal prices are measured at the local level, stocks are not held at a monetary loss, and the apparent loss is an illusion caused by spatial aggregation. Benirschka and Binkley (1995) also demonstrate that backwardation may occur when measured in prices at a central market, but not at production points where storage occurs.

Frechette and Fackler (1999) however find no evidence that location of stocks matters when examining the US corn market. Sorensen (2002) models the seasonality in corn, soybeans, and wheat futures prices and provides evidence for the theory of storage, detecting a strong negative relationship between stocks and convenience yields. Using more conventional procedures, Yoon and Brorsen (2002) investigated market spreads, aggregate US stocks, and the carrying charge for storage by producers for corn, soybeans, and wheat. Consistent with the price of storage, market inversions rarely occur during early months of the crop year when stocks levels are high. Market inversions occur most frequently across crop years and near the end of the crop year.[4]

Several research opportunities are available to develop a better understanding of backwardation in price spreads, and between cash and forward prices. Recent work offers several explanations for these inverted markets: mismeasurement and improper aggregation of data, transaction costs, and the conventional inventory/convenience yield explanation. Some evidence shows that backwardation may not exist where commodities are stored. Yet, not all studies support this conclusion. Special attention needs to be given to the data and aggregation issues.

Market efficiency

In an efficient market, prices should reflect available information such that price changes represent only random departures from previous prices. Further, if futures prices fully reflect all available information, then they provide the "best" forecast (in terms of bias and efficiency) of cash prices.[5]

Weak and semi-strong form empirical tests (Fama, 1970, 1991) have been performed to assess efficiency in agricultural futures markets. The weak-form evidence is mixed, and is heavily dependent on the sample period, the commodity tested, the type of data, and technique used (Garcia *et al.*, 1988). With regards to randomness in prices, Kamara (1984) concludes that futures prices have some degree of low-level serial correlation, but it is not clear whether these can be profitably used. Acceptance of the null that returns are serially independent means that markets are efficient, but failure to accept the null is not evidence of market inefficiency (Danthine, 1977). Efficiency requires the lack of buying and selling rules that have expected returns greater than zero.

This idea led researchers to assess the effectiveness of mechanical trading rules at generating profits. Many researchers have simulated trading and some have found profits (e.g. Peterson and Leuthold, 1982). In the most comprehensive study of agricultural markets, Lukac *et al.* (1988) simulated portfolios of 12 commodities and 12 trading systems. Out-of-sample results demonstrated that the short-run futures price movements could lead to positive net returns. Irwin *et al.* (1997) used a technical trading system to investigate trading profits for the soybean complex. Their findings support Lukac *et al.* (1988), but suggest that profits were declining in more recent periods. Further evidence that the effectiveness of technical trading is declining is provided by Hamm and Brorsen (2000) who report no significant profits from trading the wheat futures market using neural networks.[6]

The evidence on the weak-form forecasting ability of futures prices is somewhat mixed. Goss (1981) indicates that futures prices for discontinuous inventory and non-inventory commodities are not unbiased predictors, while continuous inventory commodities are better forecasters. Goss identifies that the absence of inventories may lead to gaps in the flow of information or increase errors in expectations because of the lack of close ties between cash and futures prices. Garcia *et al.* (1988) report that livestock markets do not perform as well as storable grains, and attribute the difference to storability and supply response within the year. Forecasting ability of futures prices is affected by the time-to-maturity. At longer forecast horizons, forecasts become less precise as more unexpected information enters the market.

Recently, cointegration and error-correction models have been used to test for unbiasness and efficiency. Aulton *et al.* (1997) investigated the efficiency of three UK futures markets and the results provide evidence of long-run efficiency for wheat and pigmeat, but not for potatoes. Short-run inefficiencies also occur in the pigmeat and potato markets which the authors attribute to low trading volume and possible quality differences. Kellard *et al.* (1999) assess the forecast efficiency of the soybean, live hogs, and live cattle markets. They determine that these markets are efficient in the long run, but encounter short-run inefficiencies, particularly in the live cattle market. They conclude due to the variability in returns that it would be difficult to imagine that a risk-averse trader would use these models. McKenzie and Holt (2002) extend the error-correction framework to allow for a time-varying risk premium. Their results indicate that live cattle, hogs, corn, and soybean meal are both efficient and unbiased in the long run. Soybean meal futures prices are also efficient and unbiased in the short run.

However, live cattle, hogs, and corn futures markets exhibited short-run inefficiencies and pricing biases. Risks premiums were found in cattle and hog markets.

The most popular method of semi-strong form tests with agricultural futures data compares econometrically forecasted prices generated using available public information (e.g. Leuthold and Hartmann, 1979). [Other methods employed are the forecast error approach (e.g. Goss, 1987) and the event studies approach (see *Price discovery* section below)]. The test is not sufficient to assess efficiency because it does not examine if the risk-adjusted profits from using the model exceed the cost of model construction and its use. Empirical results of studies that consider this condition are mixed. Rausser and Carter (1983), citing findings not presented, indicate that the soybean meal complex was inefficient. Garcia *et al.* (1988) and Leuthold *et al.* (1989) developed econometric models that forecast better than futures markets for cattle and hogs. For cattle, the risk-return ratios from trading were centered on zero and quite high, providing no evidence of inefficiency. In contrast, simulated trading for hogs generated volatile but high profits, suggesting inefficiency. Recently, Goss *et al.* (2001) note little evidence of price inefficiency in the cattle market using this criterion.

Overall, the findings from the efficiency tests of randomness and forecasting ability are rather consistent with economists' views that, in the long run, futures markets are efficient, but that in the short run, inefficiencies may exist for periods (Malkiel, 2003). Tomek (1997) argues that little additional resources should be spent studying efficiency, and in principal we concur. Nevertheless, new information, new techniques, and new insights will deserve consideration, but their success seems unlikely. If research is undertaken, we need to ask for more than statistical significance; consistent risk-adjusted returns are the gauge. Findings also need to pass a "reality check" for data snooping (e.g. Sullivan *et al.*, 1997; White, 2000), and post-sample assessment is essential.

Risk premium

One standard of pricing efficiency has been that the futures price is an unbiased estimate of the unobservable spot price. If this condition is not met, a source of the bias is the presence of a risk premium. The risk premium concept spawned many studies in the 1950s and 1960s, which concluded that the existence of a bias in price related to a risk premium was highly unlikely (Gray and Rutledge, 1971). In recent studies, the findings appear to be influenced by the procedure used and the model employed to represent the risk premium. For example, Fama and French (1987) and Kolb (1992) report only limited evidence of a constant risk premium based on the study of numerous commodities. However, as noted, McKenzie and Holt (2002), using an ARCH-in-mean error-correction, find time-varying risk premiums for live cattle and hogs.

The research identified above was conducted in isolated markets, but risk premiums may also exist in a portfolio framework. Dusak (1973) utilized the capital-asset pricing model to empirically test for a risk premium with futures contracts of wheat, corn, and soybeans, and found that for routine long positions systematic risk and average realized returns were close to zero, providing evidence against a systematic risk premium. Ehrhardt *et al.* (1987) and Park *et al.* (1988), using arbitrage pricing models, also report little evidence of a risk premium. In contrast, using asset-pricing models that allow expected returns and risk premiums to vary over time, Bessembinder and Chan (1992) and Bjornson and Carter (1997) discover evidence of non-trivial time-varying risk premium in several commodity futures markets. In a very different framework, de Roon *et al.* (2000) assess the effect of hedging pressure (i.e. the net position of hedgers) on futures risk premiums for 20 futures markets. Consistent with a risk premium, they observe that both own-hedging pressure and cross-hedging pressure are important in explaining returns.

The debate over the existence of risk premiums will likely continue with new theoretical models, new data, and empirical results. The measurement of a risk premium is complicated because it appears to be model-specific, and depends on the data and procedures employed. Recent evidence appears to indicate that it may be time varying in nature (McKenzie and Holt, 2002; Bjornson and Carter, 1997). The work on hedging pressure suggests that premiums may be consistent with market activities by hedgers (de Roon *et al.*, 2000), but the magnitudes and their economic significance are yet to be determined.

Changing volatility of futures prices

As early as the 1950s, Kendall (1953) noticed that Chicago wheat futures prices exhibited non-constant variances. Samuelson (1965) contended that futures prices should exhibit increased volatility as they approach their maturity, a time-to-maturity effect. Anderson and Danthine (1983) argued that volatility is related to information flows. They contend that futures prices are volatile when uncertainty is being resolved and stable when little uncertainty is resolved. Increased volatility does not have to occur as maturity approaches, but may be influenced by the commodity characteristics. This intuitive notion is consistent with observations that information shocks during important periods of crop growth and when inventories are low have differential impacts on price changes. Yang and Brorsen (1993), Chatrath *et al.* (2002), and Adrangi and Chatrath (2003) using extensive data sets confirm time-varying variances influenced by seasonal and time-to-maturity effects.[7]

Several studies have investigated the determinants of volatility. Anderson (1985) notes that seasonality, particularly for grains, is the primary factor affecting the volatility of prices. Kenyon *et al.* (1987) also find that seasonal variables capture both the seasonal and time-to-maturity effects, but not the influence of lagged volatility, and current loan rates. Peck (1981) and Ward (1974) argue that the degree of speculative behavior can affect the variability of prices. Contrary to expectations, Peck (1981) finds an inverse relationship between speculation and price variability and argues that allegations of "excess speculation" are unwarranted. Cornell (1981) discovers a relationship between daily volume and price variability. Brorsen (1989), investigating the liquidity costs and returns to scalpers in the corn market, finds that seasonality and volume are also important in explaining the variability of returns. Streeter and Tomek (1992) postulate a general model to explain the monthly volatility of soybean prices. They determine that the Samuelson effect is nonlinear, and that seasonality is important during the summer months. Speculators do not dominate hedgers, but when speculation is large, price variability declines. Concentration of open interest by large traders increases volatility, and a lag in variability exists.

Bessembinder and Seguin (1993) investigated the effects of expected and unexpected volume and open interest on price volatility for cotton and wheat. Conditional volatility is positively related to expected and unexpected volume, with the response to unexpected volume greatly exceeding the effect of expected volume. The effect of unexpected volume on volatility is asymmetric: positive unexpected volume shocks exceed the effects of negative shocks. Unexpected open interest (a proxy for market depth) reduces the variability in prices. Using conditional heteroskedasticity models, Goodwin and Schnepf (2000) analyze the determinants of price variability for US corn and wheat futures markets. Consistent with the literature, price variability is significantly influenced by inventories, futures markets variables (e.g. volume/open interest), growing conditions, and seasonality. Time-to-maturity is significant for corn but not for wheat. Crain and Lee (1996), using wheat prices for a long-time span, confirm that volatility is highly influenced by changes in government programs. They report seasonal patterns in the volatility which are small in comparison to the program effects. Volatility in futures and cash prices interact, but volatility is primarily transferred from futures to cash prices.

We need to increase our understanding of the determinants of price changes, the interaction among prices, and volatility (e.g. Goodwin and Schnepf, 2000). Clearly, a better understanding of these factors can provide private and governmental decision-makers with information to design effective policies, and may eventually lead to more effective forecasts of price volatility. This understanding may become particularly important as new markets with different levels of liquidity and different microstructures emerge in a global economy.

Price discovery and trading environment

Price discovery

Price discovery is an important aspect of understanding how markets relate, coordinate and share, and process information. For futures markets price discovery refers to how prices are "established" in the market for a particular transaction. Futures markets should generate prices that express the markets view of subsequent cash prices, and transmit that information quickly to the marketing system (Tomek, 1979–80). Garbade and Silber (1983) developed an equilibrium model of simultaneous price dynamics to investigate the transmission of information between cash and futures markets. Examining the relationship between daily cash and futures prices for four storable commodities, they conclude that futures markets generally dominate cash markets in registering and transmitting information.

Various research techniques have subsequently been used to address this topic. For example, Schroeder and Goodwin (1991) used Granger causality on live cattle and hogs, respectively, and found that information is discovered first in the futures market, and then transferred to cash markets. Koontz *et al.* (1990) extended the analysis in the live cattle market to investigate the spatial as well as temporal interaction between cash and futures markets. Their findings demonstrated a high degree of interaction between the cash and futures, with the futures tending to dominate in the pricing process, but that pricing relationships changed over time, suggesting that the price discovery process is effective and dynamic. Bessler and Covey (1991) and Schroeder and Goodwin (1991) were the first to apply the cointegration framework to examine the relationship between daily futures and cash prices. Both studies find only limited evidence of long-run cash-futures price linkages for live cattle and hogs. Recent work by Yang *et al.* (2001), and Fortenbery and Zapata (1993, 1997) confirms that futures markets play the dominant role in the price discovery process for storable and non-storable commodities.

However, further research is needed on factors affecting price transmissions. For example, insufficient volume, lack of liquidity and institutional constraints can hinder the development of long-run linkages between cash and futures prices as discovered by Fortenbery and Zapata (1997), Maynard *et al.* (2001), and Kuiper *et al.* (2002).

Alternatively, the idea that prices reflect new or unexpected information and that the information is transmitted quickly through the marketing system has been examined using event studies and by assessing the interaction between cash and futures markets in the price-discovery process. Event studies have focused on the effects of production information in the USDA reports on price behavior. Early work demonstrated that futures prices generally react quickly to the release of USDA livestock and crop reports (e.g. Sumner and Mueller, 1989). However, Sumner and Mueller (1989) and Fortenbery and Sumner (1993) identify the informational value of crop reports was declining after 1984. Garcia *et al.* (1997), focusing on the effect of corn and soybean reports on futures prices, find that much of the unexpected information appears in the August crop reports. They also demonstrate that the informational content is of value as futures traders would be willing to pay for access to the information, but that the value has been declining. Colling and Irwin (1990) and Grunewald *et al.* (1993) examined the ability of the futures markets to incorporate unexpected information in hogs and live cattle markets, respectively. They determine that prices were efficient, responding almost immediately to new information, but not to anticipated information.

In spite of the rapid response to new information, a question emerges as the unexpected information explains only a small portion of price variability. If markets are efficient, why doesn't unexpected information, in an almost experimental setting, explain more of the movement in price? For example, Baur and Orazem (1994) indicated that USDA crop reports explain less than 1 percent of the variation in orange juice futures prices. Most likely, the answer lies in the difficulty in identifying relevant information.[8] Boudoukh *et al.* (2003) reexamined the ability of fundamental information to explain the frozen concentrated orange juice (FCOJ) futures. Using a non-linear, state-dependent model to explain the relationship between the FCOJ returns and temperature, they account for approximately 50 percent of the return variation. They also demonstrate that fundamental supply information, such as USDA production reports and news of Brazilian production, generate significant return variation consistent with expectations.[9] Further work on these issues utilizing the event-study framework is warranted.

Trading funds and behavior

Changing market structure and trader composition can influence the price-discovery process and price behavior. Concern persists that trading funds exert market power, possibly forcing prices away from their "fundamental" value or increasing price volatility.[10] Large corporate hedgers in a relatively thin market could also cause price distortions.

Several studies have focused on the relationship between price movements and large-trader positions. Brorsen and Irwin (1987) estimate quarterly open interest of futures funds and do not find evidence of a relationship between fund trading and price variability. Irwin and Yoshimaru (1999), using daily commodity pool positions, also find no significant relationship between fund positions and future price volatility. Fung and Hsieh (2000) estimate monthly hedge-fund exposure during major market events and conclude that there is little evidence that hedge-fund trading caused prices to move unwarrantedly. Finally, Irwin and Holt (2005), using Commodity Futures Trading Commission (CFTC) daily trading data for large hedge funds and Commodity Trading Advisors (CTAs) in 13 different futures markets in 1994, demonstrate a small, positive relationship between trading volume of large hedge funds and CTAs and market variability. Further tests suggest that trading by large funds and CTAs is based on private fundamental information that does not destabilize markets. Nevertheless, there still remains a public perception that large traders influence prices.

It is generally conceded that most fund trading is based on technical-trading systems rather than on economic fundamentals. Noise traders respond to non-information, such as broker advice, fads, price trends, moving averages, and chart formations. They misperceive the distribution of prices, and their impact on prices is significant if their responses to non-information are correlated, or feed on each other.

Irwin *et al.* (1996) began to explore indirectly the relationship between agricultural futures prices and noise traders in a study of mean-reversion. They argue that the basis for mean-reversion is that noise traders can move prices from their fundamental values for a period of time until the market identifies the mistake and returns to its equilibrium value. Their findings provide no support for mean-reversion in corn, soybeans, wheat, and live cattle and hog markets.

Sanders *et al.* (2000) develop and utilize a theoretical model of futures price determination in the presence of rational investors and noise traders. They use a market index for each of 28 futures markets, which is based on newsletters, brokers' recommendations, etc., as a measure of noise trader sentiment. They find no evidence that noise trader sentiment causes a systematic bias in futures prices. More recently, Sanders *et al.* (2003) test the "theory of contrary opinion," which hypothesizes that traders take a market position that is opposite of the prevailing market opinion of psychology. Again, they find little evidence that sentiment indices display consistent ability to predict returns.

Berwald (2001) uses a simulation model with both positive feedback and fundamental traders. He finds no evidence that positive feedback traders cause prices to deviate from their fundamental levels, however these traders do impact price volatility. Using data for 13 commodities, but for only six months, Berwald reports that managed futures significantly impact price volatility in nine of these markets. Clearly, the overall results are somewhat mixed and will require more and better data to disentangle the impact of managed futures and noise traders on the levels and volatility of futures prices.

The amount of capital controlled by managed trading funds grows annually, raising the possibility that their influence on market prices may be growing. Despite the research cited above, we need better information concerning the impact these funds have on the market. We need to know what proportion of the trading volume and open interest is associated with trading funds, and then their impact on price behavior. Given that trading decisions made by most fund managers are based on technical trading, or that they are noise traders, more detailed data on their trading behavior and the strategies of funds is needed, followed by an assessment of how these trades affect price behavior, levels, and volatility. Do trading funds cause prices to move away from their fundamental values, or are the fund managers just reacting to noise in the system? This information could also be tied to evaluations of efficiency of futures markets and the ability of futures markets to reflect market fundamentals (e.g. Boudoukh *et al.*, 2003).

Electronic trading

The swing from open outcry trading to electronic trading is approaching completion. Most trading in futures contracts is electronic, except in the US where there remains pit trading, although it is fading rapidly for non-agricultural contracts. Agricultural contract trading may remain as open outcry for some time yet because of the assets' uniqueness. Presumably electronic trading can be done more cheaply than pit trading, although there might be some loss of information in moving from face-to-face trading. However, research is needed on the impact of this change on price discovery. In US agricultural markets, the futures exchanges have stood for years as the principal location for price discovery, generating prices used then by cash merchants in local markets. Will electronic futures markets improve this discovery and transmission of information to the cash markets, or hinder the flow of information? Will individual traders really have easier access to the markets? How will prices behave? Will there be more liquidity or less? Will volatility increase or decrease? For some products, enough data are now being gathered to assess whether the electronic trading format has any influence on price volatility, both in the futures markets and for local spot prices. The latter point is important in establishing risk-management strategies for individual managers, for studying price distributions, and for the pricing of option contracts.

The rapid expansion of electronic trading has affected futures markets in another dimension, causing considerable change in the structure and organization of exchanges. The Chicago Mercantile Exchange (CME) reorganized into a for-profit-type firm in 2000 with shares of stocks eventually being listed publicly in 2002. The Chicago Board of Trade (CBOT) is gradually following this path. Both Chicago exchanges have created alliances with exchanges in other countries to facilitate trading. Of significant impact, the CME and the CBOT, historically intense rivals, linked their clearing operations in 2003. These changes, along with the increasing proportion of trading conducted electronically, have caused exchanges to restructure their fee schedules dramatically in order to keep customers and compete internationally. We now need research on how these changes will affect trader composition, e.g. will new fees and exchange structures favor large institutional traders and funds and thereby drive small traders out of the market? And, if so, how will this affect price discovery and market efficiency?

What path will traditional exchanges such as the CME or the CBOT take as competitors, for example from Europe (EUREX US), enter their established markets and try to win over trading volume and customers? Clearly, competitors will start in the most attractive markets first – those where commissions are high and where contracts can easily be replicated and improved. But will the reduced revenue from these contracts impact transaction costs in established grain and livestock futures markets that face less competition because of the inherent difficulties of designing and maintaining agricultural contracts? Will exchanges give up their traditional product mix of financial and non-financial futures and specialize by either trading exclusively financials on a minimum costs basis or exclusively trading commodities on a product (quality) basis? Goss and Avsar (1998) suggest that "futures exchanges can be expected to become concentrated geographically in a few key locations and within exchanges in a few key contracts." Will this mean that ultimately there will be a single central market for each asset which is linked to other geographical locations by different basis contracts? Scholars need to assess the different strategic options available to exchanges and their impact on price discovery, risk transfer, liquidity, and market performance.

Effects of margins on market behavior

Futures markets are unique in that traders are allowed to take market positions after posting only 5–10 percent of the value of the underlying contract, and then their positions are "marked-to-market" daily. These margins act as performance bonds, assuring that both sides will abide by their contractual obligations.[11] This deposit helps protect the integrity and reputation of the exchange, and it protects the futures commission merchant from customer default. These margin levels in futures markets clearly increase a trader's risk and leverage relative to the full value of the contract, but the mark-to-market provisions along with daily price limits are designed to minimize the capital needed to maintain and guarantee positions, limiting the risk of counterparty default.

In futures markets the exchanges control the levels of margins, which differ from one commodity to another. Exchanges set minimum margins, but futures commission merchants can require greater margins from customers. The exchange must search for the appropriate level of margins; not too low so to encourage excessive speculation and thereby excessive price fluctuations, and not too high which would increase the costs, especially to hedgers, resulting in decreased use of the market or a thinly traded market. Theoretically, exchanges would be expected to raise margins when futures prices become more volatile, and reduce margins as volatility falls. But are exchanges responsive to these environments, and what impact does changing margin levels have on trading volume and price behavior?

Kuhn (1981) reviewed four early empirical studies and concluded there was no evidence that higher margins controlled price fluctuations. Large price fluctuations are more likely associated with low rather than high levels of speculation. Tomek (1985) could not find strong empirical relationships between margin and either trading volume or open interest because all three variables change as price volatility changes. He concluded that futures margins are a poor policy tool for controlling price behavior, but they have an excellent record of providing contract integrity. In a small sample study of four commodities, Hartzmark (1986) found that changing margin levels are inversely related to open interest, but do not affect the volume of trading. He found no systematic relationship between margins and price volatility. However, because margins impose a cost on traders, changing margin levels can affect the composition of traders in the market, but it is impossible to predict which group of traders (commercial or noncommercial) will enter or leave the market.

More recently, Fishe *et al.* (1990) utilize theoretical concepts of margin requirements to examine exchange determination of margin levels. Using data for ten commodities from 1972–88, they conclude that exchanges set margins appropriately in accordance with theory. However, they cannot state definitively whether margin changes increase or decrease volatility. Hence, they conclude, similar to Tomek (1985), that government policy which uses margins to affect price volatility (behavior) would be ill-advised. Finally, Dutt and Wein (2003) argue that the theory used in previous studies, which suggests that margin rements impose a cost to traders and will therefore reduce trading volume, rrect, but empirical estimation of this hypothesis has neglected to adjust gins for underlying price risk. That is, margin changes occur when the exchanges believe that market risk has changed, or there is an expected change to underlying volatility. Margin changes are endogenous to the system, but previous research treated these changes as exogenous. Utilizing a modified model and data for six futures markets, Dutt and Wein (2003) find that after adjusting for risk, there are economically and statistically significant negative effects from margin changes on trading volume, as predicted by theory. However, they do not specifically examine relationships with price behavior. Additional research is warranted in this area.

Liquidity

Liquidity is defined in various ways. Black (1971) perhaps provides the most comprehensive discussion. His definition centers around three dimensions: (1) tightness, the cost of buying and immediately reselling a contract, i.e. the bid–ask spread; (2) market depth, the number of contracts required to cause a change in price; and (3) resiliency, the time needed to recover from random shocks (Kyle, 1985). A liquid market is then defined as being tight, with great market depth, and generally representing the true underlying value of the asset. While Black's (1971) definition is comprehensive, it is multidimensional and difficult to implement. Information about liquidity is important to market participants because it provides traders with an estimate of the potential transactions costs. A number of studies on futures market liquidity exist, some of which focus directly on agricultural commodity markets.

By far, the bulk of the empirical work has focused on measuring bid–ask spreads and their determinants. Bid–ask spreads are usually not observed in open outcry futures markets, an issue particularly relevant for agricultural commodities. But even in the few markets with nominal bid–ask spreads, trading frequently occurs within the quoted range, necessitating estimation of the effective spreads from transactions data. Roll (1984) developed one of the most used measures of the bid–ask spread. However, the procedure which uses the first-order serial covariance of price changes to measure the effective bid–ask spread has been criticized because it assumes that consecutive buy and sell orders occur with equal probability. Research has shown that this assumption is frequently violated in futures data, leading to positive covariances between price changes and giving the estimator a clear practical disadvantage. Thompson and Waller (1987, 1988) proposed a nominal spread estimator that is based on the average absolute observed price change. This measure has been applied to investigate the transaction costs of agricultural futures trading in corn and oats (Thompson and Waller, 1988), corn and soybeans (Ma *et al.*, 1992), and in wheat (Thompson *et al.*, 1993). Several studies have proposed other covariance-type (Chu *et al.*, 1996) and absolute price change-type (Smith and Whaley, 1994; Wang *et al.*, 1997) estimators, modifying the Roll

(1984) and Thompson and Waller (1988) measures. Direct evaluation of the alternative procedures is complicated by the fact that spreads are not always observable. To date, only three studies (Locke and Venkatesh, 1997; Gwilym and Thomas, 2002; Bryant and Haigh, 2004), all based on unique data that permitted comparisons of estimated and actual spreads, have assessed the performance of the estimators. The overall results suggest that the measures have difficulty representing actual spreads, often producing significantly biased estimates. For example, Bryant and Haigh (2004), who provide the only comparative study using agricultural futures markets (coffee and cocoa), report that absolute price change estimators perform better in terms of bias and mean square error, but that covariance estimators have lower error variances. Further, they find no estimator encompasses the others, indicating that composite forecasts of bid–ask spreads may be useful. Clearly, measures of the bid–ask spread must be interpreted with caution, particularly when used as an absolute estimate of transaction costs. Nevertheless, as appropriate data become available, additional research is warranted to determine the relative ability of the alternative measures to reflect spreads, and to assess the usefulness of composite forecast procedures.

The size of the cost of liquidity in commodity futures markets has been attributed to trading volume and price volatility (Thompson *et al.*, 1993; Wang *et al.*, 1997; Wang and Yau, 2000; Locke and Sarkar, 2001) and the activity of scalpers (Thompson and Waller, 1988; Brorsen, 1989). In a particularly informative study that demonstrates how the determinants of liquidity can influence trading costs, Thompson *et al.* (1993) compare the liquidity costs between Kansas City and Chicago wheat futures and conclude that, even after accounting for differences in trading volume, trading in Kansas City is more expensive than in Chicago. Recently, in light of the advancement of electronic trading, researchers have investigated how liquidity costs are also influenced by whether trading occurs in traditional open outcry fashion or via computerized systems. In an almost experiment-like setting, Pirrong (1996) for example reports that the computerized Bund market (DTB) was more liquid and displayed no greater spreads than the open outcry Bund market (LIFFE). These findings are consistent with later studies by Blennerhassett and Bowman (1998) and Frino *et al.* (1998) on financial assets, but in contrast to Bryant and Haigh (2004) on LIFFE cocoa and coffee futures. Bryant and Haigh (2004) argue that the bid–ask spreads widen in electronic trading of agricultural commodities because of the specific nature of these markets. They contend that the greater proportion of informed traders in commodity futures markets compared to financial futures markets leads to a severe adverse selection problem which outweighs the reduced processing costs of electronic trading. While these findings are based on only the cocoa and coffee markets, they may have important implications for other agricultural commodities that are currently pit-traded and where electronic trading appears imminent. Further, research is warranted to investigate the liquidity implications of introducing automated trading for other important commodities such as grains, livestock, and metals to determine its impact on bid–ask spreads, and to assess the extent of the adverse selection problem in these markets.

Researchers have also analyzed the characteristics of intraday bid–ask spreads in futures markets, and have observed an inverse-J or U-shaped pattern, reflecting greater spreads at the open that narrow during trading, and slightly increase at the close (Ma *et al.*, 1992; Gwilym and Thomas, 2002). The authors explain this U-shape with intraday information disparities and asymmetries and varying intraday volatility and volume. However, the existing studies are limited to only four commodities, and more research is needed to gain a more thorough understanding of intraday bid–ask spreads. This insight would assist market participants to better coordinate the timing of their orders to help to minimize transaction costs.

Market depth and resiliency are two related concepts of Black's (1971) liquidity definition that have received considerably less attention. Pirrong (1996) estimates a two equation model to determine the impact of expected and unexpected volume on Roll's (1984) and Thompson and Waller's (1987) liquidity measures for LIFFE and DTB Bund futures contracts. The results indicate that absolute price changes at the automated DTB decrease in size when expected volume increases, confirming the hypothesis that the market is deeper when expected volume is large. For the open outcry LIFFE contracts, the magnitude of absolute price changes increases with large expected volume reflecting the fact that market-making capacity is constrained, and that entry of new market-making capacity is limited over short time periods. Moreover, consistent with Bessembinder and Seguin (1993) who evaluate eight financial and non-financial assets including cotton and wheat, Pirrong (1996) finds that with negative unexpected volume the market is deeper than with positive unexpected volume.

Taking an alternative perspective, Pennings *et al.* (1998) propose a model of market depth that incorporates the price path caused by temporary order imbalances. Four different phases of price adjustment are proposed, resulting in an S-shaped price path. Using hog and potato futures data from the Amsterdam Agricultural Futures Exchange, Pennings *et al.* (1998) estimate this price path with a Gompertz curve, and conclude that both markets lack market depth.

Hasbrouck (2004) proposes a measure of overall market quality that is based on a Bayseian approach and reports the greatest market depth for S&P 500 contracts and the smallest market depth for pork bellies, with currency futures displaying market depth in between the two. Furthermore, Hasbrouck (2004) observes very strong price clustering for the pork belly contract but is unable to determine whether the price clustering results from minimizing the cost of negotiation or from the market power of the floor traders. More research on other agricultural commodities is warranted here to confirm the existence of price clustering and to establish an economic explanation.

The limited number of studies on market depth leaves several important research questions unanswered. What is the impact of electronic trading on market depth? How do open outcry and automated trading systems affect market depth? Do financial assets and commodities differ in this aspect as they do in the bid–ask spreads, and how could such a possible difference be explained? Can the measures of market depth advanced by Pirrong (1996), Pennings *et al.* (1998), and Hasbrouck (2004) be compared, and if so, do they provide consistent results? Are there potential biases inherent in their procedures?

Another element of market depth that has received little to no attention is the time dimension. How long does it take to execute an entire order? The time component of market depth appears to be equally important as the quantity component because long execution times increase the risk of price changes due to the arrival of new information. Clearly, more research is needed in this area. The other aspect of market depth and the third part in the definition of market liquidity, resiliency, is also related to time. To date, little research has focused on assessing the time that the market requires to recover from random shocks. Yet this information might prove valuable to market participants when deciding on the optimal time to execute new orders following a large trade.

The successful introduction of electronic trading in some markets also opens the door to investigate other factors of liquidity. Trade-based measures are backward-looking approaches, but market participants are less interested in what liquidity was than what it will be when they execute a particular trade. Because all orders are entered into a central computer system, automated trading will, at least in theory, contain information about all orders. The information potentially allows for a construction of a forward-looking order-based liquidity measure. This research should not only focus on designing such an order-based approach but also attempt to assess its quality in terms of reduced transaction costs.

Concluding remarks

As identified, agricultural commodity markets are in a state of transition, and researchers must continue to develop an understanding of how these markets function, their uses, and their performance in a changing environment. In assessing the literature, it is clear that we have learned a lot, but we still have much to learn. Some questions that we investigate recycle as the market environment and its participants change, and as our ability to answer them changes because of new advances in theory, empirical procedures or the availability of new data. Other questions are new and emerge out of the changing environment and encourage us to think differently. Regardless of their source, relevant answers to these questions require us to be more grounded in an understanding of the specific market characteristics, producers, market participants, exchanges, and the situations faced. They also require us to develop and use new paradigms and procedures to clarify issues and provide decision-makers with useful information.

Even in a selected discussion, important topics and references are omitted, either due to oversight or space limitations. For example, we do not cover issues and research opportunities in contract design and cash settlement. Similarly, our focus on pricing efficiency and the behavior of speculative prices has been limited. Several excellent surveys of the history and research on commodity futures markets exist. An early comprehensive review of the economic literature was provided by Gray and Rutledge (1971), who noted an overview by Working in 1962 regarding "new concepts concerning futures markets and prices." The most recent comprehensive review was provided by Williams (2001). Recent reviews on specific topics include: Andreou *et al.* (2001) on the empirical behavior of speculative prices; Tomek and Peterson (2001) on risk management; Chen *et al.* (2003) on hedge ratios; and Lien and Tse (2002) on developments in hedging. Finally, our discussion has been influenced by our background and research experiences and consequently focuses primarily on US markets. We hope our discussion provides a platform for a dialogue among researchers with different experiences and interests.

Notes

1 Haigh and Holt (2002) provide an innovative hedging example of combining two distinct approaches – dynamic programming and GARCH methods – for purchasing commodities in advance.
2 Positive spread relationships are referred to as contango, and are limited in size to full carrying charge. Backwardation, the inverse charge, has no theoretical negative price spread limit.
3 See Kamara (1982), Williams (1987), and Carter (1999).
4 Chavas *et al.* (2000) model storage and arbitrage pricing under explicit (e.g. transportation costs) and implicit (opportunity costs of time spent gathering information) transaction costs, and rationalize inverse carrying charges. Application of their model to the soybean market confirms that transaction costs significantly influence storage behavior.
5 The efficient market hypothesis and the behavior of speculative prices have received considerable attention. For example, Kamara (1982) emphasized the empirical contributions on important issues post-1970. He added a more specific piece on price behavior in 1984 (Kamara, 1984). Blank (1989) and Carter (1999) also update research contributions decade by decade. Tomek (1997) examined the effectiveness of futures prices as forecasts of cash prices. Andreou *et al.* (2001) also provide a recent review on the empirical behavior of speculative prices.
6 In a related context, researchers have examined whether chaos, a non-linear deterministic process that appears random, is prevalent in commodity futures prices. The presence of chaos implies that while prices are deterministic, longer-run forecasts based on either statistical or technical procedures will not be successful because initial measurement errors multiply exponentially. Neftci (1991) and Clyde and Olser (1997), however, demonstrate that short-term technical trading systems can be useful when prices are chaotic under certain conditions. Recent studies (Yang and Brorsen, 1993; Chatrath *et al.*, 2002; and Adrangi and Chatrath, 2003) call into question the existence of chaos in agricultural futures markets.
7 Sorensen (2002), Chatrath *et al.* (2002), and Adrangi and Chatrath (2003) also find seasonality in the futures returns.
8 The use of daily data may also preclude researchers from investigating the effect of new information if markets adjust completely within the day.
9 Of course, this begs the question: what explains the other 50 percent?
10 Latest reports show money invested in funds has grown to US$50.7 billion by the end of 2002.
11 This margining procedure, and its role, is distinctly different from the margin policy in the stock market. Margins in securities, regulated by the Federal Reserve, reflect

the down payment for buying stocks, and the remaining balance must be borrowed. For most investors the margin requirement is 50 percent of the stock's market value, and it is designed to limit the role of credit in potentially destabilizing stock prices. Stocks have no daily mark-to-market provision.

References

Adrangi, B. and A. Chatrath (2003). "Non-linear Dynamics in Futures Prices: Evidence from the Coffee, Sugar, and Cocoa Exchange." *Applied Financial Economics*. 13, 245–256.

Anderson, R.W. (1985). "Some Determinants of the Volatility of Futures Prices." *Journal of Futures Markets*. 5, 331–348.

Anderson, R.W. and J.P. Danthine (1980). "Hedging and Joint Production: Theory and Illustrations." *Journal of Finance*. 35, 487–498.

Anderson, R.W. and J.P. Danthine (1983). "Time and Pattern of Hedging and the Volatility of Futures Prices." *Review of Economic Studies*. 50, 249–266.

Andreou, E., N. Pittis and A. Spanos (2001). "On Modelling Speculative Prices: The Empirical Literature." *Journal of Economic Surveys*. 15, 187–220.

Arias, J., B.W. Brorsen and A. Harri (2000). "Optimal Hedging Under Nonlinear Borrowing Cost, Progressive Tax Rates, and Liquidity Constraints." *Journal of Futures Markets*. 20, 375–396.

Aulton, A.J., C.T. Ennew and A.J. Rayner (1997). "Efficiency Tests of Futures Markets for U.K. Agricultural Commodities." *Journal of Agricultural Economics*. 48, 408–424.

Baillie, R. and R. Myers (1991). "Bivariate GARCH Estimation of the Optimal Commodity Futures Hedge." *Journal of Applied Econometrics*. 6, 109–124.

Baur, R.F. and P.F. Orazem (1994). "The Rationality and Price Effects of USDA Forecasts of Oranges." *Journal of Finance*. 49, 681–696.

Benirschka, M. and J.K. Binkley (1995). "Optimal Storage and Marketing over Space and Time." *American Journal of Agricultural Economics*. 77, 512–524.

Berwald, D.K. (2001). *The Market Impact of Managed Futures*. Unpublished Ph.D. Dissertation, University of California.

Bessembinder, H. and K. Chan (1992). "Time-Varying Risk Premia and Forecastable Returns in Futures Markets." *Journal of Financial Economics*. 32, 169–193.

Bessembinder, H. and P.J. Seguin (1993). "Price Volatility, Trading Volume, and Market Depth: Evidence from Futures Markets." *Journal of Financial and Quantitative Analysis*. 28, 21–39.

Bessler, D.A. and T. Covey (1991). "Cointegration: Some Results on US Cattle Prices." *Journal of Futures Markets*. 11, 461–474.

Bjornson, B. and C.A. Carter (1997). "New Evidence on Agricultural Commodity Return Performance under Time-Varying Risk." *American Journal of Agricultural Economics*. 79, 918–930.

Black, F. (1971). "Towards a Fully Automated Exchange, Part I." *Financial Analysts Journal*. 27, 29–34

Blank, S.C. (1989). "Research on Futures Markets: Issues, Approaches, and Empirical Findings." *Western Journal of Agricultural Economics*. 14, 126–139.

Blennerhassett, M. and R.G. Bowman (1998). "A Change in Market Microstructure: The Switch to Electronic Screen Trading on the New Zealand Stock Exchange." *Journal of International Financial Markets, Institutions and Money*. 8, 261–276.

Boudoukh, J., M. Richardson, Y. Shen and R.F. Whitelaw (2003). "Do Asset Prices

Reflect Fundamentals? Freshly Squeezed Evidence from the OJ Market." *NBER Working Paper Series*. 9515, 1–52.

Brandt, J.A. (1985). "Forecasting and Hedging: An Illustration of Risk Reduction in the Hog Industry." *American Journal of Agricultural Economics*. 67, 24–31.

Brennan, D., J.C. Williams and B.D. Wright (1997). "Convenience Yield without the Convenience: A Spatial-Temporal Interpretation of Storage under Backwardation." *The Economic Journal*. 107, 1009–1022.

Brorsen, B.W. (1989). "Liquidity Costs and Scalping Returns in the Corn Futures Market." *Journal of Futures Markets*. 9, 225–236.

Brorsen, B.W. and S.H. Irwin (1987). "Futures Funds and Price Volatility." *Review of Futures Markets*. 6, 118–135.

Bryant, H.L. and M.S. Haigh (2004). "Bid-Ask Spreads in Commodity Futures Markets." *Applied Financial Economics*. 14, 923–936.

Carter, C.A. (1999). "Commodity Futures Markets: A Survey." *Australian Journal of Agricultural and Resource Economics*. 43, 209–247.

Chatrath, A., B. Adrangi and K.K. Dhanda (2002). "Are Commodity Prices Chaotic?" *Agricultural Economics*. 27, 123–137.

Chavas, J.P., P.M. Despins and T.R. Fortenbery (2000). "Inventory Dynamics under Transaction Costs." *American Journal of Agricultural Economics*. 82, 260–273.

Chen, S.S., C.F. Lee and K. Shrestha (2003). "Futures Hedge Ratios: A Review." *Quarterly Review of Economics and Finance*. 43, 433–465.

Chu, Q.C., D.K. Ding and C.S. Pyun (1996). "Bid-Ask Bounce and Spreads in the Foreign Exchange Futures Market." *Review of Quantitative Finance and Accounting*. 6, 19–37.

Clyde, W.C. and C.L. Osler (1997). "Charting: Chaos Theory in Disguise?" *Journal of Futures Markets*. 17, 489–514.

Coble, K.H., R.G. Heifner and M. Zuniga (2000). "Implications of Crop Yield and Revenue Insurance for Producer Hedging." *Journal of Agricultural and Resource Economics*. 25, 432–454.

Colling, P.L. and S.H. Irwin (1990). "The Reaction of Live Hog Futures Prices to USDA Hogs and Pigs Reports." *American Journal of Agricultural Economics*. 72, 84–94.

Collins, R.A. (1997). "Toward A Positive Economic Theory of Hedging." *American Journal of Agricultural Economics*. 79, 488–499.

Cornell, B. (1981). "The Relationship Between Volume and Price Variability in Futures Markets." *Journal of Futures Markets*. 1, 303–316.

Crain, S.J. and J.H. Lee (1996). "Volatility in Wheat Spot and Futures Markets, 1950–1993: Government Farm Programs, Seasonality and Causality." *Journal of Finance*. 51, 325–343.

Danthine, J.P. (1977). "Martingale, Market Efficiency, and Commodity Prices." *European Economic Review*. 10, 1–17.

de Roon, F.A., T.E. Nijman and C. Veld (2000). "Hedging Pressure Effects in Futures Markets." *Journal of Finance*. 55, 1437–1456.

Dusak, K. (1973). "Futures Trading and Investor Returns: An Investigation of Commodity Market Risk Premiums." *Journal of Political Economy*. 81, 1387–1406.

Dutt, H.R. and I.L. Wein (2003). "Revisiting the Empirical Estimation of the Effect of Margin Changes on Futures Trading Volume." *Journal of Futures Markets*. 23, 561–576.

Ederington, L.H. (1979). "The Hedging Performance of the New Futures Markets." *Journal of Finance*. 34, 157–170.

Ehrhardt, M.C., J.V. Jordan and R.A. Walking (1987). "An Application of Arbitrage Pricing Theory to Futures Markets: Test of Normal Backwardation." *Journal of Futures Markets*. 7, 21–34.

Fackler, P.L. and K.P. McNew (1993). "Multiproduct Hedging: Theory, Estimation, and an Application." *Review of Agricultural Economics*. 15, 521–535.

Fama, E.F. (1970). "Efficient Capital Markets: A Review of Theory and Empirical Work." *Journal of Finance*. 25, 383–417.

Fama, E.F. (1991). "Efficient Capital Markets: II." *Journal of Finance*. 46, 1575–1617.

Fama, E.F. and K.R. French (1987). "Commodity Futures Prices: Some Evidence on Forecast Power, Premiums and the Theory of Storage." *Journal of Business*. 60, 55–73.

Fishe, R.P.H., L.G. Goldberg, T.F. Gosnell, and S. Sinha (1990). "Margin Requirements in Futures Markets: Their Relationship to Price Volatility." *Journal of Futures Markets*. 10, 541–555.

Fortenbery, T.R. and D.A. Sumner (1993). "The Effects of USDA Reports in Futures and Options Markets." *Journal of Futures Markets*. 13, 157–173.

Fortenbery, T.R. and H.O. Zapata (1993). "An Examination of Cointegration Relations Between Futures and Local Grain Markets." *Journal of Futures Markets*. 13, 921–932.

Fortenbery, T.R. and H.O. Zapata (1997). "An Evaluation of Price Linkages Between Futures and Cash Markets for Cheddar Cheese." *Journal of Futures Markets*. 17, 279–301.

Frechette, D.L. and P.L. Fackler (1999). "What Causes Commodity Price Backwardation?" *American Journal of Agricultural Economics*. 81, 761–771.

Frino, A., T. McInish and M. Toner (1998). "The Liquidity of Automated Exchanges: New Evidence from German Bund Futures." *Journal of International Financial Markets, Institutions and Money*. 8, 225–242.

Fung, W. and D. Hsieh (2000). "Measuring the Market Impact of Hedge Funds." *Journal of Empirical Finance*. 7, 1–36.

Garbade, K.D. and W.L. Silber (1983). "Price Movements and Price Discovery in Futures and Cash Markets." *Review of Economics and Statistics*. 65, 289–297.

Garcia, P. and D.R. Sanders (1996). "Ex Ante Basis Risk in the Live Hog Futures Contract: Has Hedgers' Risk Increased?" *Journal of Futures Markets*. 16, 421–440.

Garcia, P., M.A. Hudson and M.L. Waller (1988). "The Pricing Efficiency of Agricultural Futures Markets: An Analysis of Previous Research Results." *Southern Journal of Agricultural Economics*. 20, 119–130.

Garcia, P., S.H. Irwin, R.M. Leuthold and L. Yang (1997). "The Value of Public Information in Commodity Futures Markets." *Journal of Economic Behavior and Organization*. 32, 559–570.

Garcia, P., R.M. Leuthold, T.R. Fortenbery and G.F. Sarassoro (1988). "Pricing Efficiency in the Live Cattle Futures Market: Further Interpretation and Measurement." *American Journal of Agricultural Economics*. 70, 162–169.

Garcia, P., R.M. Leuthold and M.E. Sarhan (1984). "Basis Risk: Measurement and Analysis of Basis Fluctuations for Selected Livestock Markets." *American Journal of Agricultural Economics*. 66, 499–504.

Garcia, P., J.S. Roh and R.M. Leuthold (1995). "Simultaneously Determined, Time-Varying Hedge Ratios in the Soybean Complex." *Applied Economics*. 27, 1127–1134.

Gardner, B.L. (1989). "Rollover Hedging and Missing Long-Term Futures Markets." *American Journal of Agricultural Economics*." 71, 311–318.

Goodwin, B.K. and R. Schnepf (2000). "Determinants of Endogenous Price Risk in Corn and Wheat Futures Markets." *Journal of Futures Markets*. 20, 753–774.

Goss, B.A. (1981). "The Forward Pricing Function of the London Metal Exchange." *Applied Economics*. 13, 133–150.

Goss, B.A. (1987) "Wool Prices and Publicly Available Information," *Australian Economic Papers*. 26(49), 225–236.

Goss, B.A., and S.G. Avsar (1998) "Increasing Returns to Liquidity in Futures Markets," *Applied Economics Letters*. 5, 105–109.

Goss, B.A., S.G. Avsar and B.A. Inder (2001). "Simultaneity, Rationality, and Price Determination in US Live Cattle." *Australian Economic Papers*. 40, 500–519.

Grant, D. (1989). *Optimal Futures Positions for Corn and Soybean Growers Facing Price and Yield Risk*. USDA, ERS Technical Bulletin Number 1751.

Grant, D. and M. Eaker (1989). "Complex Hedges: How Well Do They Work?" *Journal of Futures Markets*. 9, 15–27.

Gray, R.W. and D.J.S. Rutledge (1971). "The Economics of Commodity Futures Markets: A Survey." *Review of Marketing and Agricultural Economics*. 39, 3–54.

Grunewald, O., M.S. McNulty and A.W. Biere (1993). "Live Cattle Futures Response to Cattle on Feed Reports." *American Journal of Agricultural Economics*. 75, 131–137.

Gwilym, A.O. and S. Thomas (2002). "An Empirical Comparison of Quoted and Implied Bid–Ask Spreads on Futures Contracts." *Journal of International Financial Markets, Institutions and Money*. 12, 81–99.

Haigh, M.S. and M.T. Holt (2000). "Hedging Multiple Price Uncertainty in International Grain Trade." *American Journal of Agricultural Economics*. 82, 881–896.

Haigh, M.S. and M.T. Holt (2002). "Combining Time-Varying and Dynamic Multi-Period Optimal Hedging Models." *European Review of Agricultural Economics*. 29, 471–500.

Hamm, L. and B.W. Brorsen (2000) "Trading Futures Markets Based on Signals From a Neural Network," *Applied Economics Letters*, 7, 137–140.

Hanson, S.D., R.J. Myers and J.H. Hilker (1999). "Hedging with Futures and Options under a Truncated Cash Price Distribution." *Journal of Agricultural and Applied Economics*. 31, 449–459.

Hartzmark, M.L. (1986). "The Effects of Changing Margin Levels on Futures Market Activity, the Composition of Traders in the Market, and Price Performance." *Journal of Business*. 59, S147–S180.

Hartzmark, M.L. (1988). "Is Risk Aversion a Theoretical Diversion?" *Review of Futures Markets*. 7, 1–26.

Hasbrouck, J. (2004). "Liquidity in the Futures Pits: Inferring Market Dynamics from Incomplete Data." *Journal of Financial and Quantitative Analysis*. 39, 305–326.

Holthausen, D.M. (1979). "Hedging and the Competitive Firm under Price Uncertainty." *American Economic Review*. 69, 989–995.

Irwin, S.H. and B.R. Holt (2005). "The Effect of Large Hedge Fund and CTA Trading on Futures Market Volatility." In *Commodity Trading Advisors: Risk, Performance Analysis and Selection*. G.N. Gregoriou, V. Karavas, F.-G. Lhabitant and F.D. Rouah, eds. New York: John Wiley & Sons.

Irwin, S.H. and S. Yoshimaru (1999). "Managed Futures, Positive Feedback Trading, and Futures Price Volatility." *Journal of Futures Markets*. 19, 759–776.

Irwin, S.H., C.R. Zulauf, M.E. Gerlow and J.N. Tinker (1997). "A Performance Comparison of a Technical Trading System with ARIMA Models for Soybean Complex Prices." In *Advances in Investment Analysis and Portfolio Management. Volume 4*. C.F. Lee, ed. London: JAI Press. 193–203.

Irwin, S.H., C.R. Zulauf and T.E. Jackson (1996). "Monte Carlo Analysis of Mean

Reversion in Commodity Futures Prices." *American Journal of Agricultural Economics*. 78, 387–399.

Johnson, L.L. (1960). "The Theory of Hedging and Speculation in Commodity Futures." *Review of Economic Studies*. 27, 139–151.

Kamara, A. (1982). "Issues in Futures Markets: A Survey." *Journal of Futures Markets*. 2, 261–294.

Kamara, A. (1984). "The Behavior of Futures Prices: A Review of Theory and Evidence." *Financial Analysts Journal*. 40(July–August), 68–75.

Kellard, N., P. Newbold, T. Rayner and C. Ennew (1999). "The Relative Efficiency of Commodity Futures Markets." *Journal of Futures Markets*. 19, 413–432.

Kendall, S. (1953). "The Analysis of Economic Time Series – Part I: Prices." *Journal of the Royal Statistical* Society. 96, (Part I), 11–25.

Kenyon, D.E. and C.V. Beckman (1997). "Multiple-Year Pricing Strategies for Corn and Soybeans." *Journal of Futures Markets*. 17, 909–934.

Kenyon, D.E. and J. Clay (1987). "Analysis of Profit Margin Hedging Strategies for Hog Producers." *Journal of Futures Markets*. 7, 183–202.

Kenyon, D.E., K. Kling, J. Jordan, W. Seale and N. McCabe (1987). "Factors Affecting Agricultural Futures Price Variance." *Journal of Futures Markets*. 7, 73–91.

Kolb, R.W. (1992). "Is Normal Backwardation Normal?" *Journal of Futures Markets*. 12, 75–91.

Koontz, S.R., P. Garcia and M.A. Hudson (1990). "Dominant-Satellite Relationships Between Live Cattle Cash and Futures Markets." *Journal of Futures Markets*. 10, 123–136.

Kuhn, B.A. (1981). "Margins: A Review of Literature." *Research on Speculation*. Chicago: Chicago Board of Trade. 84–93.

Kuiper, W.E., J.M.E. Pennings, and M.T.G. Meulenberg (2002). "Identification by Full Adjustment: Evidence from the Relationship Between Futures and Spots Prices." *European Review of Agricultural Economics*. 29, 67–84.

Kyle, A.S. (1985). "Continuous Auctions and Insider Trading." *Econometrica*. 53, 1315–1336.

Lapan, H. and G. Moschini (1994). "Futures Hedging under Price, Basis, and Production Risk." *American Journal of Agricultural Economics*. 76, 465–477.

Lence, S.H. (1995). "The Economic Value of Minimum-Variance Hedges." *American Journal of Agricultural Economics*. 77, 353–364.

Lence, S.H. (1996). "Relaxing the Assumptions of Minimum-Variance Hedging." *Journal of Agricultural and Resource Economics*. 21, 39–55.

Lence, S.H., Y. Sakong and D.J. Hayes (1994). "Multiperiod Production with Forward and Options Markets." *American Journal of Agricultural Economics*. 76, 286–295.

Leuthold, R.M. and P.A. Hartmann (1979). "A Semi-Strong Form Evaluation of the Efficiency of the Hog Futures Market." *American Journal of Agricultural Economics*. 61, 482–489.

Leuthold, R.M., P. Garcia, B.D. Adam and W.I. Park (1989). "An Examination of the Necessary and Sufficient Conditions for Market Efficiency: The Case of Hogs." *Applied Economics*. 21, 193–204.

Lien, D. and Y.K. Tse (2002). "Some Recent Developments in Futures Hedging." *Journal of Economic Surveys*. 16, 357–396.

Locke, P.R. and A. Sarkar (2001). "Liquidity Supply and Volatility: Futures Market Evidence." *Journal of Futures Markets*. 21, 1–17.

Locke, P.R. and P.C. Venkatesh (1997). "Futures Market Transaction Costs." *Journal of Futures Markets*. 17, 229–245.

Lukac, L.P., B.W. Brorsen and S.H. Irwin (1988). "Similarity of Computer Guided Technical Trading Systems." *Journal of Futures Markets*. 8, 1–13.

Ma, C.K., R.L. Peterson and R.S. Sears (1992). "Trading Noise, Adverse Selection, and Intraday Bid-Ask Spreads in Futures Markets." *Journal of Futures Markets*. 12, 519–538.

McKenzie, A.M. and M.T. Holt (2002). "Market Efficiency in Agricultural Futures Markets." *Applied Economics*. 34, 1519–1532.

McKinnon, R.I. (1967). "Futures Markets, Buffer Stocks, and Income Stability for Primary Producers." *Journal of Political Economy*. 75, 844–861.

Mahul, O. (2003). "Hedging Price Risk in the Presence of Crop Yield and Revenue Insurance." *European Review of Agricultural Economics*. 30, 217–239.

Malkiel, B.G. (2003). "The Efficient Market Hypothesis and Its Critics." *Journal of Economic Perspectives*. 17, 59–82.

Manfredo, M.R., R.M. Leuthold and S.H. Irwin (2001). "Forecasting Fed Cattle, Feeder Cattle, and Corn Price Volatility: The Accuracy of Time Series, Implied Volatility, and Composite Approaches." *Journal of Agricultural and Applied Economics*. 33, 523–538.

Martinez, S.W. and K.D. Zering (1992). "Optimal Dynamic Hedging Decisions for Grain Producers." *American Journal of Agricultural Economics*. 74, 879–888.

Mathews, K.H. and D.M. Holthausen (1991). "A Simple Multiperiod Minimum Risk Hedge Model." *American Journal of Agricultural Economics*. 73, 1020–1026.

Maynard, L.J., S. Hancock and H. Hoagland (2001). "Performance of Shrimp Futures Markets as Price Discovery and Hedging Mechanisms." *Aquaculture Economics and Management*. 5, 115–128.

Miller, S.E. (1985). "Simple and Multiple Cross-Hedging of Millfeeds." *Journal of Futures Markets*. 5, 21–28.

Neftci, S.N. (1991). "Naïve Trading Rules in Financial Markets and Weiner-Kolmogorov Prediction Theory: A Study of Technical Analysis." *Journal of Business*. 64, 549–571.

Noussinov, M.A. and R.M. Leuthold (1999). "Optimal Hedging Strategies for the U.S. Cattle Feeder." *Journal of Agribusiness*. 17, 1–19.

Park, H.Y., K.C.J. Wei and T.J. Frecka (1988). "A Further Investigation of the Risk-Return Relation for Commodity Futures." In *Advances in Futures and Options Research. Volume 3*, F.J. Fabozzi, ed. Greenwich, CT: JAI Press. 357–377.

Park, W.I., P. Garcia, and R.M. Leuthold (1989). "Using a Decision Support Framework to Evaluate Forecasts." *North Central Journal of Agricultural Economics*. 11, 233–242.

Peck, A.E. (1981). "Measures and Price Effects of Changes in Speculation on the Wheat, Corn, and Soybean Futures Markets." *Research on Speculation*. Chicago: Chicago Board of Trade. 138–149.

Peck, A.E. and A.M. Nahmias (1989). "Hedging Your Advice: Do Portfolio Models Explain Hedging?" *Food Research Institute Studies*. 17, 599–615.

Pennings, J.M.E. and P. Garcia (2004). "Hedging Behavior in Small and Medium-Sized Enterprises: The Role of Unobserved Heterogeneity." *Journal of Banking and Finance*. 28, 951–978.

Pennings, J.M.E. and R.M. Leuthold (2000). "The Role of Farmer's Behavioral Attitudes and Heterogeneity in Futures Contract Usage." *American Journal of Agricultural Economics*. 82, 908–919.

Pennings, J.M.E., W.E. Kuiper, F.T. Hofstede and M.T.G. Meulenberg (1998). "The Price Path Due to Order Imbalances: Evidence from the Amsterdam Agricultural Futures Exchange." *European Financial Management*. 4, 47–64.

Peterson, P.E. and R.M. Leuthold (1982). "Using Mechanical Trading Systems to Evaluate the Weak Form Efficiency of Futures Markets." *Southern Journal of Agricultural Economics*. 14, 147–151.

Pirrong, C. (1996). "Market Liquidity and Depth on Computerized and Open Outcry Trading Systems: A Comparison of DTB and LIFFE Bund Contracts." *Journal of Futures Markets*. 16, 519–543.

Rausser, G.C. and C.A. Carter (1983). "Futures Market Efficiency in the Soybean Complex." *Review of Economics and Statistics*. 65, 469–478.

Roll, R. (1984). "A Simple Implicit Measure of the Effects of Bid-Ask Spread in an Efficient Market." *Journal of Finance*. 23, 1127–1139.

Samuelson, P. (1965). "Proof that Properly Anticipated Prices Fluctuate Randomly." *Industrial Management Review*. 6, 41–49.

Sanders, D.R., S.H. Irwin and R.M. Leuthold (2000). "Noise Trader Sentiment in Futures Markets." In *Models of Futures Markets*. B.A. Goss, ed. New York: Routledge. 86–116.

Sanders, D.R., S.H. Irwin and R.M. Leuthold (2003). "The Theory of Contrary Opinion: A Test Using Sentiment Indices in Futures Markets." *Journal of Agribusiness*. 21, 39–64.

Schroeder, T.C. and B.K. Goodwin (1991). "Price Discovery and Cointegration for Live Hogs." *Journal of Futures Markets*. 11, 685–696.

Smith, T. and R.E. Whaley (1994). "Estimating the Effective Bid-Ask Spread from Time and Sales Data." *Journal of Futures Markets*. 14, 437–455.

Sorensen, C. (2002). "Modeling Seasonality in Agricultural Commodity Futures." *Journal of Futures Markets*. 22, 393–426.

Stein, J.L. (1961). "The Simultaneous Determination of Spot and Futures Prices." *American Economic Review*. 51, 1012–1025.

Streeter, D.H. and W.G. Tomek (1992). "Variability in Soybean Futures Prices: An Integrated Framework." *Journal of Futures Markets*. 12, 705–728.

Sullivan, R., A. Timmermann and H. White (1997). "Data Snooping, Technical Trading Rule Performance, and the Bootstrap." *Working Paper 97/31*. Department of Economics, University of California, San Diego.

Sumner, D.A. and R.A.E. Mueller (1989). "Are Harvest Forecasts News? USDA Announcements and Futures Market Reactions." *American Journal of Agricultural Economics*. 71, 1–8.

Thompson, S. and M.L. Waller (1987). "The Execution Cost of Trading in Commodity Futures Markets." *Stanford Food Research Institute Studies*. 20, 141–163.

Thompson, S. and M.L. Waller (1988). "Determinants of Liquidity Costs in Commodity Futures Markets." *The Review of Futures Markets*. 7, 110–126.

Thompson, S., J.S. Eales and D. Seibold (1993). "Comparison of Liquidity Costs Between the Kansas City and Chicago Wheat Futures Contracts." *Journal of Agricultural and Resource Economics*. 18, 185–197.

Tomek, W.G. (1979–80). "Futures Trading and Market Information: Some New Evidence." *Food Research Institute Studies*. 17, 351–359.

Tomek, W.G. (1985). "Margins on Futures Contracts: Their Economic Roles and Regulation." In *Futures Markets: Regulatory Issues*. A.E. Peck, ed. Washington, D.C.: American Enterprise Institute for Public Policy Research. 143–209.

Tomek, W.G. (1993). "Dynamics of Price Changes: Implications for Agricultural Futures Markets." *Research Frontiers in Futures and Options: An Exchange of Ideas*." Proceedings of a Symposium in Recognition of T.A. Hieronymus. Urbana, IL: Office for Futures and Options Research. 45–55.

Tomek, W.G. (1997). "Commodity Futures Prices as Forecasts." *Review of Agricultural Economics*. 19, 23–44.

Tomek, W.G. and H.H. Peterson (2001). "Risk Management in Agricultural Markets: A Review." *Journal of Futures Markets*. 21, 953–985.

Veld-Merkoulova, Y.V. and F.A. de Roon (2003). "Hedging Long-Term Commodity Risk." *Journal of Futures Markets*. 23, 109–133.

Wang, G.H.K. and J. Yau (2000). "Trading Volume, Bid-Ask Spread, and Price Volatility in Futures Markets." *Journal of Futures Markets*. 20, 943–970.

Wang, G.H.K., J. Yau and T. Baptiste (1997). "Trading Volume and Transactions Costs in Futures Markets." *Journal of Futures Markets*. 17, 757–780.

Ward, R.W. (1974). "Market Liquidity in the FCOJ Futures Market." *American Journal of Agricultural Economics*. 56, 150–154.

White, H. (2000). "A Reality Check for Data Snooping." *Econometrica*. 68, 1097–1126.

Williams, J.C. (1987). "Futures Markets: A Consequence of Risk Aversion or Transaction Costs?" *Journal of Political Economy*. 95, 1000–1023.

Williams, J.C. (2001). "Commodity Futures and Options." In *Handbook of Agricultural Economics, Vol. 1*. B. Gardner and G. Rausser, eds. Amsterdam: Elsevier Press. 745–816.

Working, H. (1948). "Theory of the Inverse Carrying Charge in Futures Markets." *Journal of Farm Economics*. 30, 1–28.

Working, H. (1949). "The Theory of Price of Storage." *American Economic Review*. 39, 150–166.

Working, H. (1962). "New Concepts Concerning Futures Markets and Prices." *American Economic Review*. 52, 431–459.

Wright, B.D. and J.C. Williams (1989). "A Theory of Negative Prices for Storage." *Journal of Futures Markets*. 9, 1–13.

Yang, J., D.A. Bessler and D.J. Leathan (2001). "Asset Storability and Price Discovery in Commodity Futures Markets: A New Look." *Journal of Futures Markets*. 21, 279–300.

Yang, S. and B.W. Brorsen (1993). "Nonlinear Dynamics of Daily Futures Prices." *Journal of Futures Markets*. 13, 175–191.

Yoon, B. and B.W. Brorsen (2002). "Market Inversion in Commodity Futures Prices." *Journal of Agricultural and Applied Economics*. 34, 459–476.

5 Currency futures volatility during the 1997 East Asian crisis

An application of Fourier analysis

Vanessa Mattiussi and Giulia Iori[1]

Abstract

We analyze a recently proposed method to estimate volatility and correlation when prices are observed at a high frequency rate. The method is based on Fourier analysis and does not require any data manipulation, leading to more robust estimates than the traditional methodologies proposed so far. In the first part of the paper, we evaluate the performance of the Fourier algorithm to reconstruct the time volatility of simulated univariate and bivariate models; in the second part, the Fourier method is used to investigate the volatility and correlation dynamics of futures markets over the Asian crisis period, with the purpose of detecting possible interdependencies and volatility transmissions across countries amid a period of financial turmoil. Keywords: high frequency data, Fourier analysis, Asian crisis, volatility spillover.

Introduction

In recent years, high-frequency data have become increasingly available for a wide range of securities allowing for a deeper understanding of complex intraday volatility and correlation dynamics. Within a high-frequency domain the price formation is followed in real time, or tick-by-tick, resulting in a large number of observed values and, therefore, in a virtually continuous process.

In the last decade, temporal dependencies in financial markets have been mainly analyzed by means of parametric GARCH models (Bollerslev *et al.*, 1992, 1994; Shephard, 1996). High-frequency data provide novel insights into the main features of these models. For instance, Andersen and Bollerslev (1998a) found that a better ex-post measure of the underlying daily latent volatility factor, usually estimated by the daily (absolute or squared) returns, can be computed by exploiting the entire sequence of absolute or square intraday returns. Andersen and Bollerslev (1998b), building on the continuous time stochastic volatility framework developed by Nelson (1990) and Drost and Werker (1996), applied the same idea to improve the forecasting performance of the popular GARCH(1,1), showing that the volatility forecasts closely correlate with the future latent daily volatility. Andersen *et al.* (2001) extended and theoretically characterized this new measure, termed realized volatility. This methodology is nonetheless based on the strong assumption of regularly spaced data, whereas tick-by-tick quotes are, by nature, observed at uneven intervals over time. For implementation purposes, the observed series of prices are then synchronized or homogenized by imputation techniques such as linear interpolation and previous-tick interpolation. However, Barrucci and Renò (2002b) showed that the former, also employed in Andersen *et al.* (2001), induces a downward bias in the realized volatility estimator that intensifies as the sampling frequency increases.

Regarding the analysis of volatility within the context of non-synchronous data, several contributions can be found in the financial and econometric literature. By moving backward to the years preceding the large diffusion of high-frequency databases, we can refer to the works of Scholes and Williams (1977) and Cohen *et al.* (1983); for more recent papers, see Martens (2002), Oomen (2002), Barndorff-Nielsen and Shephard (2002), Brandt and Diebold (2003), Barndorff-Nielsen and Shephard (2004), among many others. Although very valid, all these approaches require, either directly or in a less explicit way, synchronization of the original data to be applied. An exception can be found in De Jong and Nijman (1997) where the cross products of returns are regressed on the number of common time units to these returns. Nevertheless, the estimation method is based on a discrete time model and yet no further developments have explored the possibility to extend it to a continuous time setting. Very recently, Hayashi and Yoshida (2005), also Hayashi and Yoshida (2006), have proposed a new approach to estimate the covariance of two diffusion processes when they are observed at discrete and asynchronous times. The method is an alternative, but similar in spirit, to the realized covariance. The resulting estimator is proved to be unbiased and consistent as the observation interval shrinks to zero and it does not require any manipulation of the observed data.

In this paper, we will study an alternative, non parametric approach suggested by Malliavin and Mancino (2002) where the estimate of the variance–covariance matrix $\Sigma(t)$ of a multivariate process is computed via Fourier analysis. Being based on integration rather than on differentiation, the method adapts well to the non-homogeneous time structure of high-frequency data. The procedure employs the observations in their original form, as in Hayashi and Yoshida, but it also allows recovering the time evolution of $\Sigma(t)$ over a fixed window, an appealing feature that is not shared, to our knowledge, by any other estimator in the field. Early recognition of the validity of the method can be found in Barrucci *et al.* (2000) where, by Monte Carlo experiments on equally spaced data, it was possible to estimate the volatility of a univariate process and the cross-volatilities of a multivariate process. Further applications have been evaluated in a more recent literature. Barrucci and Renò (2002a) measure ex-post volatility through the Fourier algorithm and found an improvement in the forecasting performance of the GARCH(1,1) model in respect to the usual volatility measure given by the cumulative sum of square intraday returns. Renò (2003) exploits the Fourier approach to prove that the so-called Epps effect (Epps, 1979), namely the tendency of correlation to decrease as sampling frequency increases, can be explained by asynchronous trading and lead-lags relationships. Precup and Iori (2006) show that the Fourier estimator generates more accurate results in respect to interpolation-based methods such as the standard Pearson coefficient and the co-volatility weighted measure proposed in Dacorogna *et al.* (2001).

We initially use the Fourier estimator to reconstruct volatility trajectories of simulated univariate and bivariate models. Monte Carlo experiments are also performed to analyze the correlation behavior between two tick-by-tick asset prices as a function of the frequency scale. In a second stage of the study, we apply the method to the time series of three futures contracts continuously recorded from April to December 1997, which includes the Asia crisis. In particular, our dataset contains high frequency prices for two currency futures, the Australian dollar and the Japanese yen (both in terms of the US dollar), and for the S&P 500 index future. The currency futures were chosen because of the geographical proximity of these countries to the center of the East Asian Crisis and the index future because of the role of the underlying index as the leading indicator of the US stock market performance. The objective is to extend the knowledge of price dynamics in futures markets by looking at possible volatility transmissions among currencies during a period of financial turmoil.

Several studies have focused on the properties of futures returns and volatility and temporal relationships between spot and futures markets. For example, Kawaller *et al.* (1987) have shown that S&P 500 index futures returns lead S&P 500 spot returns by up to 40 minutes, while the spot market rarely leads the futures market beyond one minute, in accordance with the hypothesis that investors with better market-wide information prefer to trade in stock index futures. Chan and Karolyi (1991), Abhyankar (1995), Tse (1999) and Min and Najand (1999) report that unlike a lead-lag relation, there is a bi-directional or contemporaneous relationship among the spot and the futures markets volatility, with innovations in either market spilling onto the other. However, while contagion has been so far investigated by analyzing the behavior of several asset classes such as stocks, bonds and exchange rates, most of the studies have focused on spot rather than on futures markets. A notable exception is the paper by Najand *et al.* (1992) where the authors study volatility spillover in five daily currency futures prices over the period January 1980 and December 1989. They find that ARCH and spillover effects are both present but tend to alternate over time. Tai (2003) looks at contagion effects in both conditional means and volatilities among British pound, Canadian dollar, Deutsche mark, and Swiss franc futures markets detecting spillover in coincidence of the 1992 ERM crisis.

The remainder of the paper is organized as follows. The next section introduces the Fourier algorithm and briefly outlines its implementation. Numerical experiments are performed in the third section to test the reliability of the method. The fourth section presents a literature review of the most common methods used to test for contagion during the Asian crisis. Results are discussed in the fifth section while the final section concludes.

The Fourier method: theory and implementation

The estimator proposed in Malliavin and Mancino (2002) is a fully non-parametric method to compute the time-varying correlation matrix between two or more assets. It is based on the only a priori assumption that the log-price $p_i(t) = \log S_i(t)$ of an asset i at time t follows a diffusion process of the form

$$dp_i(t) = \sum_{j=1}^{d} \sigma_{ij}(t) dW_j(t) + \mu_i(t)dt, \quad i = 1, ..., d \tag{1}$$

where $\sigma(t)$ and $\mu(t)$are time-dependent random functions and W_t are independent Brownian motions. For this kind of model, we define the volatility matrix as

$$\Sigma_{ij}(t) = \sum_{k=1}^{d} \sigma_{ik}(t)\sigma_{kj}(t)$$

typically estimated through the well-known pathwise formula, due to Norber Wiener (see, for instance, Karatzas and Shreve, 1991),

$$\langle p_i, p_j \rangle_t = \int_0^t \Sigma_{ij}(u)du,$$

where $\langle p_i, p_j \rangle_t$ is the quadratic covariation of the process. Although the latter is an unbiased estimator of $\Sigma_{ij}(t)$, it is based on a differentiation procedure that can lead to unstable results when observations are missed at the selected mesh points, as is usually the case working with tick-by-tick data. Alternatively, the linear and previous tick interpolation methods then adopted to synchronize the series have the drawback of reducing the number of observations and inducing spurious autocorrelations among the returns. The Fourier algorithm is instead based on integration and can be directly applied to the tick-by-tick data, including all the observations, two important features that highlight its natural adaptability to the high-frequency framework.

The volatility matrix $\Sigma_{ij}(t)$ is reconstructed on a fixed time window through the Fourier coefficients of dp_i defined as

$$a_0(dp_i) = \frac{1}{2\pi} \int_0^{2\pi} dp_i$$

$$a_k(dp_i) = \frac{1}{\pi} \int_0^{2\pi} \cos(kt)dp_i$$

$$b_k(dp_i) = \frac{1}{\pi} \int_0^{2\pi} \sin(kt)dp_i.$$

Note that by changing the origin and rescaling the unit of time we can always reduce the observed time window $[0, T]$ to $[0, 2\pi]$. Malliavin and Mancino (2002) derived a mathematical expression for the Fourier coefficients of $\Sigma_{ij}(t)$ based upon the coefficients of dp_i. The result is reported below without proof.

Theorem: *For a fixed integer* $n_0>0$ *the Fourier coefficients of the volatility matrix are given by*

$$a_0(\Sigma_{ij})=\lim_{N\to\infty}\frac{\pi}{N+1-n_0}\sum_{s=n_0}^{N}[a_s(dp_i)a_s(dp_j)+b_s(dp_i)b_s(dp_j)]$$

$$a_k(\Sigma_{ij})=\lim_{N\to\infty}\frac{\pi}{N+1-n_0}\sum_{s=n_0}^{N}[a_s(dp_i)a_{s+k}(dp_j)+b_s(dp_i)b_{s+k}(dp_j)] \tag{2}$$

$$b_k(\Sigma_{ij})=\lim_{N\to\infty}\frac{\pi}{N+1-n_0}\sum_{s=n_0}^{N}[a_s(dp_i)b_{s+k}(dp_j)-b_s(dp_i)a_{s+k}(dp_j)].$$

The integer n_0 represents the number of coefficients it is advisable to omit, should they be affected by the drift term in equation (1). By the Fourier–Féjer inversion formula, $\Sigma_{ij}(t)$ can then be obtained pointwise as

$$\Sigma_{ij}(t)=\lim_{M\to\infty}\sum_{k=0}^{M}[a_k(\Sigma_{ij})\cos(kt)+b_k(\Sigma_{ij})\sin(kt)]. \tag{3}$$

The use of this formula allows us to keep the characteristics of the volatility matrix, i.e. the partial sums on the right-hand side in the above expression are still symmetric, positive definite matrices.

The implementation is carried out by computing the Fourier coefficients of dp_i via integration by parts as follows

$$a_k(dp)=\frac{1}{\pi}\int_0^{2\pi}\cos(kt)dp=\frac{p(2\pi)-p(0)}{\pi}-\frac{k}{\pi}\int_0^{2\pi}\sin(kt)p(t)dt. \tag{4}$$

However, a price does not evolve continuously but, instead, it is observed at uneven intervals in the form of tick-by-tick quotes $p(t_i)$, $i=1,\ldots,$ where n corresponds to the number of observations in the re-scaled interval $[0, 2\pi]$. Therefore, to implement the method and in particular the integration, we need an assumption on the way data are connected. A possible option is to set $p(t_i)=p(t_{i+1})$, in other words, to consider piecewise constant prices over the interval $[t_i, t_{i+1}]$. Under this assumption, the integral in (4) becomes

$$\frac{k}{\pi}\int_{t}^{t_{i+1}}\sin(kt)p(t)dt=p(t_i)\frac{k}{\pi}\int_{t}^{t_{i+1}}\sin(kt)dt=p(t_i)\frac{1}{\pi}(\cos(kt_i)-\cos(kt_{i+1})).$$

In the integration by parts formula (4), the constant term $\frac{p(2\pi)-p(0)}{\pi}$ can be set to zero by adding a drift term in the diffusion equation (1) so that

$$\tilde{p}(t)=p(t)-\frac{p(2\pi)-p(0)}{\pi}t.$$

This change of variable will not have any effect on the final estimates and will also remove a possible source of bias.

Another aspect of the computation is related to the choice of a convenient frequency at which to stop the expansions (2). The smallest Fourier wavelength that can be evaluated to avoid aliasing is twice the smallest distance between two consecutive prices, here denoted with τ. It can also be seen as the minimum frequency rate at which tick-by-tick data are sampled, i.e. τ usually equal to 1 second. In the frequency domain, this corresponds to the highest frequency $\frac{n}{2\tau}$, also known as Nyquist frequency (see Priestley, 1979), where n is the number of observations. We can then conclude that a reasonable value for N is given by $\frac{n}{2}$.

Numerical analysis

The performance of the Fourier algorithm as volatility estimator was initially tested on the short-interest rate model introduced in Chan *et al.* (1992). This is a broad class of processes that includes the mean reverting version of the Ornstein–Uhlenbeck process proposed by Vasicek (1977) and the one-factor general equilibrium model developed in Cox *et al.* (1985). It is defined as the solution of the following stochastic differential equation (SDE)

$$dr(t) = \beta(\alpha - r(t))dt + \eta r^{\gamma}(t)dW(t). \tag{5}$$

To simulate the process, we have used the parameters estimated in Jiang (1998) on the three-month Treasury Bill rates via an indirect inference approach and given by $\hat{\alpha}=0.079(0.044)$, $\hat{\beta}=0.093(0.100)$, $\hat{\gamma}=1.474(0.008)$ and $\hat{\eta}=0.794(0.019)$, where the numbers in the parentheses are the standard deviations of the estimates.

In order to estimate the volatility path, we have adopted the technique suggested in Malliavin and Thalmaier (2005) to obtain positive volatility terms despite only a finite number of coefficients being employed in the summation (3). It follows that the volatility is estimated by taking instead

$$\sigma^2(t) = \sum_{k=0}^{M} \xi(\delta k)[a_k(\sigma^2)\cos(kt) + b_k(\sigma^2)\sin(kt)],$$

with $\sigma^2 = \Sigma_{ii}$ in equations (2) and where $\xi(\cdot)$ is a variant of the Fejer kernel (see Priestley, 1979) defined as

$$\xi(x) = \frac{\sin^2(x)}{x^2},\ \xi(0) = 0.$$

The original Fejer kernel is a smoother method responsible for eliminating a well-known problem in Fourier analysis, namely the Gibbs phenomenon.[2]

To mirror the inherent non-homogeneous nature of the high-frequency data, we have simulated an uneven series of ticks by extracting the transaction times between contiguous trades, the so-called durations, from an Exponential (λ) with $\lambda=10$. The choice of the Exponential was motivated by a simple statistical analysis of the differences $t_i - t_{i-1}$ for the three-month futures contracts used in the fifth section. In all cases the empirical distribution is well approximated by an Exponential, despite the different level of liquidity of the three contracts.

Figure 5.1 illustrates the temporal behavior of the diffusion coefficient $\sigma^2(t)=\hat{\eta}^2 r^{2\gamma}(t)$ on 10 days of trading of 8 hours each with a time step of 1 second. The estimate is consistent with the simulated path leading to a good reconstruction of the trajectory with $\delta=\frac{1}{50}$.

It is important to note that the trajectory was estimated directly from the generated values of the interest rates and not from the simulated volatility time series.

In the model (5) employed so far, the randomness of the volatility component originated from the state variable itself with the parameter γ measuring the degree of dependence of the variance from the interest rate level. A natural step in the analysis now involves applying the estimation methodology to a more complex structure, where the volatility is characterized by its own latent

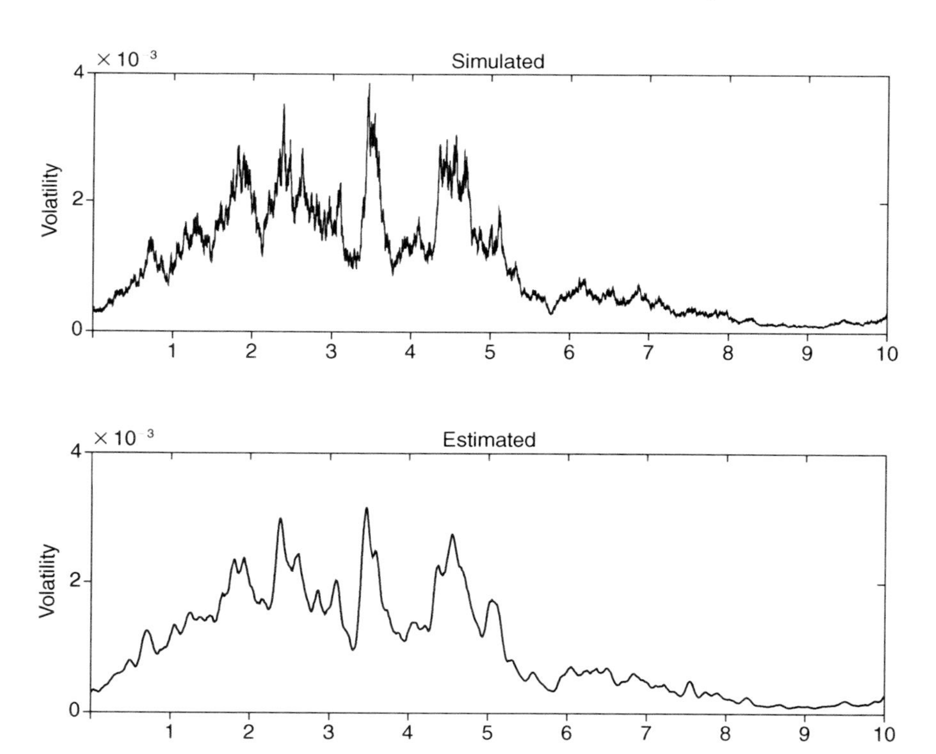

Figure 5.1 Top panel: squared diffusion coefficient $\hat{\eta}^2 r^{2\hat{\gamma}}(t)$ as simulated by model (5). Bottom panel: estimated trajectory via Fourier method (unevenly high frequency data) (source: simulated data).

stochastic process. In particular, we suppose that a stock price S and its variance ν satisfied the following SDEs

$$dS(t) = \mu(t)S(t)dt + \sqrt{\nu(t)}\,S(t)dW_1 \qquad (6)$$

and

$$dv(t) = \lambda(\text{v} - v(t))dt + \eta\sqrt{\nu(t)}\,dW_2 \qquad (7)$$

with

$$\langle dW_1, dW_2 \rangle = \rho dt,$$

where λ is the speed of reversion of $v(t)$ to its long-term mean $\text{v}(t)$. This bivariate stochastic volatility process is well known in finance as the Heston model (Heston, 1993). The process followed by $v(t)$ may be recognized as belonging to the class (5) introduced at the beginning of the section when $\gamma = \frac{1}{2}$.

We have simulated 10 days of trading of 8 hours each with a time step of 1 second in the same fashion as we did before. Figure 5.2 plots the trajectory of

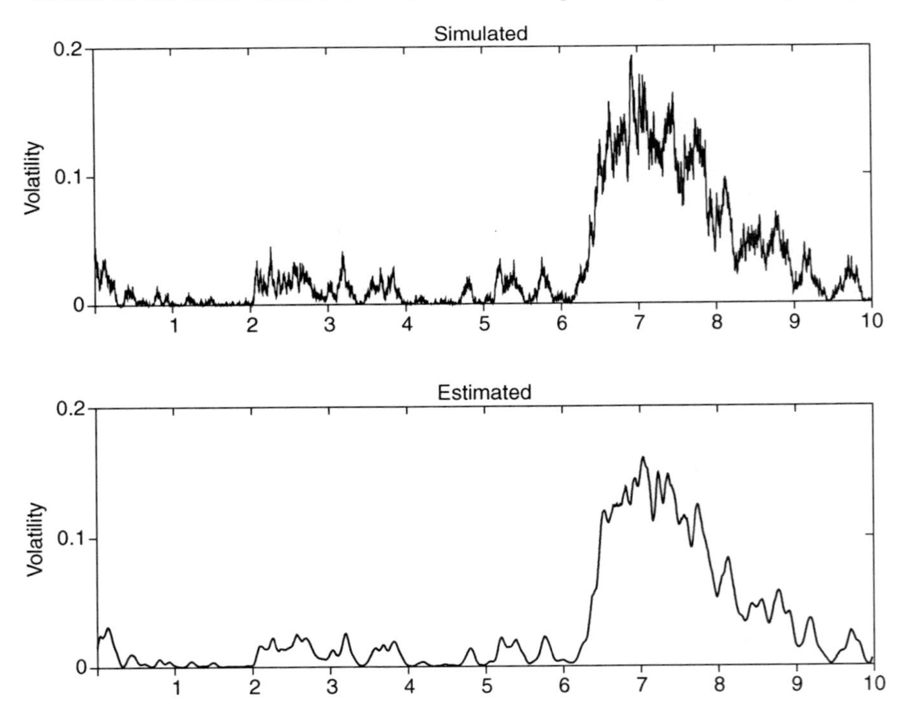

Figure 5.2 Top panel: one simulated path of $\sigma^2(t)$ by model (7). Bottom panel: volatility reconstruction with Fourier method (unevenly high frequency data) (source: simulated data).

the historical volatility with exponential sampling. Although the Heston framework is quite complex, the obtained reconstruction follows the dynamics of the original process (7) with a good representation of both the abrupt changes and the more regular sections in the volatility path. The value of the smoothing parameter was set to $\frac{1}{25}$.

Another noteworthy application of the Fourier algorithm consists in estimating the integrated volatility matrix σ_{ij}^2 by

$$\hat{\sigma}_{ij}^2 = \frac{1}{2\pi}\int_0^{2\pi} \Sigma_{ij}(s)ds$$

over a fixed time window $[0, 2\pi]$. With a minimum computational effort, it can be proved that

$$\hat{\sigma}_{ij}^2 = 2\pi a_0(\Sigma_{ij}) \Rightarrow \rho_{ij} = \frac{\hat{\sigma}_{ij}^2}{\hat{\sigma}_{ii}\hat{\sigma}_{jj}},$$

with the Fourier correlation coefficient ρ_{ij} on the right-hand side. Borrowing the idea in Renò (2003), we performed a numerical test on the bivariate stochastic model

$$\begin{aligned}
dp_1(t) &= \sigma_1(t)dW_1(t)\\
dp_2(t) &= \sigma_2(t)dW_2(t)\\
d\sigma_1^2(t) &= \lambda_1[\omega_1 - \sigma_1^2(t)]dt + \sqrt{2\lambda_1\theta}\sigma_1^2(t)dW_3(t)\\
d\sigma_2^2(t) &= \lambda_2[\omega_2 - \sigma_2^2(t)]dt + \sqrt{2\lambda_2\theta}\sigma_2^2(t)dW_4(t)
\end{aligned} \tag{8}$$

with $\langle dW_1, dW_2\rangle = \rho dt$. This is the bivariate continuous time limit of the popular GARCH(1,1) model, whose parameters were estimated in Andersen and Bollerslev (1998a, b) on the daily return times series of the DEM–US$ and JPY–US$ exchange rates as follows

$$\theta_1 = 0.035 \quad \theta_2 = 0.054$$

$$\omega_1 = 0.636 \quad \omega_2 = 0.476$$

$$\lambda_1 = 0.296 \quad \lambda_2 = 0.480$$

To gain a deeper insight into the accuracy of the estimates provided by the Fourier algorithm, we have compared the method with the well-known Pearson correlation estimator. The results are illustrated in Figure 5.3. Model (8) was run 1,000 times with a time step of 1 second over a period of 24 hours (86,400 seconds) trading. As before, the durations are extracted from an exponential

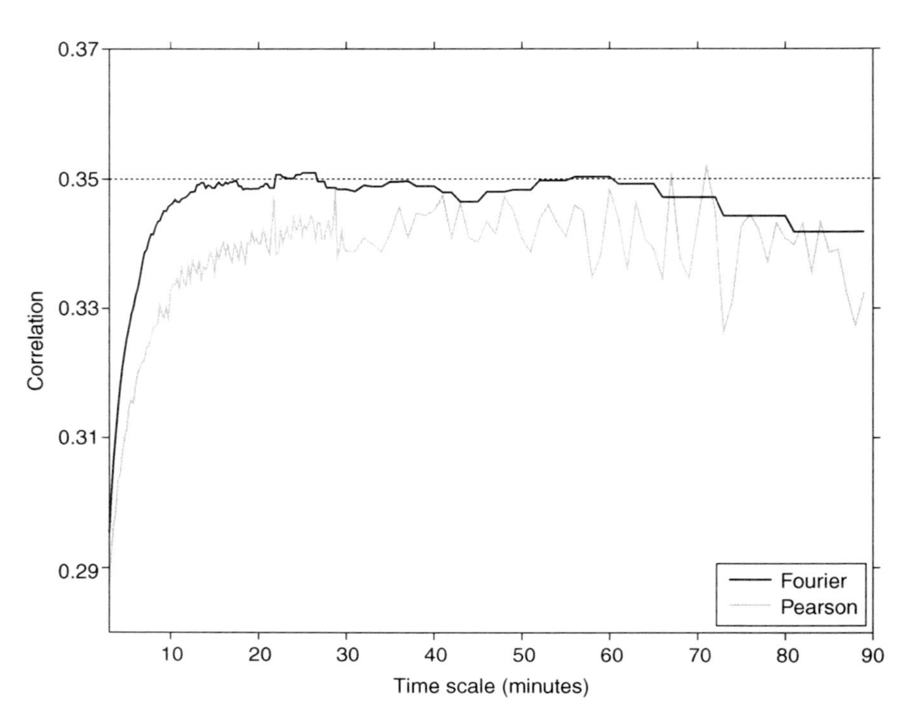

Figure 5.3 Fourier correlation and Pearson correlation between two simulated asset prices according to model (8). The dotted line represents the true correlation level set to 0.35. The results are obtained with 1,000 simulations (source: simulated data).

distribution with $\lambda = 15$ and $\lambda = 40$. Up to 30 minutes, we have sampled every 25 seconds, instead of every minute, to ensure a more detailed representation. From the plot, we observe that at short timescales (less then 10 minutes), which correspond to high frequencies,[3] the correlation is well beyond the benchmark to converge very fast towards it as the frequency decreases. It can be inferred that the frequency scale N in equations (2) must be chosen with care in order to obtain a stable correlation spectra. It is also apparent that the Fourier method, in contrast to the Pearson estimate, is able to provide a much smoother correlation trajectory. Moreover, the Pearson approach can only be applied to homogeneous and synchronous series whereas the Fourier correlation is directly calculated from the observed prices without any previous data manipulation.

Asian crisis and contagion

The last decade has witnessed dramatic movements in financial markets starting with the ERM breakdown in 1992, followed by the 1994–95 Mexican peso crisis, which spawned the so-called "tequila effect", the East Asian crisis in 1997 and the Russian virus of 1998. However, it is since the financial turbulence in Asia that policy-makers and economists have engaged in considerable research to identify and analyze the causes of financial contagion.

The term contagion has been an evolving concept in the academic literature but there is still disagreement on its precise meaning. The most common definition splits contagion into two categories: fundamental-based contagion and "pure" contagion (see Calvo and Reinhart, 1996). The first category refers to the transmission of shocks between countries or market routes through real links such as trade, macroeconomic similarities and financial connections. Under the second category, contagion arises when co-movements cannot be explained in terms of fundamentals, and common shocks and all channels of potential interconnection are either not present or controlled for.

Three major approaches have been applied by researchers in order to identify contagion: correlation of asset prices, transmission of volatility changes and conditional probability of currency crises (Dornbusch *et al.*, 2000; Pericoli and Sbracia, 2003). The estimation of correlation coefficients among stock returns is the most common method used to uncover contagion effects. While high correlations among countries are not necessarily evidence of contagion, but purely a reflection of cross-country dependence, a significant increase in the correlation coefficient after a shock to one country is usually interpreted as a sign of contagion. King and Wadhwani (1990) were among the first to define contagion as a significant increase in the correlation between assets returns and, by implementing this measure, offered supporting evidence for contagion during the October 1987 crash. Baig and Goldfajn (1998) show that the cross-country correlations among currencies and sovereign spreads of Indonesia, Korea, Malaysia, the Philippines and Thailand significantly increased during the East Asian crisis period compared to other periods. They also provide evidence of cross-border contagion in the currency market after employing dummy variables to control for own-country news and other fundamentals. However, Forbes and Rigobon (2001, 2002) prove that the correlation coefficient underlying traditional tests for contagion is biased upward during periods of market turmoil. Indeed, being conditional on the variance of one of the two markets under analysis, an increase in the market volatility, which is likely to happen after a crisis, can lead to the incorrect acceptance that cross-market correlations have also increased and, therefore, that contagion has occurred. They suggest a simple way to account for this effect and show that, once the adjusted coefficient is applied to the 1997 East Asian crisis, the 1994 Mexican peso collapse, and the 1987 US stock market crash data, the correlation across multicountry returns is no longer significant. In a recent paper, Arestis *et al.* (2005), after correcting for the heteroskedasticity bias, extend this study by employing the sequential dummy test proposed in Caporale *et al.* (2005), which is based on a set of less restrictive over-identifying assumptions than the one used by Forbes and Rigobon (2002) to test for contagion. They find some evidence of contagion from Indonesia to the UK and from Korea and Thailand to France during the Asian crisis, mainly concentrated in the second semester of 1997.

Several studies have also attempted to explore how, during a crisis period, changes of volatility in one market preceded changes of volatility in another, a phenomenon referred to as volatility spillover. A methodology commonly used to assess such changes is based on the estimation of multivariate GARCH models. Park and Song (2001) apply a GARCH framework to provide empirical evidence of volatility spillover among foreign exchange markets in East Asian countries during the crisis period. They find that the effects of the crisis in Indonesia and Thailand were transmitted to the Korean foreign exchange market, while the Korean crisis was not contagious to the two Southeast Asian countries. Dungey *et al.* (2003) use a bivariate GARCH model between the Asian equity markets and the Australian equity market to show that the former contributed poorly to the total volatility in the Australian market over the period, leading to little significant evidence of contagion.

The final approach aims to estimate the probability that one country is reached by the crisis given that other countries have already experienced it. Eichengreen *et al.* (1996), by means of a panel of quarterly macroeconomic and political data covering 20 industrial economies from 1959 through 1993, relate the probability of a crisis to a set of explanatory variables through a probit model across countries and prove that contagion appears to spread more easily to countries which are closely tied by international trade linkages than to countries in similar macroeconomic circumstances.

Using a similar approach, Caramazza *et al.* (1999) investigate the Mexican, Asian and Russian crises. The results indicate that fundamentals such as trade spillovers, common creditors and financial fragility are highly significant in explaining the three crises, while exchange rate regimes and capital controls do not seem to matter.

Data analysis

As an application of the Fourier method, we have investigated return correlations and volatility dynamics of futures contracts over the Asian crisis period. Our analysis is based on the three-month S&P 500 index futures, the three-month JPY–US$ futures and the three-month AU$–US$ futures, all observed tick-by-tick over the period April–December 1997. In particular, the futures on the S&P 500 is the most liquid contract with 702,165 tick prices followed by the AU$–US$ currency futures with 226,360 and the JPY–US$ contract with 19,027 available quotes. The Australian market is therefore characterized by the smaller turnover of transactions. We analyze only near-to-maturity contracts, which are the most liquid ones, and apply a rolling-over mechanism to construct the actively traded times series shown in Figure 5.4 (left-hand panels) together with their relative log returns series (right-hand panels). The effect of the Hong Kong stock market crash, also known as the "mini-crash", caused by the Asian crisis on October 27 is evident and translates into a clear price drop for both the AU$–US$ and the S&P 500 index futures. On the other side, by looking at the graphs for the JPY–US$ contract, it appears that the Asian events did not have a remarkable effect on the Japanese market.

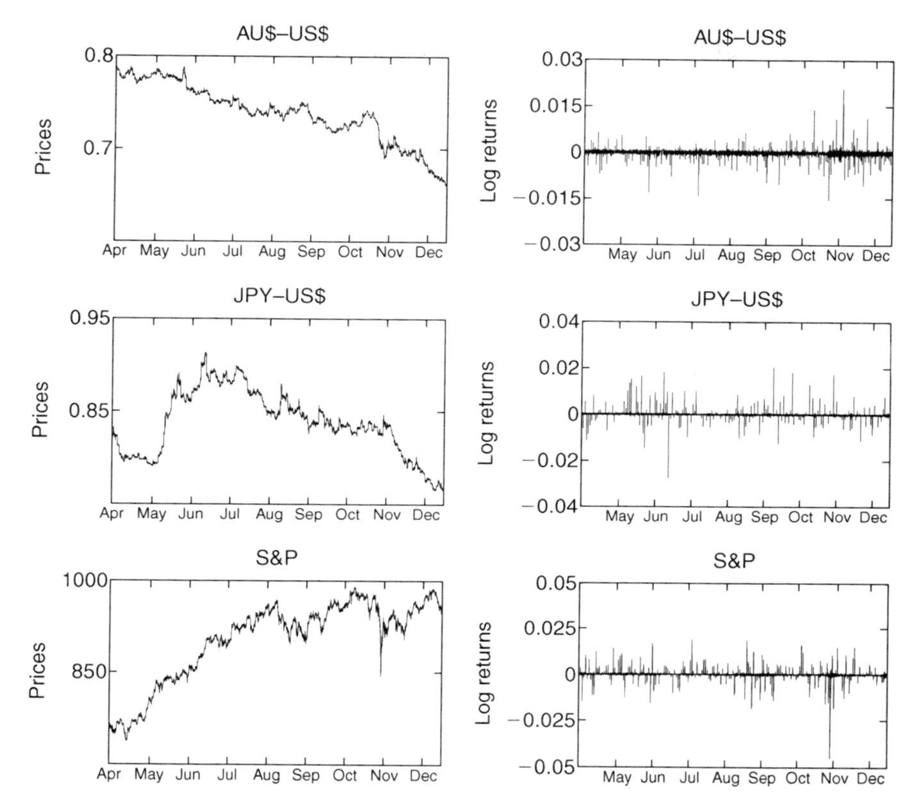

Figure 5.4 Times series of the tick prices (left-hand panels) and of the log returns (right-hand panels) for the future contracts under study (source: S&P index futures, AU$–US$ currency futures and JPY–US$ currency futures).

In Figure 5.5 we plot the volatility estimates for the three contracts in hand over the period under consideration. Note that the trajectory for the Australian futures (middle panel) is thinner compared to the other contracts due to the low liquidity of the asset. We observe that the volatilities of the AU$–US$ and the S&P 500 futures follow each other rather closely between July and November 1997 and in particular around the mini-crash of October 27. A peak on May 21, following Thailand's announcement on May 15 of wide-ranging capital controls, is detected on the AU$–US$ futures but not on the other two contracts. The JPY–US$ futures also present a spike on October 27, but not a persistently high volatility after the event. The volatility of the JPY–US$ is highest during the end of May and mid-June 1997, before the crisis properly started, and clusters of high volatility are also detected around June 10. A second period of increased volatility is observed from August to September 1997. The Japanese economy was only marginally affected by the 1997 turmoil (Dungey *et al.*, 2004). Milton Friedman (1999) argued that the severe period of recession and

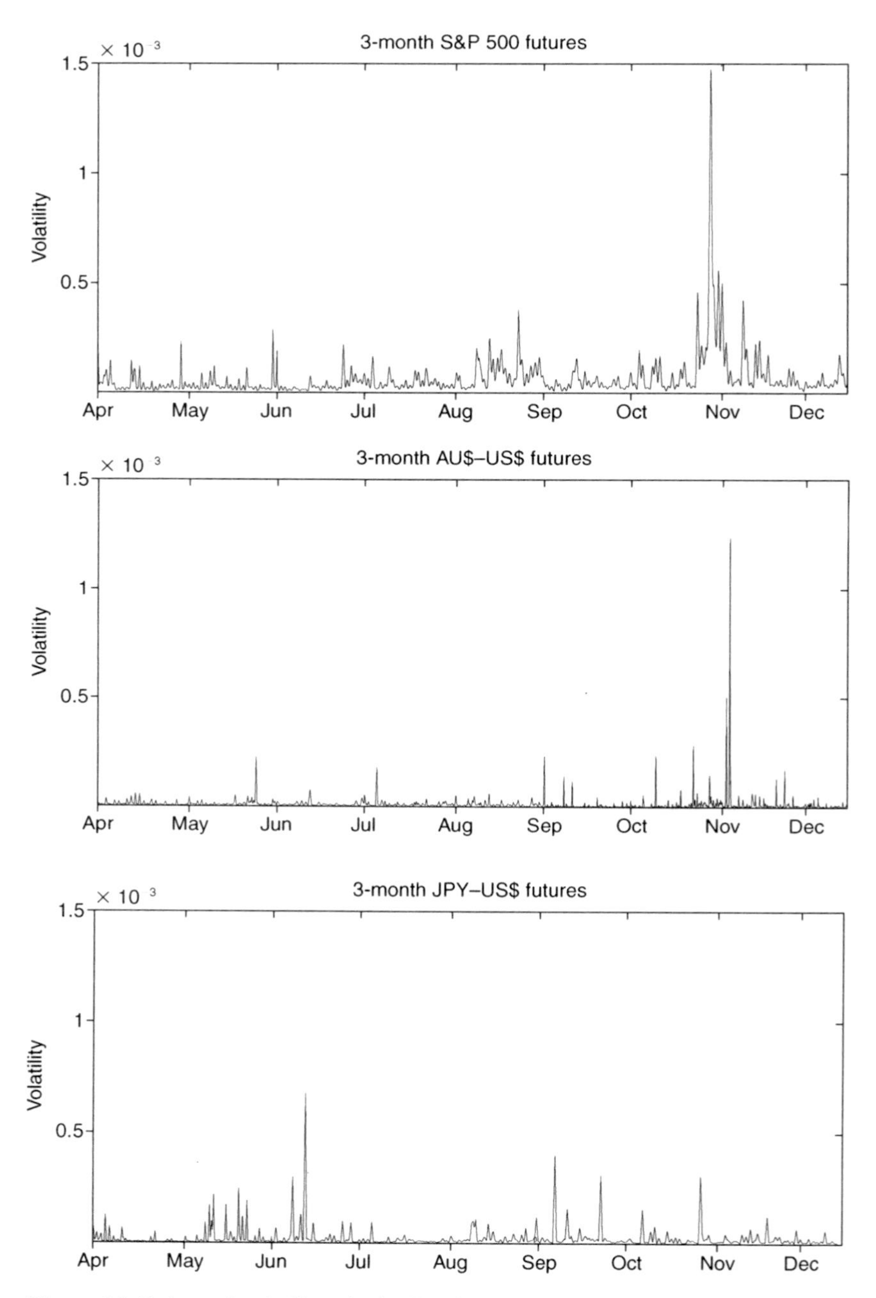

Figure 5.5 Estimated volatility via the Fourier method for the S&P 500 (top panel), the AU$–US$ (middle panel) and the JPY–US$ (bottom panel) futures over the period April–December 1997 (source: S&P index futures, AU$–US$ currency futures and JPY–US$ currency futures).

stagnation Japan was going through actually predated and transcended the Asian crisis.

Ellis and Lewis (2001), by analyzing daily market-close data for stock prices, bond futures prices and exchange rates, found that developments in the US market generally had a much greater influence on price movements and volatility than cross-market shocks originating in the Asian crisis economies. They also provide evidence that stock markets reacted to the developments in Asia after the United States did, instead of responding directly to the news itself. Volatility of both the Australian dollar and the New Zealand dollar exchange rates against the US dollar increased remarkably during the Asian crisis, building towards the end of the period, and remained high into the world crisis period.

Our results seem to strengthen the analysis of Ellis and Lewis and show that the volatility of the AU$–US$ futures follows closely the volatility of the S&P 500 index futures. This conclusion is well supported by the clear, large spike in the volatility trajectory of the Australian futures which occurs soon after a similar level of volatility is detected for the futures on the index.

Finally, we have derived the integrated weekly correlations across the three contracts for the period April–November 1997. The frequency scale was set to a value corresponding to 30 minutes in the time domain. Figure 5.6 illustrates the obtained trajectories. This value is a trade-off between short and long timescales where non-synchronicity and a lack of statistics respectively, may generate downward biases in the estimated correlations (see Figure 5.3). We also checked that the correlations patterns reconstructed are stable when changing the frequency scale around the chosen value.

Figure 5.4 and Figure 5.6 are consistent with each other. Starting from mid-July, both the currency futures curves are downward sloping, whereas the S&P 500 index performance is overall positive. By looking at the correlation time series, the trajectory relative to the currency futures shows an increasing level of mutual dependence. An opposite pattern can instead be observed between the JPY–US$ futures and the S&P 500 index futures, with the lowest correlation value reached towards the end of October. There is no clear evidence that a spike in the correlation spectra may be due to structural changes affecting cross-market linkages, and as such to contagion. Indeed, periods of high volatility that characterized crucial stages of the Asian crisis do not seem to have played a significant role in driving the correlation up or down. For instance, the largest correlation value between the Australian and US market is detected around mid-September, during a relative calm period for the S&P 500 index futures, and not soon after the October mini-crash, as expected. Similarly, the futures on the AU$–US$ and JPY–US$ exchange rates show a high degree of correlation around mid-June when the volatilities of the two contracts are relatively low.

Conclusions

In this chapter we have implemented the Fourier methodology proposed by Malliavin and Mancino (2002) to compute historical volatility and correlation.

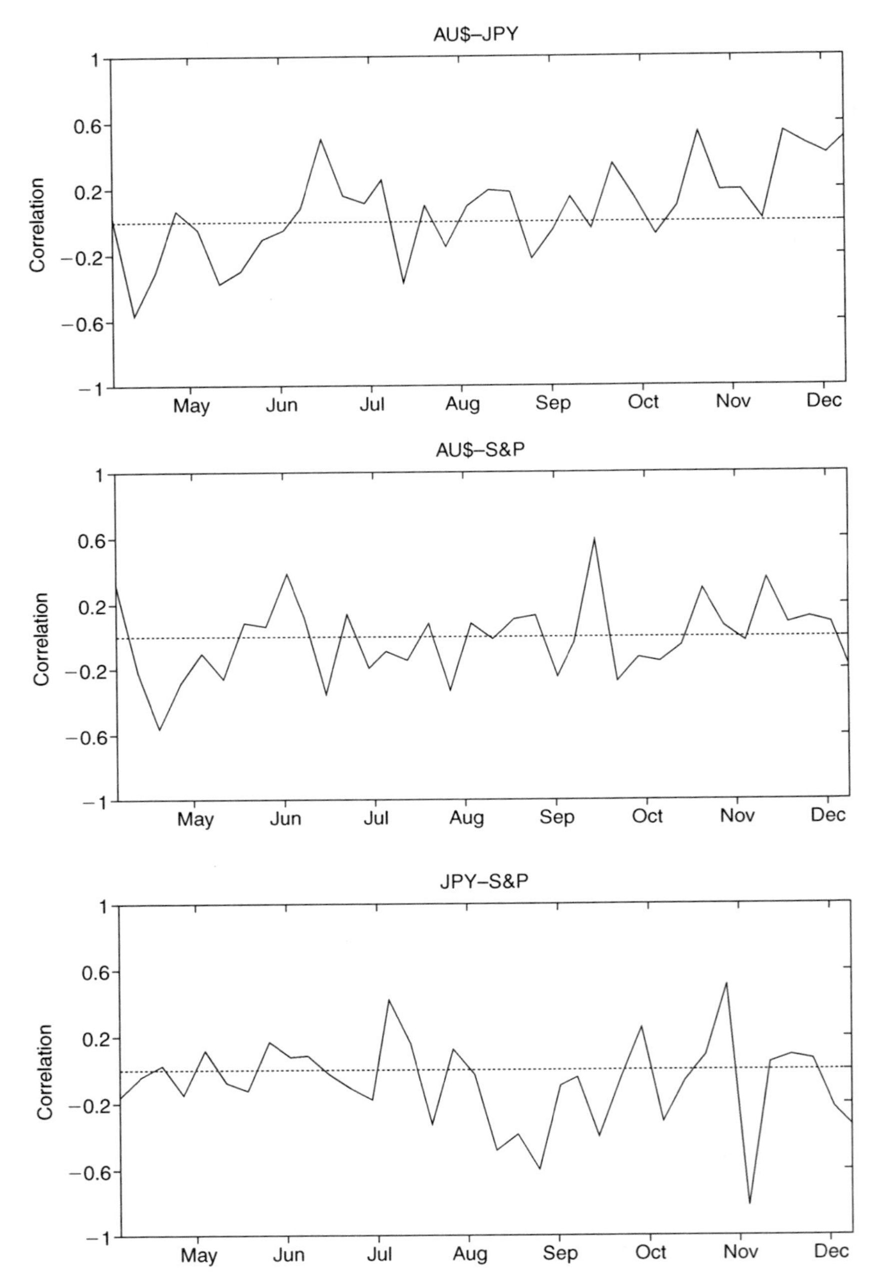

Figure 5.6 Weekly correlation estimated via the Fourier method over the period April–December 1997: AU$–JPY (top panel), AU$–S&P (middle panel) and JPY–S&P (bottom panel). The timescale was set to 30 minutes (source: S&P index futures, AU$–US$ currency futures and JPY–US$ currency futures).

Whilst classical methods require equally spaced observations, the Fourier estimator, being based on integration rather than on differentiation, naturally exploits the non-homogeneous time structure of the high-frequency prices without any prior data manipulation.

We have first tested the performance of the method through numerical experiments obtaining volatility reconstructions that very well match the simulated volatility dynamics. Further evidence is provided by computing the integrated correlation of a bivariate diffusion process. We have then applied the estimator to futures time series, observed at a high-frequency level, during the East Asian crisis of 1997. Our results are coherent with the existing literature. We have found that the Australian economy was not impacted by the Asian events directly but its reaction was rather driven by the developments in the US market. Also, we have observed that the Asian turmoil did not have a noticeable effect on the Japanese market.

We believe that our analysis would benefit from a more complete dataset including pre-crisis and post-crisis samples to gain a deeper insight into the contagion problem. Our correlation reconstruction considers only a symmetric contemporaneous relationship across markets, whereas a wider range of data would allow for a better outline of the inherently non-symmetric nature of contagion by capturing the lead-lag relationship between returns or volatilities across markets. Nonetheless, our method based on time-varying estimates has the advantage of looking at contagion from a more dynamical perspective compared with existing approaches.

Notes

1 The authors are indebted to Barry A. Goss for providing the data employed in this study, for his helpful suggestions and his kind encouragement during the preparation of this manuscript. All errors and omissions are our own responsibility.

2 The Gibbs phenomenon arises when a piecewise continuously differentiable function is approximated by a Fourier series. It can be shown, for instance by applying the method to a simple sawtooth function, that the series displays an overshoot in the left-hand side interval of the discontinuity and a symmetric undershoot in the right-hand side of the interval. The overshoot does not vanish as the frequency increases but, instead, approaches a finite limit, i.e. the height of the overshoot does not decrease by increasing the number of terms in the series.

3 The conversion can be obtained easily by taking $N=\frac{86400}{2\tau}$ where $\tau=1, 2,\dots,T$ are minutes.

References

Abhyankar, A.H. (1995): "Return and volatility dynamics in the FT-SE 100 stock index and stock index futures markets". *Journal of Futures Markets*, 15(4), 457–488.

Andersen, T.G. and T. Bollerslev (1998a): "Deutsche Mark–Dollar volatility: intraday activity patterns, macroeconomics announcements and longer run dependencies". *Journal of Finance*, 53, 219–265.

Andersen, T.G. and T. Bollerslev (1998b): "Answering the skeptics: yes, standard volatility models do provide accurate forecasts". *International Economic Review*, 39, 885–905.

Andersen, T.G., T. Bollerslev, F.X. Diebold and P. Labys (2001): "The Distribution of realized exchange rate volatility". *Journal of American Statistical Association*, 96, 42–55.

Arestis, P., G.M. Caporale, A. Cipollini and N. Spagnolo (2005): "Testing for financial contagion between developed and emerging markets during the 1997 East Asian Crisis". *International Journal of Finance and Economics*, 10(4), 359–367.

Baig, T. and I. Goldfajn (1998): "Financial market contagion in the Asian Crisis". Working Paper 98–155, International Monetary Fund, Washington.

Barndorff-Nielsen, O.E. and N. Shephard (2002): "Estimating quadratic variation using realized variance". *Journal of Applied Econometrics*, 17, 457–477.

Barndorff-Nielsen, O.E. and N. Shephard (2004): "Econometric analysis of realized covariation: high frequency based covariance, regression and correlation in financial economics". *Econometrica*, 27, 885–925.

Barrucci, E. and R. Renò (2002a): "On measuring volatility and the GARCH forecasting performance". *Journal of International Financial Markets, Institutions and Money*, 12, 182–200.

Barrucci, E. and R. Renò (2002b): "On measuring volatility of diffusion processes with high frequency data". *Economics Letters*, 74, 371–378.

Barrucci, E., M. Mancino and R. Renò (2000): "Volatility estimate via Fourier analysis". *Finanza Computazionale, Atti della Scuola Estiva 2000*, Università Ca' Foscari, Venezia, 273–291.

Bollerslev, T., R.Y. Chou and K.F. Kroner (1992): "ARCH modeling in finance: a review of the theory and empirical evidence". *Journal of Econometrics*, 52, 5–59.

Bollerslev, T., R.F. Engle and D.B. Nelson (1994): "ARCH models". *Handbook of Econometrics Volume IV*, in Engle and McFadden eds, North Holland Press.

Brandt, M.W. and F.X. Diebold (2003): "A no-arbitrage approach to range-based estimation of return covariances and correlations". Working Paper 03–013, Penn Institute for Economic Research, Philadelphia.

Calvo, S. and C.M. Reinhart (1996): "Capital flows to Latin America: is there evidence of contagion effects?", in Calvo, Goldstein and Hochreitter eds, *Private Capital Flows to Emerging Markets*, Institute for International Economics, Washington.

Caporale, G.M., A. Cipollini and N. Spagnolo (2005): "Testing for contagion: a conditional correlation analysis", *Journal of Empirical Finance*, 12(3), 476–489.

Caramazza, F., L. Ricci and R. Salgado (1999): *Trade and financial contagion in currency crises*. IMF Working Paper.

Chan, K. and A. Karolyi (1991): "Intraday Volatility in the Stock Index and Stock Index Futures Markets". *Review of Financial Studies*, 4, 657–684.

Chan, K., A. Karolyi, F. Longstaff and A. Sanders (1992): "An empirical comparison of alternative models of the short-term interest rate". *Journal of Finance*, 47(3), 1209–1227.

Cohen, K.J., G.A. Hawawini, S.F. Maier, R.A. Schwartz and D.K. Whitcomb (1983): "Friction in the trading process and the estimation of systematic risk". *Journal of Financial Economics*, 12, 263–278.

Cox, J., J. Ingersoll and S. Ross (1985): "A theory of the term structure of interest rates". *Econometrica*, 53, 385–406.

Dacorogna, M.M., R. Gençay, U.A. Müller, R.B. Olsen and O.V. Pictet (2001): *An Introduction to High-Frequency Finance*. Academic Press, San Diego, CA.

de Jong, F. and T. Nijman (1997): "High frequency analysis of lead-lag relationships between financial markets". *Journal of Empirical Finance*, 4, 259–277.

Dornbusch, R., Y.C. Park and S. Claessens (2000): "Contagion: understanding how it spreads". *The World Bank Research Observer*, 15(2), 177–197.

Drost, F.C. and B.J.M Werker (1996): "Closing the GARCH gap: continuous time GARCH modeling". *Journal of Econometrics*, 74, 31–57.

Dungey, M., R.A. Fry and V.L. Martin (2003): "Equity transmission mechanisms from Asia to Australia: interdependence or contagion?" *Australian Journal of Management*, 28(2), 157–182.

Dungey, M., R.A. Fry and V.L. Martin (2004): "Currency market contagion in the Asia-Pacific region". *Australian Economic Papers*, 43(4), 379–395.

Eichengreen, B., A. Rose and C. Wyplosz (1996): *Contagious currency crisis*. NBER Working Paper W5681.

Ellis, L. and E. Lewis (2001): *The response of financial markets in Australia and New Zealand to news about the Asian crisis*. RBA Research Discussion Papers RDP2001–03, Reserve Bank of Australia.

Epps, T. (1979): "Comovements in stock prices in the very short run". *Journal of the American Statistical Association*, 74, 291–298.

Forbes, K.J. and R. Rigobon (2001): "Measuring contagion: conceptual and empirical issues", in S. Claessens and K. Forbes eds, *International Financial Contagion*, Kluwer Academic Publishers.

Forbes, K.J. and R. Rigobon (2002): "No contagion, only interdependence: measuring stock market comovements". *Journal of Finance*, 57(5), 2223–2261.

Friedman, M., (1999): "How Asia Fell", *Hoover Digest No 2*, Hoover Institution, Stanford University.

Hayashi, T. and N. Yoshida (2005): "On covariance estimation of non synchronously observed diffusion processes". *Bernoulli*, 11, 359–379.

Hayashi, T. and N. Yoshida (2006): *Estimating correlations with non synchronous observations in continuous diffusion models*. Preprint (2005), Submitted.

Heston, S.L. (1993): "A closed-form solution for option with stochastic volatility with applications to bond and currency options". *The Review of Financial Studies*, 6(2), 327–343.

Jiang, G.J. (1998): "Nonparametric modeling of U.S. interest rate term structure dynamics and implications on the prices of derivative securities". *Journal of Finance and Quantitative Analysis*, 33(4), 465–497.

Karatzas, I. and S.E. Shreve (1991): *Brownian Motion and Stochastic Calculus (2 edn)*. Volume 113 of Graduate Texts in Mathematics, Springer-Verlag, Berlin.

Kawaller, I.G., P.D. Koch and T.W. Koch (1987): "The temporal relationship between S&P 500 futures and the S&P 500 index". *Journal of Finance*, 42, 1309–1329.

King, M. and S.B. Wadhwani (1990): "Transmission of volatility between stock markets". *Review of Financial Studies*, 3(1), 5–33.

Malliavin, P. and M. Mancino (2002): "Fourier series method for measurement of multivariate volatilities". *Finance and Stochastics*, 6(1), 49–61.

Malliavin, P. and A. Thalmaier (2005): *Stochastic Calculus of Variations in Mathematical Finance*. Springer Finance.

Martens, M. (2002): "Measuring and forecasting S&P index-futures volatility using high-frequency data". *Journal of Futures Markets*, 22, 497–518.

Min, J.H. and M. Najand (1999): "A further investigation of the lead-lag relationship between the spot market and stock index futures: early evidence from Korea". *Journal of Futures Markets*, 19(2), 217–232.

Najand, M., H. Rahaman and K. Yung (1992): "Inter-currency transmission of volatility in foreign exchange futures". *The Journal of Financial Markets*, 12(6), 609–620.

Nelson, D.B. (1990): "ARCH models as diffusion approximations". *Journal of Econometrics*, 45, 7–38.

Oomen, R. (2002): *Modeling realized variance when returns are serially correlated.* Technical Report, Warwick Business School, University of Warwick.

Park, Y.C. and Song, C.Y. (2001): "Financial contagion in the East Asia Crisis with special reference to the Republic of Korea", in S. Claessens and K. Forbes eds, *International Financial Contagion*, Kluwer Academic Publishers.

Pericoli, M. and M. Sbracia (2003): "A primer on financial contagion." *Journal of Economic Surveys*, 17(4), 571–608.

Precup, O. and G. Iori (2006): "Cross-correlation in the high-frequency domain". *European Journal of Finance*, 12 (November).

Priestley, M. (1979): *Spectral Time Series Analysis*. Wiley.

Renò, R. (2003): "A closer look at the Epps effect". *International Journal of Theoretical and Applied Finance*, 6(1), 87–102.

Scholes, M. and J. Williams (1977): "Estimating betas from non synchronous data". *Journal of Financial Economics*, 5, 309–327.

Shephard, N. (1996): "Statistical aspects of ARCH and stochastic volatility", in Cox, Hinkley and Barndorff-Nielsen eds, *Likelihood, Time Series with Econometric and Other Application*, Chapman and Hall, London.

Tai, C. (2003): "Looking for Contagion in Currency Futures Markets". *Journal of Futures Market*, 23(10), 957–988.

Tse, Y. (1999): "Price discovery and volatility spillovers in the DJIA Index and futures Markets". *Journal of Futures Markets*, 19(8), 911–930.

Vasicek, O. (1977): "An equilibrium characterization of the term structure". *Journal of Financial Economics*, 5, 177–188.

6 Distributional properties of returns in thin futures markets

The case of the US$/AU$ contract

Volker Schieck[1]

Abstract

Using high-frequency data on US$/AU$ exchange rate futures, we construct realized volatility models. We investigate whether return, standardized return, variance and logarithmic standard deviation series are normally distributed in a thinly traded market. The behaviour of these series is analysed with the help of statistical normality tests. We find that logarithmic realized standard deviations, as opposed to variances, are fairly normally distributed. For returns as well as for standardized returns we cannot reject a normal distribution for roughly half of the series under inspection. This is an unexpected result as it is not in line with earlier results obtained with this methodology. The Asian crisis, falling into the time period covered by our data sample, is not found to have a significant impact on the distributional characteristics of the series.

Introduction

The volatility of financial markets is one of the most widely researched topics in finance, which, given the size of these markets, is not surprising. The foreign exchange market, in particular, is regarded as the largest of all financial markets, with a turnover estimated at US$1.5 trillion per day (Lyons, 2001 p. 13). The recognition that volatility is not constant over time, and thus the search for a way to forecast the movements of financial instruments, has fuelled research in this area for decades. Over the years, markets for new types of financial instruments have evolved as well as new tools to analyse them. The main focus of these newly developed methods and products are the major financial markets where global capital flows are greatest. Analytical and empirical results for large and liquid markets are established and serve as the basis for decision-making. Numerous important features of the volatility process have been identified in recent years, such as long memory (e.g. Ding *et al.*, 1993; Breidt *et al.*, 1998) and the volatility clustering effect (Bollerslev *et al.*, 1992; and Bollerslev *et al.*, 1994, provide helpful reviews). In recent years, a new approach to the analysis of volatility has been established. Closely linked to the increasing availability of ever more detailed financial market data, the analysis of intraday trading patterns has led eventually to the development of realized volatility models. One important result due to these models states that series of standardized returns and logarithmic realized standard deviations obtained from tick data are approximately normally distributed, whereas series of raw returns and realized variances are not (see, e.g., Andersen *et al.*, 2003a, henceforth ABDL, 2003). This is an influential result, since the distribution of financial market returns is one of the most important topics for the financial industry. As a key variable in the measure of expected risk it gains importance in countless applications in the industry.

To our knowledge, this methodology so far has been implemented mainly for the major financial market places. Whether and how these results carry over to markets with much lower trading volumes is not so well known. Numerous studies have documented a significant relationship between price variability and trading volume. The correlation between these two quantities is generally considered positive (e.g. Epps and Epps, 1976; Admati and Pfleiderer, 1988; and Varian, 1989), but under certain market conditions it can also be negative (Tauchen and Pitts, 1983).[2] It is therefore not evident that the results, which have been obtained with realized volatility models, remain valid also in comparatively smaller markets. In general, not much is known about return behaviour in thin futures markets, and it is thus interesting to investigate it with this new methodology. The futures market for the US dollar (US$)/Australian dollar (AU$) exchange rate is a prime example for the target market we want to analyse. It is a comparatively small market, and is representative of other thinly traded futures contracts in both developed and emerging markets. The main focus of our study lies on the analysis of return and realized volatility series for a number of different maturities of this specific futures contract. In particular, we employ high-frequency, tick-by-tick data and the methods developed by ABDL (2003) to determine whether the established findings of normally distributed standardized returns and log-realized standard deviations apply in this special case.

A second, minor focus of this study lies on the crisis that hit Asian financial markets in 1997–98. As our data set spans the years from 1997 through 1999, we have the opportunity to analyse whether this crisis is reflected in the distributional properties of these data. In particular, this means that we analyse whether it is possible to trace out significant abnormalities in the various series in the period in which the crisis was taking place. Any systematically deviating behaviour of the early series in our data set could potentially add some knowledge of financial crisis warning mechanisms.

Literature review

Financial market volatility is essentially an unobservable variable and there have been suggested many different methodological approaches in order to grasp its determining features. They range from parametric econometric models (such as models of the (G)ARCH type) to attempts to "extract" the volatility implied by options prices, which are based on option-pricing models (see, for example, Lamoureux and Lastrapes, 1993; Canina and Figlewski, 1993; or Christensen and Prabhala, 1998). Another prominent alternative is provided by more simple methods, such as the use of squared returns as approximations. Each of these approaches has limitations. Parametric specifications are always hampered by potential misspecification, since the unique and ultimately correct parameterization does not exist. Option-price-based models suffer from similar drawbacks. The simpler approaches using squared or absolute returns as indicators for the latent volatility theoretically deliver model-free and unbiased volatility estimates. At the "usual" daily, weekly or monthly frequencies, however, these estimates often tend to suffer severely from noise in the data which renders the outcomes unreliable (Andersen and Bollerslev, 1998a). One line of research that has been followed in order to try to avoid these problems is the use of intraday data, which eventually led to the establishment of realized volatility models. Recently, application of these models has become more frequent, following the increased availability of high-frequency data.

In an early work exploiting intraday data, Bollerslev and Melvin (1994) explore the link between exchange rate volatility and inherent bid–ask spreads, aiming at enhancing the understanding of the data's microstructure. Andersen and Bollerslev (1997a, b) investigate the relationships between long memory in intraday and daily data. They show that knowledge of intraday volatility patterns helps in understanding the volatility clustering effect, which is present in data with lower frequencies. In a similar spirit, Andersen and Bollerslev (1998b) then provide an instructive work in which they characterize systematically the volatility process of exchange rates. They analyse the process at different frequencies and again conclude for the significance of the information present in high-frequency data. In their analysis, they consider intraday activity patterns, macroeconomic announcements as well as volatility persistence. In a recent paper, Andersen *et al.* (2003b) have linked such high-frequency exchange rate dynamics to fundamental determinants of the volatility process. Building on works by French *et al.* (1987), Schwert (1989) and Schwert and Seguin (1990) who employ daily data in constructing monthly realized volatility models, ABDL (2003) formally establish the framework for realized volatility models. According to their work, it becomes possible to construct ex-post daily realized volatilities by accumulating intraday return data and "volatility estimates so constructed are model-free, and as the sampling frequency of the returns approaches infinity, they are also, in theory, free from measurement error."[3] Their article, together with later works involving the same methodologies for different data sets, is promising for modelling and forecasting financial volatility. Consider Andersen *et al.* (2001b), henceforth ABDL (2001), Andersen *et al.* (2001a), henceforth ABDE (2001), and Thomakos and Wang (2003) for helpful applications using foreign exchange, stock and futures markets data respectively. One common result of these studies is that series of raw returns, normalized by realized standard deviations, as well as series of logarithmic realized standard deviations are close to normally distributed, whereas series of simple returns and realized variances are not.

Following this approach, we determine whether the finding of normality holds for the data series under investigation. By treating volatility as actually observable we can rely on basic statistical methods to endeavour to reproduce these results with our new data set. Following Thomakos and Wang (2003) we will also apply formal statistical tests for normality, in order to check the validity of the results so obtained.

The Asian crisis

In the years following the Asian (financial) crisis, many studies have been conducted in order to investigate how far such a crisis could have been prevented had it been foreseen. There have been various attempts to establish early warning mechanisms that go beyond traditional warning signals such as alarming levels of budget deficit, inflation and/or current account deficit (Stein and Lim, 2004), which often did not indicate the crisis. Kaminsky *et al.* (1997) advocate the use of a signals approach by monitoring different indicators that, altogether, tend to behave differently in advance of a crisis. Their study, however, does not include the Asian Crisis. Kaminsky (1999) then distinguishes between currency and banking crises and analyses the links between the two. Evaluating more than 100 financial crises that broke out between 1975 and 1990 and comparing them to the Asian crisis, she develops a new set of indicators, mainly based on general financial distress. Bustelo (2000), however, while comparing the ERM crisis of the European Monetary System in 1992–93, the Mexican crisis of 1994–95 and the Asian Crisis, argues that financial crises rarely feature common patterns, underlining the difficulties involved in singling out generally applicable warning signals. Kaminsky and Reinhart (2000) and, more recently, Kaminsky *et al.* (2003) begin their analyses from a similar starting point in that they also compare different crises that have hit financial markets over the last 30 years. Their main focus, though, lies on the analysis of financial contagion, the mechanisms with which it spreads over different, not necessarily closely related, economies and the possibilities for detecting the eventual relevance of such phenomena in advance. Contagion is an effect that is also addressed by Stein and Lim (2004). In their article, they develop new means aimed at establishing an early warning system that helps detect financial crises before they can spread out and gain momentum. As in Kaminsky (1999), Stein and Lim (2004) distinguish between effects that may lead to a currency crisis and those that could induce a banking crisis. Accordingly, two different methods are applied in searching for indicative results. In order to identify meaningful results, they are, however, only partially successful: they do not achieve the desired outcome for all of the countries analysed and hence also refer to the presence of contagious effects.

A common feature of financial crises that appears in many of these studies, especially the more recent ones, is the presence of massive capital flows. These have a strong impact on the local currencies and the related financial systems have not always succeeded in coping with them. Compared to the most adversely affected economies, Australia was not as severely hit by the consequences of the Asian crisis, but according to Henry and Summers (1999), "the recent Asian economic downturn has led to significant turbulence in the US$/AU$ exchange rate," with the AU$ depreciating by over 7 per cent against the US$ in nominal terms.[4] We will see whether we can detect any traces of such developments in our data set.

Data discussion

In the empirical part of this study we employ data on futures of the US$/AU$ exchange rate. We use a tick-by-tick data set from which we construct intraday returns, suitable for the realized volatility modelling. The data originate from the Chicago Mercantile Exchange (CME) and cover the years 1997 through 1999. For each year we have data on four different contracts maturing in March, June, September and December of the respective years, which gives us a total of 12 series. Each series consists of time-stamped "time and sales" data, which record the price of a transaction only if the price is different from the previously recorded price.

An inspection of the data set revealed that it had to be truncated considerably in order to be appropriate for the analyses. We encountered two main problems: first, we found that the series for some days exhibit zero trading, in particular early in the series, far from the contracts' maturity dates. As these sample points might distort the analyses by adding to the sample size but not carrying any information, we decided to include only the observations of the three calendar months preceding the month of maturity (e.g. for the March contract analysis we employ data from December onward, deleting all earlier sample points; the remaining series received analogous treatment). By doing so, we hope to avoid any problems that might arise from no trading at all in the market.

Second, futures and spot prices converge as the futures contracts approach maturity. This could lead to distortions in futures prices during the delivery month, as these are expected to take over some of the spot market dynamics towards the end of their duration period. We thus decided to also exclude the month in which a futures contract matures. This can be seen as another safety measure employed to minimize confusion in the data to be analysed. We are then left with data covering three months of trading in each contract.

In order to implement the realized volatility method, we want to construct X-minute return series, where X should be chosen discriminately.[5] On the one hand, it needs to be small enough in order to reflect the high frequency of the data and to justify the asymptotic theory underlying the realized volatility measurement. On the other hand, X needs to be large enough to avoid microstructure frictions of the underlying price data, such as inherent bid–ask price spreads and discrete clustering.[6]

Inspecting the (truncated) data set, however, it becomes apparent that, rather than having a dense data set, we sometimes observe large gaps between the single ticks, where returns would have to cover intervals of over 60 minutes, making it hard to construct, for example, five-minute return series, and confirming thus ABDL (2001) in saying that "ultimately it [the choice of the sampling frequency] is an empirical issue that hinges on market liquidity."[7] Since the subject of our study is a market characterized by its low trading volumes, this is a problem that was to be expected. The inherent challenge is therefore to optimally make use of what is available in terms of data.

One obvious response would be to enlarge the return horizon in order to circumvent the biggest gaps in the series. We do not consider this to be helpful, however, as this way we lose a good deal of the information from the high frequency of the underlying price data. The asymptotic treatment of the return series would become questionable since, as discussed in the Methodology section, the theoretical results for the realized volatility modelling hinge on sufficiently finely sampled data.

An alternative solution is to further limit the sample, that is, to restrict ourselves to the first 40 minutes of each trading day (i.e. from 7:20 a.m. until 8:00 a.m.). Although it now appears to be more appropriate to speak of "early-morning volatility" instead of daily volatility, we choose this option. The reasons why this is indeed the preferable choice will become clear in the next paragraph. Considering the distribution of trades in these further shortened samples, we separate each trading day (i.e. each 40-minute morning period) into four ten-minute intervals. It seems that for the great majority of the series in this period, this choice of interval size is justifiable in the sense that the single ticks are dense enough for our purposes; five-minute returns, for example, are still too narrow and not enough meaningful intervals could be obtained this way. It is obvious that this treatment limits the size of the data set significantly. We only have four observations per day, corresponding to four ten-minute intervals. Given that all prior studies employ much larger data sets, it is not guaranteed that the quality of the data allows for a meaningful application of the realized volatility models.[8]

We are nevertheless convinced that this option is more promising than increasing the interval size. Given that the original price data cover trading from 7:20:00 a.m. to 2:00:00 p.m., an interval size of more than 60 minutes would give us at most six intraday observations. This, admittedly, is more than the four we have now, but the crucial point is that we lose considerably more information from the microstructure of the data. It is therefore more appealing to restrict the data set under investigation to the early morning part. It will be shown later that indeed some sensible results can be obtained with such a limited data set. Notwithstanding some difficulties that arise from the short time series used, some established findings can be reproduced.

Methodology

In this section we will explain in more detail how we arrived at the results, which we will present below. We do not intend to provide here a detailed discussion of the theoretical issues involved in the realized volatility measurements. A more thorough treatment of such issues is given in ABDL (2001). We restrict ourselves instead to presenting the basic ideas underlying the methodology we apply. In doing so, we move along the lines of ABDE (2001), who provide a short but comprehensive discussion of the main issues to be considered.

The underlying theory

To begin with, we assume a logarithmic Nx1 vector price process, p_t, to follow a continuous time stochastic volatility diffusion,

$$dp_t = \mu_t dt + \Omega_t dW_t, \tag{1}$$

where W_t denotes a N-dimensional Brownian motion and Ω_t, the process of the NxN diffusion matrix, is strictly stationary. The unit time interval is normalized to represent one trading day, i.e. $h=1$. We then determine the return process, which is evidently conditional on the sample path realizations of μ_t and Ω_t. The distribution of the continuously compounded h-period returns, $r_{t+h,h} \equiv p_{t+h} - p_t$ is given by

$$r_{t+h,h} \,\big|\, \sigma(\mu_{t+\tau}, \Omega_{t+\tau})^{h}_{\tau=0} \sim N\left(\int_0^h \mu_{t+\tau} d\tau, \int_0^h \Omega_{t+\tau} d\tau\right), \tag{2}$$

where $\sigma(\mu_{t+\tau}, \Omega_{t+\tau})^{h}_{t+0}$ denotes the sigma field generated by the sample paths of μ_t and Ω_t. By integrating the diffusion matrix Ω we are thus able to obtain a measure of the true latent h-period volatility of the return process. From the theory of quadratic variation, it holds that, under weak regularity conditions,

$$\sum_{j=1,\ldots,[h/\Delta]} r_{t+j\Delta,\Delta} r'_{t+j\Delta,\Delta} - \int_0^h \Omega_{t+\tau} d\tau \quad \stackrel{a.s.}{\rightarrow} \quad 0 \quad \forall t \quad as \quad \Delta \rightarrow 0. \tag{3}$$

Thus, as the sampling frequency of returns increases, we achieve an ever more exact result for the volatility until we achieve asymptotically a volatility measurement that is free of measurement error.[9] The availability of high-frequency data enables us to elegantly circumvent some of the problems that normally arise with the use of squared return series as an ex-post volatility measure. It becomes possible to avoid the noise induced by measurement error in return series that are sampled at a lower frequency (see ABDE, 2001, for a more detailed discussion and for related references).

Implementation

The practical proceedings aimed at the implementation of these concepts comprise the following: first, we want to construct ten-minute interval return series and aggregate those in order to artificially form daily return series, each one consisting thus of four observations. From these, we can calculate the realized variance and standard deviation series. Following ABDE (2001) we then normalize the return series by dividing by the realized standard deviations and put the series of standard deviations in logarithms.[10] Second, we look at the four series' distributional properties (i.e. we employ a simple graphical analysis and consider descriptive statistics). Third, following Thomakos and Wang (2003), we use more formal testing means, such as statistical normality tests, in order to determine how far the series' distributions can be considered to approach a standard normal distribution.

We shall consider each of these points in more detail. To begin with, we note that price data have been transformed to natural logarithms. We further assume that returns are independent and have a zero-expected value. Actual returns are then calculated as the difference between the last observations in each interval, that is, the last observation before the next ten-minute mark. The return for the second interval is then given by the difference between log prices of, say, 7:39:59 a.m. and 7:29:59 a.m. This is the usual way to proceed in order to ensure that returns do not overlap the endpoints of the sampling intervals and hence do not violate the independence assumption. Note that this is also the approach followed by, for example, ABDE (2001). It is important to emphasize here that our trading day consists of the first 40 minutes of the day only. The first return for each day is therefore the difference between the last observation in the first interval and the last observation in the last interval on the previous day. More explicitly, it is the difference between log prices at, say, 7:29:59 a.m. on day one and at 7:59:59 a.m. on day zero. This way we obtain 12 series of 200 (March 1997) up to 260 (September 1998) ten-minute returns. Given that we have four observations per day, this corresponds to roughly 60 trading days for each contract with the exception of the March 1997 series with only 50 trading days.

We then calculate the daily realized volatilities, that is, we sum the squares of the artificially constructed ten-minute intervals and use that as volatility measure. Under the aforementioned assumptions, the variance of the sum is equal to the sum of the variances and is hence given by

$$VAR_{i,t} = \sum_{j=1,\ldots,1/\Delta} r^2_{i,t+j\Delta}, \tag{4}$$

where i indicates the contract, $t=1,\ldots,T$ denotes the trading day and T takes on a value in [50,65] for the respective contracts; $\Delta=1/4$ indicates the intraday sampling frequency and $r_{i,t}$ denotes the series of daily returns, incorporating the ten-minute return observations. Accordingly, logarithmic realized standard deviations are given by $l\sigma_{i,t}=\ln(\sqrt{VAR_{i,t}})$. We standardize returns by the simple realized standard deviation: $r^*_{i,t}=r_{i,t}/l\sigma_{i,t}$. This way, we obtain series of about 60 observations for each variable and contract, each based on the four intraday observations.

In order to improve reliability of our results, it is necessary that these time series are stationary. [This is the more important since in a different, but related, research project in which we employed daily data (original daily quotes, not accumulated tick data) of the same futures contracts, we found that one of the return series was close to non-stationary.] We therefore conducted unit root tests of the series of aggregated daily observations. Employing augmented Dickey–Fuller (ADF) and Phillips–Perron (PP) tests, we find that for all of the series we have to reject the hypothesis of a unit root. Only for one series (December 1997 contracts), the ADF statistic comes close to indicating a significant unit root at a 5 per cent confidence level. As this is not confirmed by the PP test, we decide to keep the series as they are and conclude for overall stationarity.

Normality tests

As Thomakos and Wang (2003) have found, the standard Jarque–Bera (JB) test tends to over-reject the null hypothesis of normality in the presence of long memory in the series, which in our case is to be expected. Hence, we also employ two additional tests for normality: the Crámer–von Misses (CVM) and the Anderson–Darling (AD) tests.[11] These tests are similar in nature and compare the empirical distribution's order statistics with the theoretical distribution tested, which in our case is a standard normal distribution. They also conduct a simulation study, which indicates that these two tests give reliable results in comparison to the JB test, even in the presence of serial correlation. In particular, they show that for those tests, for a Gaussian series with long memory in a large sample, it is possible to use the critical values derived under independence for all tests, except for the JB test. As we face a very small sample here, the adverse effects on the JB test may not be as pronounced as for their sample. We will, however, present combined results and see whether the outcomes of the three tests differ qualitatively from each other.

Results

In the following two subsections we analyse the results from the realized volatility modelling. We consider the realized variances together with the logarithmic standard deviations as well as the return series together with the standardized return series. Our main interest lies with the series' unconditional distributions and we try to determine how far it is justifiable to state that they are approaching a standard normal distribution.

Realized variances and logarithmic standard deviations

The summary statistics in Table 6.1 give a first impression of the results we obtained. We notice that the realized variance series are highly leptokurtic with

Table 6.1 Descriptive statistics of realized variances and logarithmic standard deviations

Realized variances

	March 97	*June 97*	*Sep. 97*	*Dec. 97*	*March 98*	*June 98*	*Sep. 98*	*Dec. 98*	*March 99*	*June 99*	*Sep. 99*	*Dec. 99*
Mean	3.98E-06	3.84E-06	3.58E-06	4.45E-06	5.33E-06	2.70E-06	4.22E-06	4.71E-06	4.07E-06	2.03E-06	3.63E-06	2.46E-06
Std. dev.	4.60E-06	4.42E-06	4.37E-06	6.73E-06	5.24E-06	3.17E-06	6.03E-06	5.74E-06	4.11E-06	2.05E-06	6.63E-06	2.71E-06
Skewness	1.832536	2.091036	2.33872	2.793575	1.272604	2.109083	3.225919	2.844999	1.499078	2.248785	4.422138	2.273048
Kurtosis	5.809408	8.004302	9.219146	11.67102	4.516892	7.468585	16.68111	11.67032	5.080131	9.016896	24.94284	9.717575
Observations	50	63	64	62	61	63	65	62	60	64	65	61

Logarithmic standard deviations

	March 97	*June 97*	*Sep. 97*	*Dec. 97*	*March 98*	*June 98*	*Sep. 98*	*Dec. 98*	*March 99*	*June 99*	*Sep. 99*	*Dec. 99*
Mean	–6.550342	–6.573864	–6.556412	–6.579255	–6.365597	–6.708226	–6.56616	–6.419279	–6.508423	–6.752463	–6.680557	–6.746861
Std. dev.	0.625037	0.659303	0.588923	0.686626	0.67978	0.617416	0.667046	0.630839	0.681847	0.487123	0.656605	0.593456
Skewness	–0.236837	–0.457579	–0.390779	–0.218647	–0.982627	–0.603824	–0.324589	–1.47851	–1.27354	–0.547951	–0.128211	–0.505467
Kurtosis	2.416733	2.521222	3.001032	3.223109	3.7637	3.148865	3.031541	8.095858	5.744142	3.650945	3.207985	3.072369
Observations	50	63	64	62	61	63	65	62	60	64	65	61

kurtosis values ranging from 4.52 to 24.94 (mean: 10.32) whereas the logarithmic standard deviations have much thinner tails with kurtosis ranging from 2.42 to 8.1 (mean: 3.74). A second observation regards the series' skewness statistics: the realized variance series are very strongly skewed to the left, values ranging from 1.27 to 4.42 (mean: 2.41), whereas the logarithmic standard deviation series are skewed much less and to the right, values ranging from –1.48 to –0.13 (mean: –0.6).

For both series we thus observe a three- to fourfold decrease in these curvature measures, after transforming the simple realized variances. Turning to Figure 6.1, which pictures the kernel density of the March 1997 contracts' volatility series along with that of a N(0,1) distribution, the transformation's effects become apparent. We present the graphics of this specific contract as here the "improvement" in terms of closeness to a standard normal distribution of the log realized standard deviations are best visible.

The impressions from the descriptive statistics are confirmed and fit our initial expectations. The change in the distributional properties in favour of a normal distribution after transforming the series is obvious. Especially the skewness of the realized variances has been eliminated almost completely. The peakedness still prevails but to a much smaller degree, such that the graph

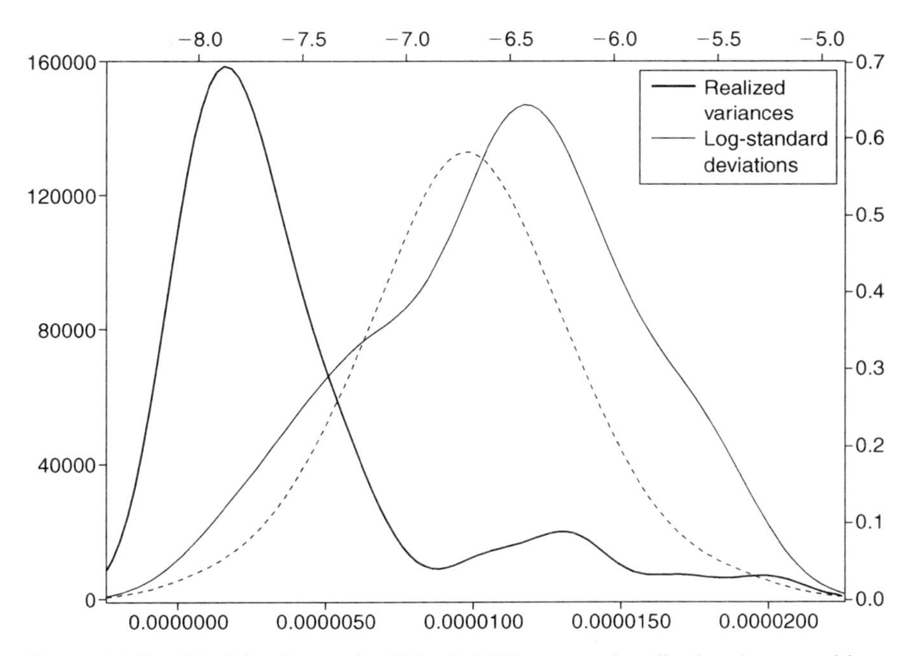

Figure 6.1 Empirical density graph of March 1997 contracts' realized variances and logarithmic standard deviation series.

Notes

Top/right scale is for the series of logarithmic standard deviations, and the dotted line represents a standard normal distribution graph.

vaguely resembles a standard normal distribution density. The graphs of the other contracts' series exhibit similar patterns. A complete set of all series' empirical kernel density graphs is given in Figures 6.A.1 through 6.A.4 in the Appendix.

In order to formalize our conclusions, we consider statistical normality tests. Table 6.2 summarizes their outcomes.

Starting with the results for the realized variances, we observe that the null hypothesis of normality has to be rejected for all series at a significance level of 1 per cent. All three different tests deliver results that are consistent with each other. There is no doubt that these series are far from approaching a normal distribution.

Turning to the results of the logarithmic standard deviations, we find very different results. At a 1 per cent significance level the tests' outcomes clearly indicate that only for two series, the June 1998 and December 1998 contracts, we have to reject normality according to the AD and CVM tests (in the case of the June 1998 contracts also according to the JB tests). For all the other series we do not. Changing the significance level, however, leads us to realize that the actual results are somewhat weaker than that. At a 5 per cent significance level we find that for four of the series (March, June and December 1998 and March 1999), we have to reject the hypothesis of normality. For the June 1998 series, the JB test is not significant. As, however, the other two tests delivered highly significant results, we reject the hypothesis of normality for the series. Further lowering the confidence levels, we find that for the June 1997 and 1999 series we have to reject the hypothesis of normality at a 10 per cent level according to the AD test (June 1997) and both AD and CVM tests (June 1999), respectively. This leaves us with just six series for which we cannot reject normality at all.

We therefore conclude at this point that the series' transformations have led to the expected results in roughly 50 per cent of the cases at a reasonable significance level. Whereas the realized variance distributions behave as expected, not all the log-realized standard deviation distributions do so. Unfortunately, these results are not as strong as anticipated and we are thus not quite in a position to confirm results from the aforementioned earlier works. A possible explanation might lie in our very limited data set. The results we obtain, however, are encouraging in the sense that they point in the right direction and in our opinion it is safe to say that the applied methodology has also in our case proven to be valid. The qualitative conclusions we are able to draw until now are the same. The size of the effects, however, does not appear to be as strong.

Impact of the Asian crisis

As mentioned above, we also want to examine our data with respect to the financial crisis that hit Asian economies in the late 1990s. Inspecting our outcomes, it appears very difficult, if not impossible, to make out any significant pattern that

Table 6.2 Results from the normality tests of the realized variances' and logarithmic standard deviations' distributions

Realized variances

	March 97	*June 97*	*Sep. 97*	*Dec. 97*	*March 98*	*June 98*	*Sep. 98*	*Dec. 98*	*March 99*	*June 99*	*Sep. 99*	*Dec. 99*
JB	44.42818*	111.6485*	161.4833*	274.8739*	22.3134*	99.1231*	619.6641*	277.8389*	33.28972*	150.4831*	1515.88*	167.2234*
p-value	0	0	0	0	0.000014	0	0	0	0	0	0	0
CVM	0.769145*	0.688645*	1.022649*	1.493796*	0.380635*	0.930467*	1.309136*	1.294066*	0.564845*	0.977332*	1.881213*	0.71965*
p-value	0	0	0	0	0	0	0	0	0	0	0	0
AD	4.293907*	4.162265*	5.536558*	7.826268*	2.35704*	5.28135*	6.812106*	7.029831*	3.209863*	5.240508*	10.02532*	4.119647*
p-value	0	0	0	0	0	0	0	0	0	0	0	0

Logarithmic standard deviations

	March 97	*June 97*	*Sep. 97*	*Dec. 97*	*March 98*	*June 98*	*Sep. 98*	*Dec. 98*	*March 99*	*June 99*	*Sep. 99*	*Dec. 99*
JB	1.176184	2.800204	1.628894	0.622592	11.29888*	3.886508	1.144075	89.67197*	35.04482*	4.332616	0.295236	2.610863
p-value	0.555386	0.246572	0.442884	0.732497	0.003519	0.143237	0.564374	0	0	0.1146	0.862761	0.271056
CVM	0.050984	0.096532	0.057178	0.033756	0.169875^{+}	0.181036*	0.061351	0.234224*	0.136996$^{\#}$	0.117568^{+}	0.044294	0.055559
p-value	0.4973	0.1256	0.4122	0.7917	0.0131	0.0094	0.3632	0.002	0.0355	0.0647	0.6027	0.4329
AD	0.303592	0.652133^{+}	0.37384	0.263021	1.11647*	1.096155*	0.353143	1.367736*	0.885905$^{\#}$	0.750902$^{\#}$	0.268538	0.397483
p-value	0.5725	0.0888	0.4169	0.7013	0.0064	0.0071	0.4651	0.0015	0.0235	0.0507	0.6827	0.3675

Notes

1 The statistics of the Crámer–von Misses and of the Anderson–Darling tests have a finite sample correction and are adjusted for parameter uncertainty. The assigned probabilities correspond to these adjusted values.

2 We indicate significance of the various test statistics by the following:

Significance at the 1% level – *

Significance at the 5% level – $^{\#}$

Significance at the 10% level – $^{+}$

would state a considerable anomaly in that time period. We can see from the descriptive statistics in Table 6.1 that the mean volatility associated with the crisis period (September 1997 up to and including December 1998) is not significantly higher than during the rest of the sample period. The same holds for the dispersion of volatility throughout that period, measured by the standard deviation of the realized volatility series. None of the statistics given in Table 6.1 shows a clear time-pattern throughout the years which makes it even more difficult to state deviations from such a pattern.

One notable observation is that in the series of logarithmic-realized standard deviations, we find that in the six periods from March 1998 up to and including June 1999 the hypothesis of normality is rejected significantly more often than for the rest of the series. In fact, five out of the five cases where we reliably have to reject normality fall into this period with the exception being the September 1998 series, which is considered normally distributed. What we observe is not a very strong result that we can also attribute to pure chance. It might, however, also be some indication for significant abnormalities that are worth exploring with a more complete data set. One could speculate, for example, that the irregularities in our findings could indicate effects from the Asian crises that hit Australian markets with a lag of a few months.

Given the fact that the Australian currency had been affected significantly by the crisis, as reported in Henry and Summers (1999), these results, overall, do not indicate a significant impact of the Asian crisis. A possible explanation might lie in the time horizon of our data set – it spans only the years 1997–1999, and hence it might be possible that all of our series show behaviour, deviating from the "normal" behaviour. We are, however, not in a position to further examine these ideas, as the data set does not allow for this.

Returns and standardized returns

What remains now in this section is to look at the results from the other two series, the raw return series and the return series normalized by the realized standard deviations. We introduce Table 6.3, which presents the summary statistics for these two series.

Given our promising results from the volatility series above, the results for the return series are somewhat sobering. In fact, we observe that the results are quite different from what we expected. They are surprising in two ways: first, looking at the descriptive statistics, the return series' distributions seem to be already close to a standard normal one in roughly half of the cases. Kurtosis and skewness statistics do not seem to be too far away from their "normal" values, ranging from 2.66 to 11.85 (mean: 4.51) and from –1.93 to 1.21 (mean: –0.14), respectively. Second, turning now to the standardized return series, we find similar results in that also here for roughly half of the series we observe descriptive statistics that tend towards those of a standard normal distribution. For the normalized returns we find that the kurtosis and skewness statistics take values from 1.64 to 2.24 (mean: 1.9) and from –0.34 to 0.35 (mean: –0.1), respectively.

Table 6.3 Descriptive statistics of return and standardized return series

Returns

	March 97	*June 97*	*Sep. 97*	*Dec. 97*	*March 98*	*June 98*	*Sep. 98*	*Dec. 98*	*March 99*	*June 99*	*Sep. 99*	*Dec. 99*
Mean	0.000034	–0.000402	–0.0000547	0.000219	–0.000308	0.000214	–0.00000615	–0.000223	0.000313	0.000195	0.000178	0.000143
Std. dev.	0.001814	0.001816	0.001834	0.00167	0.002113	0.001464	0.001774	0.002164	0.001892	0.001384	0.00205	0.001588
Skewness	0.327519	0.175558	–0.468264	–0.069046	0.135687	0.615416	–0.598228	1.206643	0.130825	–1.006356	–1.935122	–0.139092
Kurtosis	4.684312	3.303	3.287516	3.409162	2.747892	3.809688	3.851235	5.802431	2.656632	4.775644	11.85099	3.985708
Observations	50	63	64	62	61	63	65	62	60	64	65	61

Standardized returns

	March 97	*June 97*	*Sep. 97*	*Dec. 97*	*March 98*	*June 98*	*Sep. 98*	*Dec. 98*	*March 99*	*June 99*	*Sep. 99*	*Dec. 99*
Mean	0.031925	–0.172035	0.069124	0.124006	–0.07696	0.064983	0.031548	–0.242141	0.227994	0.178404	0.130561	0.107689
Std. dev.	0.847002	0.938444	0.901788	0.914545	0.953567	0.868494	0.91724	0.938842	0.925832	0.899822	0.982943	1.015774
Skewness	–0.021504	–0.027148	–0.122886	–0.3356	0.172865	–0.115911	–0.215874	0.346502	–0.305068	–0.241112	–0.285727	–0.001024
Kurtosis	1.903041	2.02771	1.64479	1.895103	1.709841	1.832001	1.999929	2.066905	1.859043	2.244149	1.900936	1.737617
Observations	50	63	64	62	61	63	65	62	60	64	65	61

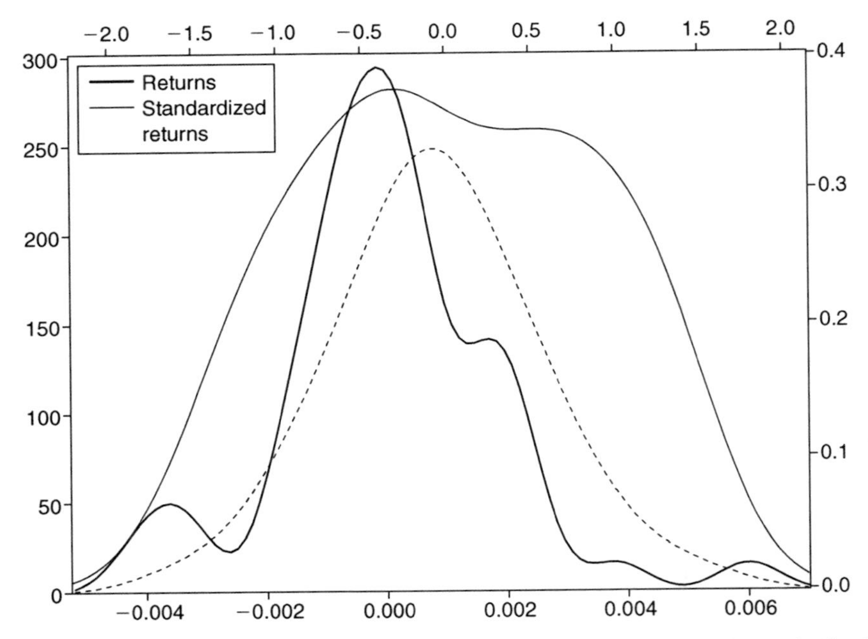

Figure 6.2 Empirical density graph of March 1997 contracts' raw and standardized return series.

Notes
The top/right scale is for the series of standardized returns, and the dotted line represents a standard normal distribution graph.

As for the other pair of series, we observe a significant reduction of kurtosis and skewness values following normalization. Here, however, kurtosis values fall below levels to be expected for a standard normal distribution. From the descriptive statistics presented in Table 6.3, therefore, the series of standardized returns appears "as normal" as the series of raw returns.

In order to confirm this initial impression from the basic statistics, we turn to Figure 6.2, which sketches again the March 1997 contracts' density graph, this time for the two return series, again together with a standard normal distribution density graph.

The graph confirms our expectations. The density of the raw returns is leptokurtic and slightly skewed. The density of the standardized returns appears somewhat deformed, which is attributable to the low kurtosis. The two graphs are neither very similar nor does one of them strongly resemble a standard normal distribution density. In order to statistically support our visual impressions, and such that we can arrive at a more definite conclusion, we turn to the normality tests. The tests results are summarized in Table 6.4 below.

Consider first the test results for the raw return series. At a 1 per cent significance level, we have to reject normality for only two of the series, namely for the December 1998 and September 1999 series. According to all three tests, the

Table 6.4 Results from the normality tests of the returns' and standardized returns series' distributions

Returns

	March 97	*June 97*	*Sep. 97*	*Dec. 97*	*March 98*	*June 98*	*Sep. 98*	*Dec. 98*	*March 99*	*June 99*	*Sep. 99*	*Dec. 99*
JB	6.804126	0.564614	2.559337	0.481749	0.348722	5.697677	5.839463	35.33373	0.465906	19.21046	252.7384	2.666225
p-value	$0.033304^{\#}$	0.754042	0.278129	0.78594	0.839994	0.057912^{+}	0.053948^{+}	0^{*}	0.792191	0.000067^{*}	0^{*}	0.263655
CVM	0.124059	0.124664	0.102833	0.047513	0.031718	0.067205	0.064648	0.285686	0.058406	0.112343	0.181023	0.047319
p-value	0.0529^{+}	0.0519^{+}	0.1028	0.5475	0.8232	0.3043	0.3287	0.0005^{*}	0.3971	0.0762^{+}	0.0094^{*}	0.5506
AD	0.784761	0.724965	0.565885	0.272311	0.209477	0.480732	0.451421	1.657272	0.371716	0.872335	1.276642	0.293754
p-value	$0.0418^{\#}$	0.0587	0.1429	0.67	0.8624	0.2326	0.2739	0.0003^{*}	0.4217	$0.0254^{\#}$	0.0026^{*}	0.6009

Standardized returns

	March 97	*June 97*	*Sep. 97*	*Dec. 97*	*March 98*	*June 98*	*Sep. 98*	*Dec. 98*	*March 99*	*June 99*	*Sep. 99*	*Dec. 99*
JB	2.51077	2.489277	5.058664	4.31754	4.534438	3.722153	3.213567	3.489878	4.185121	2.143601	4.155941	4.050437
p-value	0.284966	0.288045	0.079712^{+}	0.115467	0.1036	0.155505	0.200532	0.174656	0.123371	0.342391	0.125184	0.131965
CVM	0.065173	0.084614	0.210648	0.19857	0.167416	0.105529	0.085293	0.11505	0.211862	0.059812	0.14798	0.144101
p-value	0.3235	0.1806	0.004^{*}	0.0056^{*}	$0.0141^{\#}$	0.0945^{+}	0.177	0.07^{+}	0.0038^{*}	0.3805	$0.0253^{\#}$	$0.0285^{\#}$
AD	0.459933	0.48633	1.44146	1.2316	1.180449	0.845934	0.610589	0.850373	1.213631	0.388023	1.018104	1.04812
p-value	0.2612	0.2254	0.001^{*}	0.0033^{*}	0.0044^{*}	$0.0295^{\#}$	0.1125	$0.0288^{\#}$	0.0037^{*}	0.3866	$0.0111^{\#}$	0.0094^{*}

Notes

1 The statistics of the Crámer–von Misses and of the Anderson–Darling tests have a finite sample correction and are adjusted for parameter uncertainty. The assigned probabilities correspond to these adjusted values.

2 We indicate significance of the various test statistics by the following:
Significance at the 1% level – *
Significance at the 5% level – $^{\#}$
Significance at the 10% level – $^{+}$

hypothesis of normality is untenable. Reducing the confidence level to 5 per cent and then to 10 per cent, we find that we now also have to reject normality for the March and June 1997 series as well as for the June 1999 series. According to the Jarque-Bera test, we also have to reject normality for the June and September 1998 series at a 10 percent confidence level. Due to the aforementioned problems with this test and the strongly deviating results from the other two tests, we do not take this into account and conclude that for seven out of the 12 series of raw returns we cannot reject the hypothesis of a normal distribution. This confirms our earlier impressions and is an unexpected finding: it is usually found that return distributions are comparably fat tailed and are therefore not normal, and this is also what is found by all the aforementioned studies making use of realized volatility models. We attribute this result to the small sample size. It is likely that the short time series do not allow us to observe statistically significant non-normality. Whether the normality of the price changes is, in fact, due to the sample size, or whether it constitutes a new result and can be attributed to the particular type of data, needs to be verified with the help of a larger data set. Given the results for the volatility series, however, we regard this latter possibility as rather improbable.

The type of distribution that is justifiable to assume for financial returns is central to the financial industry, for example in setting their deposit margins. Whether the returns in thin markets are indeed systematically closer to normally distributed compared to more liquid markets or whether they comply with the usual assumption of a fat-tailed distribution (such as a Student t-distribution) when analysed with a bigger sample size, is of great interest. It would therefore be illuminating to repeat the present exercise with a richer data set, such that we can draw stronger conclusions in this respect.

We then turn to the returns, which are standardized by the realized standard deviations. Although the descriptive statistics were not very promising, we expect the series to be normally distributed, as follows from earlier research. Results from the normality tests are to be found in the lower half of Table 6.4. Against our expectations, we find a similar picture as for the raw returns above: at a 1 per cent significance level we have to reject normality for three of the series (September and December 1997, March 1999), according to the AD and CVM tests. The JB test is significant only at 10 per cent for two of these contracts, and referring again to the problems associated with this test, we base our conclusions mainly on the other two tests. Reducing the confidence level, we observe that we have to reject normality for at least six out of the 12 series (additionally, the March 1998 as well as September and December 1999 series) at a 5 per cent significance level. At 10 per cent, normality is also rejected according to both AD and CVM for the June and December 1998 series. We therefore find expected results in at most six cases, not accounting for the latter two series due to the comparably low significance of the CVM test in both cases. These results are clearly in contrast to previous results. It is, however, very likely that these results are again affected by the short span of the data set: the fact that we base our calculations of the daily realized variance on four intraday observations implies that we might have a rather poor estimator of the daily variance. The original theory states that the realized variance estimator approaches the true daily variance as the number of intraday observations increases. As the number of observations grows, over which the daily variance is calculated (that is, the smaller Δ becomes in equation (4)), the more reliable becomes the realized variance measure. Since we calculate it over only four observations, we cannot rule out the possibility that the estimator obtained is somewhat unreliable. Hence, standardizing by the logarithm of that estimator is not standardizing at all. This is exactly what we observe: the standardized return series are even less normally distributed than the raw return series. In only three cases (March, June 1997 and December 1999) the normalization led to the expected result. In six cases, however, (September, December 1997; March, June 1998; and March, December 1999) the opposite result was obtained: standardization of normally distributed returns leads to non-normally distributed standardized returns. In the remaining three cases, the series are either both normally or both non-normally distributed. This leads us to conclude that the series' transformations either did not have a significant effect at all or they did not have the expected effects in the majority of the cases.

Overall, these results are inconclusive and prevent us from obtaining results similar to those in ABDL (2001), ABDE (2001) or Thomakos and Wang (2003). In contrast with the results for the volatility series, here the qualitative conclusions also remain ambiguous. It is surprising that the method produced anticipated results for the volatility series, although it did not do so for the return series.

Impact of the Asian crisis

Even more than for the volatility series, it holds that we cannot determine any clear patterns in the data for the return series over the course of time. This makes it impossible to determine any irregularities that would possibly be induced by the Asian crisis. Interestingly, we again do not find any signs for elevated volatility in the series, associated with the months around the supposed outbreak of the crisis in the second half of 1997.

These findings could, as before, be attributed to the time horizon of our data set, being too short in order to uncover distinctive patterns in the data that could have led to predicting the turmoil in financial markets.

Conclusions

In our analysis of US$/AU$ exchange rate futures, we implemented realized volatility models so as to determine whether daily return and volatility series, constructed from intraday data, can be considered normally distributed. Following earlier work with these types of models, we investigated whether the established findings of normally distributed log-realized standard deviations and returns, standardized by realized standard deviations, can be reproduced for a thin futures market. Our results imply that we were only partially successful in doing so. On the one hand, outcomes for the log-realized standard deviations are promising in that we achieved the expected result in at least half of the cases. The fact that we could not fully reproduce here the results from earlier work is most probably attributable to our limited data set. For this variable we thus conclude that the method proved valid. It might, however, be necessary to reconfirm these findings with a larger data set. Our results for the raw and standardized returns, on the other hand, are not as expected. Standardized returns are even less close to a normal distribution than raw return series, both of which are unusual outcomes. It appears that our calculations here are severely hampered by the small sample, and we therefore cannot confirm previous results.

Although the empirical findings we obtain do not fully coincide with our expectations, we are tempted to conclude that the method applied is valid also in small markets and that therefore similar results can be expected as were achieved in earlier research. The results for the volatility series especially move in the right direction and indicate the proper working of the methodology. In order to provide stronger support for this claim, it might be necessary to repeat the current exercise with a larger data set.

Regarding the Asian crisis, we conclude that our data set and the methodology we apply are not likely to help establish new warning mechanisms for financial crises. Besides the observation of increased non-normality of the volatility series a few months after the outbreak of the crisis, we cannot make out any irregularities in the return series. Although this might be an indication of the impact of the crisis on Australian currency markets, it obviously does not constitute a signal of the *arrival* of unrest in financial markets.

Appendix

In Figure 6.A.1, the series denominated VAR_ADH97, VAR_ADM97, VAR_ADU97, VAR_ADZ97 are the realized variance series for March 1997, June 1997, September 1997 and December 1997, respectively. An analogous identification applies for Figures 6.A.2 to 6.A.4.

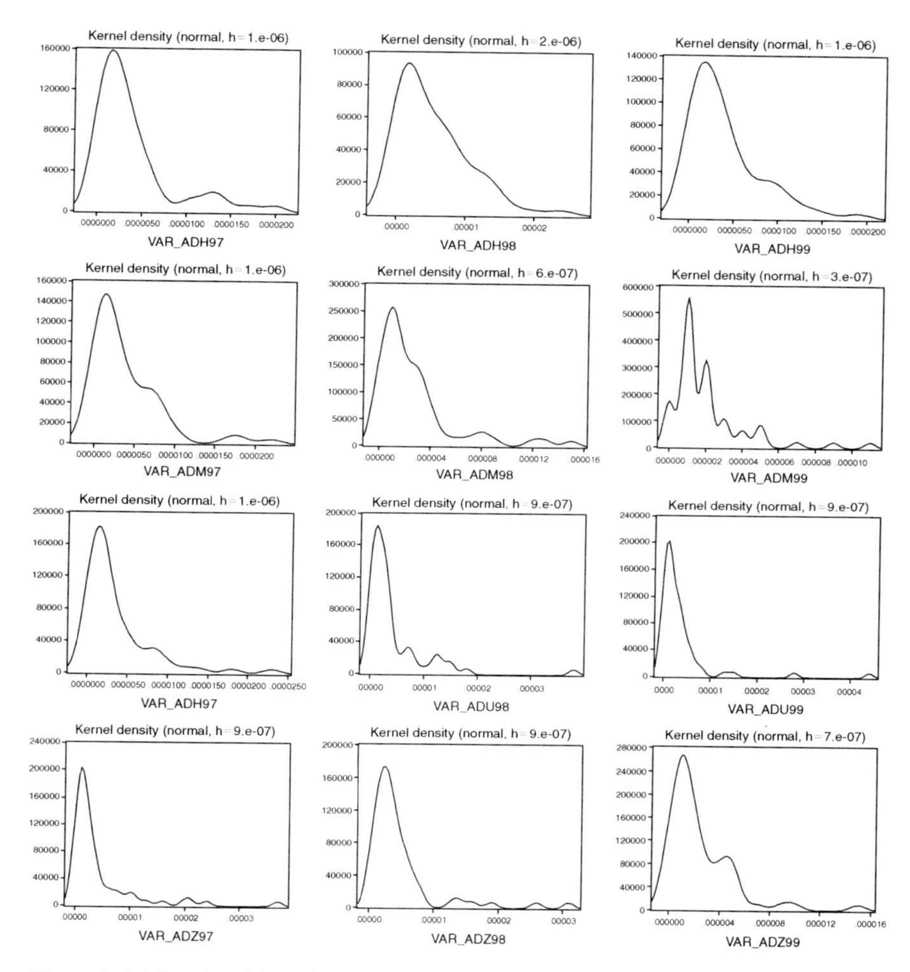

Figure 6.A.1 Empirical kernel densities of realized variances.

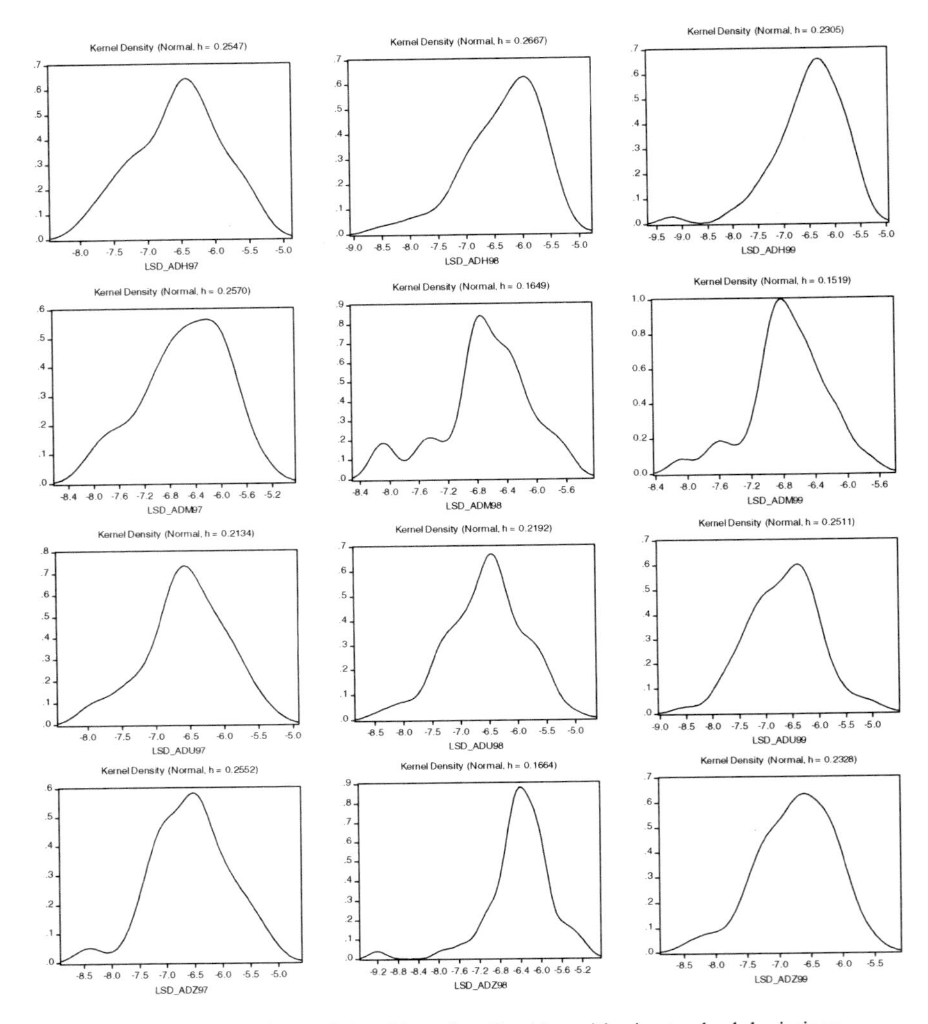

Figure 6.A.2 Empirical kernel densities of realized logarithmic standard deviations.

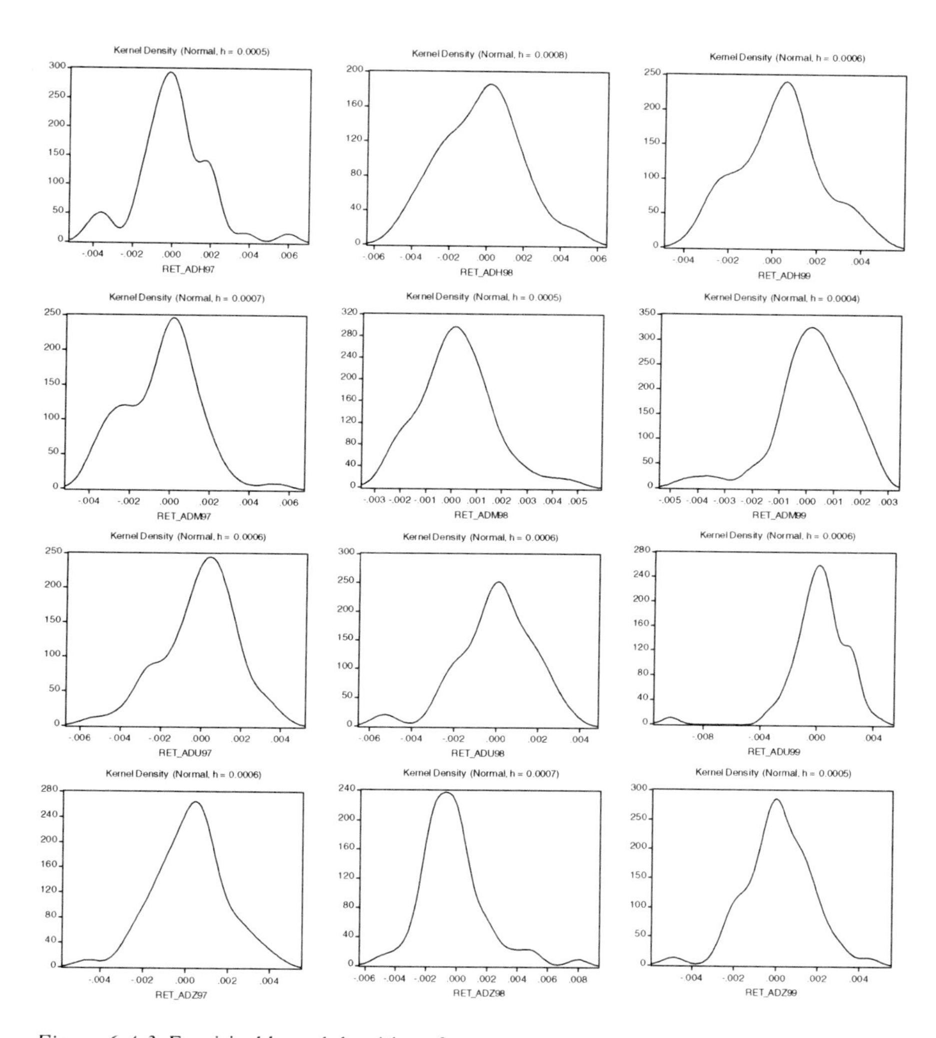

Figure 6.A.3 Empirical kernel densities of returns.

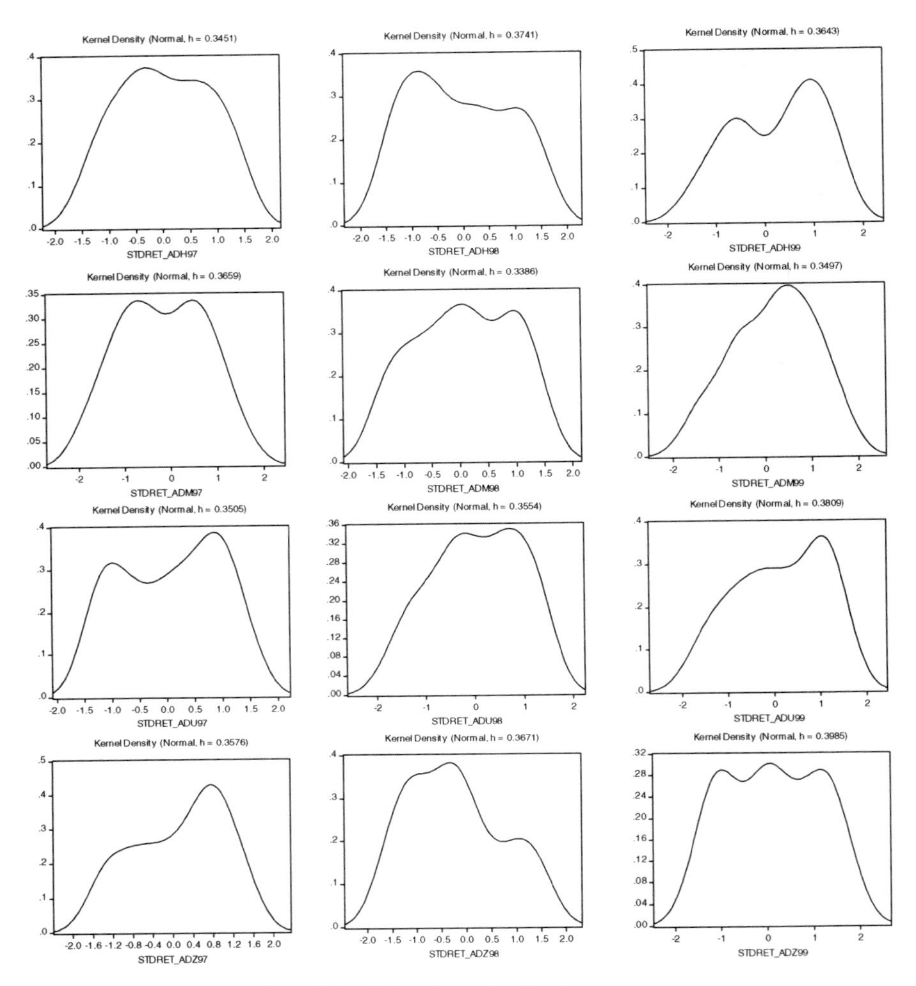

Figure 6.A.4 Empirical kernel densities of standardized returns.

Notes

1 Volker Schieck is at the University of Maastricht, 6200 MD Maastricht, The Netherlands. I am very grateful to Barry Goss for providing the data as well as for his invaluable help in the form of comments and ideas. I would further like to thank Thorsten Egelkraut, Jean Wen as well as an anonymous referee for their many helpful comments. An earlier version of this paper was submitted in the course "Topics in International Finance" at LUISS Guido Carli University, Rome, when I was an exchange student at LUISS. I would like to gratefully acknowledge the hospitality of LUISS in Rome, where a great part of this work was completed. Thanks are also due to the European Union's Erasmus program for financial support. All remaining errors are, of course, mine.

2 On the relative importance of the different components influencing this relation, such as number of trades, trade size, etc., see, for example, Chan and Fong (2000).
3 Taken from ABDE (2001), p. 45.
4 Thailand, Malaysia, Indonesia, the Philippines and South Korea suffered negative GDP growth rates between –5 and –12 per cent during the first six months of 1998; exchange rates depreciated by 29 to 52 per cent over the course of 1997 (Stein and Lim, 2004).
5 ABDL (2001), ABDE (2001), as well as Thomakos and Wang (2003), use five-minute return series, whereas ABDL (2003) use 30-minute returns.
6 See ABDE (2001) for an overview or ADBL (2001) for further treatment of the issues involved in choosing the sampling frequency.
7 By now there are also sophisticated data-based methods available that help determine the optimal sampling frequency, such as that suggested by Aït-Sahalia *et al.* (2005). A proper implementation of their methodology, however, is beyond the scope of this paper.
8 The number of observations in the series ranges from 1298 (March 1997 contracts) to 1762 (September 1998 contracts). These numbers correspond to the single trades occurring during three months of trading, where trading is restricted to the first 40 minutes of the day.
9 In order to support the basic intuition of the concept outlined, consider the case of a univariate discretely sampled i.i.d. return variable that is normally distributed with mean zero, i.e. $N=1$, $\mu_t=0$ and $\Omega_t=\sigma^2$. By standard arguments it holds that $E(h^{-1}\Sigma_{j+1,\ldots,[h/\Delta]} r^2_{t+j\Delta.\Delta})=\sigma^2$ and $Var(h^{-1}\Sigma_{j+1,\ldots,[h/\Delta]} r^2_{t+j\Delta.\Delta})=(\Delta/h)2\sigma^4 \rightarrow 0$, as $\Delta \rightarrow 0$.
10 Note that Thomakos and Wang (2003) standardize their return series on futures data somewhat differently: they first subtract the daily mean and then divide by the realized standard deviation. We try that, too, but do not observe any significant qualitative changes in results.
11 In addition to these, Thomakos and Wang (2003) make use of the Kolmogorov–Smirnov test and a test based on the quintile–quintile correlation coefficient that we do not consider here.

References

Admati, A., and Pfleiderer, P. (1988). "A Theory of Intraday Patterns: Volume and Price Variability," *Review of Financial* Studies, 1, 3–40.

Aït-Sahalia, Y., Mykland, P.A., and Zhang, L. (2005). "How Often to Sample a Continuous-Time Process in the Presence of Market Microstructure Noise," *Review of Financial Studies*, 18(2), 351–416.

Andersen, T.G., and Bollerslev, T. (1997a). "Intraday Periodicity and Volatility Persistence in Financial Markets", *Journal of Empirical Finance*, 4, 115–158.

Andersen, T.G., and Bollerslev, T. (1997b). "Heterogeneous Information Arrivals and Return Volatility Dynamics: Uncovering the Long-run in High-Frequency Returns," *The Journal of Finance*, 52(3), Papers and Proceedings of the Fifty-Seventh Annual Meeting, American Finance Association, New Orleans, Louisiana January 4–6, 1997, 975–1005.

Andersen, T.G., and Bollerslev, T. (1998a). "Answering the Skeptics: Yes, Standard Volatility Models Do Provide Accurate Forecasts," *International Economic Review*, 39, 885–905.

Andersen, T.G., and Bollerslev, T. (1998b). "Deutsche Mark–Dollar Volatility: Intraday Activity Trading Patterns, Macroeconomic Announcements and Longer Run Dependencies," *The Journal of Finance*, 53(1), 219–265.

Andersen, T.G., Bollerslev, T., Diebold, F.X., and Ebens, H. (2001a). "The Distribution of Realized Stock Return Volatility," *Journal of Financial Economics*, 61, 43–76.

Andersen, T.G., Bollerslev, T., Diebold, F.X., and Labys, P. (2001b). "The Distribution of Realized Exchange Rate Volatility," *The Journal of the American Statistical Association*, 96(453), 42–55.

Andersen, T.G., Bollerslev, T., Diebold, F.X., and Labys, P. (2003a). "Modelling and Forecasting Realized Volatility," *Econometrica*, 71(2), 579–625.

Andersen, T.G., Bollerslev, T., Diebold, F.X., and Vega, C. (2003b). "Micro Effects of Macro Announcements: Real-Time Price Discovery in Foreign Exchange," *The American Economic Review*, 93(1), 38–62.

Bollerslev, T., and Melvin, M.T. (1994). "Bid–ask Spreads and Volatility in the Foreign Exchange Rate: An Empirical Analysis," *Journal of International Economics*, 36, 355–372.

Bollerslev, T., Chou, R.Y., and Kroner, K.F. (1992). "ARCH Modeling in Finance," *Journal of Econometrics*, 52, 5–59.

Bollerslev, T., Engle, R.F. and D.B. Nelson (1994) "ARCH Models," *Handbook of Econometrics*, 4, 2959–3038.

Breidt, F.J., Crato, N., and de Lima, P. (1998). "The Detection and Estimation of Long Memory in Stochastic Volatility," *Journal of Econometrics*, 83, 325–348.

Bustelo, P. (2000). "Novelties of Financial Crises in the 1990s and the Search for New Indicators," *Emerging Markets Review*, 1, 229–251.

Canina, L., and Figlewski, S. (1993). "The Informational Content of Implied Volatility," *Review of Financial Studies*, 6, 659–681.

Chan, K., and Fong, W-M. (2000). "Trade Size, Order Imbalance and the Volatility–Volume Relation," *Journal of Financial Economics*, 57, 247–273.

Christensen, B.J., and Prabhala, N.R. (1998). "The Relation between Implied and Realized Volatility," *Journal of Financial Economics*, 50, 125–150.

Ding, Z., Engle, R.F., and Granger, C.W.J. (1993). "A Long Memory Property of Stock Market Returns and a New Model," *Journal of Empirical Finance*, 1, 83–106.

Epps, T.W., and Epps, M.L. (1976). "The Stochastic Dependence of Security Price Changes and Transaction Volumes: Implications for the Mixture-of-Distributions Hypothesis," *Econometrica*, 44(2), 305–321.

French, K.R., Schwert, G.W., and Stambaugh, R.F. (1987). "Expected Stock Returns and Volatility," *Journal of Financial Economics*, 19, 3–29.

Henry, O.T. and P.M. Summers (1999). "The Volatility of Real Exchange Rates: The Australian Case," *Australian Economic Papers*, 18(2), 79–90.

Kaminksy, G.L. (1999). "Currency and Banking Crises: The Early Warnings of Distress," *IMF Working Paper No. 99/178*, December.

Kaminsky, G.L., and Reinhart, C.M. (2000). "On Crises, Contagion, and Confusion," *Journal of International Economics*, 51, 145–168.

Kaminsky, G.L., S. Lizondo, and C.M. Reinhart (1997). "Leading Indicators of Currency Crises," *IMF Working Paper No. 97/79*, July.

Kaminsky, G.L., Reinhart, C.M., and Végh, C.A. (2003). "The Unholy Trinity of Contagion," *The Journal of Economic Perspectives*, 17(4), 51–74.

Lamoureux, C.G., and Lastrapes, W.D. (1993). "Forecasting Stock-Return Variance: Toward an Understanding of Stochastic Implied Volatilities," *Review of Financial Studies*, 6(2), 293–326.

Lyons, R.K. (2001). *The Microstructure Approach to Exchange Rates*, Cambridge, MA: The MIT Press.

Schwert, G.W. (1989). "Why Does Stock Market Volatility Change Over Time?," *Journal of Finance*, 44, 1115–1153.

Schwert, G.W., and Seguin, P.J. (1990). "Heteroskedasticity in Stock Returns," *Journal of Finance*, 45, 1129–1155.

Stein, J.L., and Lim, G.C. (2004). "Asian Crises: Theory, Evidence, Warning Signals," Invited Eminent Paper Series, *The Singapore Economic Review*, 49(2), 135–161.

Tauchen, G.E., and Pitts, M. (1983). "The Price Variability–Volume Relationship on Speculative Markets," *Econometrica*, 51(2), 485–506.

Thomakos, T., and Wang, T. (2003). "Realized Volatility in the Futures Markets," *Journal of Empirical Finance*, 10, 321–353.

Varian, H. (1989). "Differences of Opinion in Financial Markets," in Stone, C. (ed.), *Financial Risk: Theory, Evidence and Implications, Proceedings of the Eleventh Annual Economic Policy Conference of the Federal Reserve Bank of St. Louis*, Kluwer: Boston.

7 Simultaneity, forecasting and profits in the US dollar/ Deutschemark futures market

Barry A. Goss and S. Gulay Avsar[1]

Abstract

One and a half decades ago critics emphasized the poor post-sample forecasting performance of traditional economic models of exchange rates, which it was claimed, could not outperform a naïve random walk. In the past decade the focus of exchange rate research has shifted to the study of microstructure issues with intraday data. Nevertheless, the forecasting failure of traditional models has not been fully addressed. This paper demonstrates that a trading routine, based on post-sample forecasts by the authors' simultaneous model (Goss and Avsar, 2000), can produce risk-adjusted profits for a seven-day holding period, but not for positions held for one month. While this result may be interpreted as evidence against market efficiency, it does not imply that agents should discontinue the use of currency futures markets for risk management purposes. Keywords: exchange rates; trading routine; futures market; risk-adjusted profit. JEL Codes: G13, G14, F31.

Introduction

A little more than one and a half decades ago critics emphasized the poor post-sample forecasting performance of traditional economic models of exchange rates, such as the monetary model, which it was claimed, could not outperform a naïve random walk. Perceived deficiencies included undue reliance on single-equation methods, inadequate representation of expectations and insufficient attention to capital flows (e.g. Meese, 1990; Isard, 1987). In the past decade foreign exchange research has focused on the study of microstructure issues with intraday data. Nevertheless, the inability of traditional models to forecast exchange rates out of sample has not been fully addressed.

Goss and Avsar (2000) developed a simultaneous model of the US dollar/Deutschemark (US$/DEM) market, using information from both spot and futures markets. This model represents expectations in a manner consistent with the structure of the model, and is one of the very few which can surpass the random walk benchmark in post-sample forecasts (see also Goss and Avsar, 1996). It has not been demonstrated, however, that this model could be employed to produce risk-adjusted profits. This chapter addresses this issue, and shows that a trading routine, based on post-sample forecasts by an extended version of the model, can yield significant profits for a seven day holding period, but not when the positions are held for one month. Such a demonstration is in the spirit of the sufficient condition for informational inefficiency of Rausser and Carter (1983).

Foreign exchange research of the 1980s focused on the informational efficiency of these markets. Generally, it would seem that the likelihood of rejection of the efficiency hypothesis varied directly with the breadth of the information set. For example, authors such as Frenkel (1981) and Baillie *et al.* (1983) did not reject the unbiasedness hypothesis with single-equation estimation for individual currencies. In contrast, other authors rejected the efficiency hypothesis with wider information sets (e.g. Bilson, 1981, and Bailey *et al.*, 1984, who used SURE estimation, and Geweke and Fiege, 1979 and Hansen and Hodrick, 1980, who employed prior forecast errors of related currencies). Excellent surveys of this research can be found in Hodrick (1987), Baillie and McMahon (1989) and Taylor (1995). In the past decade empirical research on foreign exchange markets has focused on the study of microstructure issues, such as the relationships between exchange rates, order flow, trading activity, volatility, liquidity and information, with intraday data. For example, Bollerslev and Melvin (1994) found a positive relationship between the bid–ask spread and the conditional volatility of the Deutschemark/US dollar (DEM/US$) spot rate. Ito *et al.* (1998) found that the lunchtime variance of the Japanese yen/US dollar (JPY/US$) and DEM/US$ spot rates is higher when the Tokyo foreign exchange market is open. They argue that this outcome cannot be due to public information, the flow of which is unaffected by exchange closure, and must therefore be due to private information. Andersen *et al.* (2003) studied the impact of macroeconomic announcement surprises on the conditional means of five key spot rates (see also Lyons, 2001).

Returns to speculators and hedgers in futures markets have long been of interest to researchers. Houthakker (1957) employed open position data, from the US Commodity Exchange Authority, and found that large speculators in the wheat, corn and cotton markets gained at the expense of large hedgers in all three markets. Rockwell (1967) employed open position data from the Commodity Futures Trading Commission (CFTC) for 25 US markets, and found that large speculators gained at the expense of small (non-reporting) traders (mostly long), with large hedgers (mostly short) breaking even. He attributed the gains of large speculators to their forecasting ability. Hartzmark (1987) calculated the returns for 4,567 large traders from confidential CFTC files, for nine markets, two of which referred to financial instruments, and found inter alia that large traders made significant profits at the expense of non-reporting traders. In the sample of Hartzmark (1987), 85 per cent of large traders' profits were received by large hedgers ("commercials"), who were mainly net short, and the top five traders earned more than half of total profits. Yoo and Maddala (1991) studied the gains of speculators in 11 futures contracts, including five currencies, and found inter alia that large speculators made profits which were at least equal to large hedgers' losses, and which were received mainly at times of relatively high volatility. Dusak (1973) found the systematic risk, in the sense of the Sharpe (1964)–Lintner (1965) capital asset pricing model (CAPM), to be near zero, in markets for wheat, corn and soybeans. Lee and Leuthold (1986) reached a similar conclusion for a range of commodities, which included livestock and precious metals.

Recently the relationship between speculator behaviour and exchange rates has been a subject of renewed interest, with studies by researchers from two central banks. Klitgaard and Weir (2004), from the Federal Reserve Bank of New York, studied the relationship between the change in foreign currency per US$ and the weekly change in net long positions of foreign currency futures speculators on the Chicago Mercantile Exchange, for a group of seven currencies, and found a significant negative relationship. They attributed this relationship to the release of private information by speculators. Nevertheless, this relationship was not useful in predicting exchange rate changes during the following week. Kearns and Manners (2004), from the Reserve Bank of Australia, studied the profits of speculators with weekly CFTC open position data, and found that large speculators earned significant profits, after allowing for transaction costs, especially in the euro and Japanese yen markets. These profits, the authors argue, can be interpreted as partly a reward for risk-bearing, and partly a return to forecasting ability. While the majority of these studies found large speculators to be profitable, the outcomes are mixed, and are no doubt influenced by the sample periods and futures contracts studied.

In the model of Goss and Avsar (2000) the risk premium was assumed to be exogenous. This assumption is unduly restrictive, because it does not permit uncertainty in the market under review to influence the risk premium demanded by speculators. Accordingly, in this paper the risk premium is endogenized, which will permit uncertainty both within and outside the US$/DEM futures market to impact on the risk premium. This extension will necessitate re-modelling the conditional variance of residuals, re-estimation of structural parameters, and re-calculation of diagnostic test statistics and exchange rate forecasts by the model. The second section of this paper presents the re-specified model, while issues of data, stationarity and estimation are discussed in the third section. Results, relevant forecasts and outcomes of trading are presented in the fourth section, and the final section presents some conclusions and policy implications.

Model specification

This model contains functional relationships for short hedgers, long hedgers, net short speculators in futures and agents with unhedged spot market commitments. *Short hedgers* have long commitments in spot DEM, such as US exporters to Germany, or German agents planning to acquire US assets, and hedge their spot market risks with short positions in DEM futures. They are assumed to pursue the joint objectives of risk reduction and profit. They may be fully hedged, or alternatively their futures positions (H) may represent a variable hedge ratio. The first alternative corresponds to "carrying charge hedgers" of Working (1953a) and the latter to Working's (1953a) "selective hedgers". Preliminary estimation favoured the second alternative, and the futures market commitments of short hedgers, therefore, are made a direct function of the current futures exchange rate, a negative function of the expected futures rate and a direct function of US exports to Germany, which are employed as a proxy for the spot market commitments of short hedgers:

$$H_t = \theta_1 + \theta_2 P_t + \theta_3 P^*_{t+1} + \theta_4 X_t + e_{1t} \tag{1}$$

where H = futures market commitments of short hedgers
P_t = current futures rate in US$ per DEM[2]
P^*_{t+1} = rational expectation of futures rate at $(t+1)$ formed at time t
X = US exports to Germany
e = error term
t = time in months
θ_1 = constant; $\theta_2, \theta_4 > 0$; $\theta_3 < 0$.

It should be emphasized that the rational expectations hypothesis (REH) implies that economic agents have this economic model in mind in forming their expectations, so that any test of the REH is a joint test of the expectations hypothesis and of the validity of the model (Maddock and Carter, 1982).

Long hedgers are committed to acquire DEM spot at a later date, such as US importers from Germany or US agents planning to acquire German assets, and manage their spot market price risks with long positions (L) in DEM futures contracts. Preliminary estimation indicated that they should be treated as fully hedged, which corresponds to Working's (1953b) category of "operational hedgers". Accordingly, long hedgers' futures positions are made a negative function of the current forward premium (futures minus spot rate), and a direct function of the expected forward premium, and of US GDP, the last variable acting as a proxy for the spot market commitments of these agents

$$L_t = \theta_5 + \theta_6(P_t - A_t) + \theta_7(P^*_{t+1} - A^*_{t+1}) + \theta_8 GDP_t + e_{2t} \tag{2}$$

where A = current spot rate in US$ per DEM
A^*_{t+1} = rational expectation of spot rate at (t+1) formed at time t
GDP = US gross domestic product
and $\theta_6 < 0$; $\theta_7, \theta_8 > 0$.

This asymmetry in the specification of short and long hedging equations may reflect asymmetry between short and long hedging activities (for example, delivery is only at seller's option), or it may reflect asymmetry between arbitrage on the forward premium and arbitrage on the spot premium.

Net short speculators: short speculators in futures expect the futures rate to fall, while long speculators expect the futures rate to rise. Both groups are assumed to maximize a logarithmic utility function, which exhibits diminishing absolute risk aversion, and constant relative risk aversion, as wealth increases. This assumption seems appropriate, especially for large speculators, because it has been shown that this strategy asymptotically attracts all wealth of the economy (see Blume and Easley, 1992). The logarithmic function is a member of the HARA (hyperbolic absolute risk aversion) class of utility functions. It is convenient to represent the futures positions of speculators in a "net short speculation" function (i.e. commitments of short speculators minus commitments of long speculators, in futures). The futures market commitments of net short speculators are assumed to vary directly with the current futures rate, and negatively with the expected futures rate and the marginal risk premium. The risk premium is a subjective variable and is not observable. It is assumed to be measured here by the conditional variance of the residuals of the speculation equation, and enters the mean equation as an M-GARCH term, following Engle, Lilien and Robins (1987)

$$NSS_t = \theta_9 + \theta_{10} P_t + \theta_{11} P^*_{t+1} + \theta_{12} r_t + e_{3t} \tag{3}$$

where NSS = futures market commitments of net short speculators
r = marginal risk premium

and $\theta_{10} > 0$; θ_{11}, $\theta_{12} < 0$.

Unhedged long positions in spot DEM are effectively speculative, and can be represented by a speculative demand function (U). These positions are assumed to vary negatively with the current spot rate, directly with the expected spot rate and negatively with the US–German nominal interest differential; in this equation the risk premium did not perform:

$$U_t = \theta_{13} + \theta_{14} A_t + \theta_{15} A^*_{t+1} + \theta_{16} ID_t + e_{4t} \tag{4}$$

where ID = US–German nominal interest differential

and θ_{14}, $\theta_{16} < 0$; $\theta_{15} > 0$.

The model contains six endogenous variables, and is completed with two identities. Unhedged long positions in spot DEM are unobservable and are defined in identity (5), as all long commitments minus long hedging, while (6) is a futures market clearing identity.

$$U_t \equiv (M_t + AKO_t) - L_t \tag{5}$$

$$NSS_t \equiv L_t - H_t \tag{6}$$

where M=US imports from Germany, and AKO=US capital outflow to Germany.

The risk premium (r) in equation (3) also is an endogenous variable, and is defined in the equation for the conditional variance of the error term in the mean equation (see below). While conventional identification conditions do not apply to simultaneous rational expectations models with forward expectations (see Pesaran, 1989, pp. 120, 157–60), this model satisfies the order condition derived by Pesaran (1989, p. 160) that the number of predetermined variables in the model should be at least equal to the total number of endogenous, predetermined and expectational variables in the equation under consideration minus one.

Data, stationarity and estimation

Data

The intrasample period is 1983 (02) to 1989 (12), while the post-sample forecast period is 1990 (02) to 1992 (11). Data sources are as follows:

- H, L and NSS data are end-of-month open positions, in contracts of DEM125,000 each from the Commodity Futures Trading Commission, Washington, DC.
- Spot price data (A) are daily observations on the last trading day of the month, interbank rate in US$/DEM from Deutschebundesbank *Statistical Supplement to Monthly Reports* Series 5.
- Futures price data (P) are daily observations, last trading day of the month, in US$/DEM, for a contract two months from maturity on average, selected according to the rule defined in endnote 2, and obtained from the Chicago Mercantile Exchange, via the Futures Industry Institute in Washington, DC.
- X, M and AKO data are monthly observations, in million DEM converted to contracts of 125,000 DEM, from the same source as A, Series 4 (X, M) and Series 3 (AKO).
- ID data are monthly observations, US nominal interest rate, day-to-day money, minus German nominal interest rate, day-to-day loans, from OECD *Main Economic Indicators*, Tables R2/07 and R2/01 respectively.
- GDP data are US Gross Domestic Product in million US dollars, quarterly, interpolated to monthly observations, from *Survey of Current Business*.
- GKI is German capital inflow to US, comprising unofficial direct and portfolio investment, in million DEM per month, from the same source as AKO (although not included in the model, this variable is in the information set, and was employed in preliminary estimation).

In practice, traders would be unlikely to rely on data on macroeconomic and financial variables published by official sources, as a basis for their decision-making, because these data would be released only after a significant lag. Instead, they would more likely employ contemporaneous estimates and short-term forecasts provided by analysts, investment banks, specialist agencies, internal company forecasts and other pieces of information, some of which may be private when first released to the market. Many of these sources are not accessible to the researcher, who must have recourse to official figures, which act as proxies for the information sets traders use to make their decisions.

Stationarity

Augmented Dickey Fuller (ADF) and Phillips–Perron (P–P) tests for a single unit root were conducted. Both tests address the null of non-stationarity. The results of the ADF test suggest that the following variables are non-stationary and are I(1): P, A, H, X, M and ID, all other variables being stationary (these results are not reported here). In comparison, the P–P test indicates that only P, A and ID are I(1). The P–P tests are preferred because of their generally greater power (see Banerjee *et al.*, 1993, p. 113), and the results of these tests, using a 5 per cent level of significance, are reported in Table 7.1.

Cointegration can be presumed between P and P^* in equations (1) and (3), and between A and A^* in equation (4), and the results of the Johansen maximum eigenvalue test, reported in Table 7.2, indicate there is one cointegrating relationship between A and ID in equation (4). This test addresses the hypothesis that the number of cointegrating vectors m is at most equal to q (where $q<n$, the

Table 7.1 Unit root tests: Phillips–Perron

Variable	*Calculated test statistic*	*5% critical value*	*Order of integration*
H	–5.0240	–2.8963	I(0)
L	–9.7394	–3.4639	I(0)
NSS	–4.6961	–2.8967	I(0)
U	–9.1823	–3.4639	I(0)
P-A	–7.5169	–2.8963	I(0)
P	–1.9586	–3.4639	I(1)
A	–1.9919	–3.4639	I(1)
X	–3.4400	–2.8963	I(0)
M	–4.7838	–2.8963	I(0)
AKO	–4.5712	–2.8963	I(0)
GKI	–2.9695	–2.8963	I(0)
ID	–2.0039	–2.8963	I(1)
GDP	–4.4872	–3.4652	I(0)

Table 7.2 Johansen maximum eigenvalue test

Equation: I(1) variables	*Test statistic*	*5% critical value*	*No. of cointegrating vectors: m*
(4)	28.557	25.32	$m=0$
A_t, ID_t	9.005	12.25	$m\leq 1$

number of I(1) variables in the relationship) against the specific alternative $m = q + 1$. It can be expected, therefore, that the residuals of the structural equations will be stationary, although this will be confirmed following estimation.

Estimation

Instruments for rational expectations of endogenous price variables were obtained as fitted values, using Ordinary Least Squares (OLS), on an information set comprising all pre-determined (i.e. current exogenous and lagged endogenous) variables in the model at time t, following McCallum (1979). The risk premium was estimated as an M-GARCH variable following Engle, Lilien and Robins (1987). Lagrange Multiplier tests indicated the presence of autoregressive conditional heteroskedasticity (ARCH), and the conditional variances of the residuals in equations (1), (2) and (3) were represented as EGARCH (1,0), (3,2) and (1,1) processes respectively, following Nelson (1991). The EGARCH model is capable of taking account of the asymmetric impact of positive and negative news. The choice of model and lag length, in the representation of these conditional volatilities, were determined by Akaike and Schwartz Bayesian information criteria, and general to specific modelling.

The model was estimated by limited information and full information maximum likelihood (FIML) methods. While full information estimates are potentially more efficient, they are also less robust to specification errors (see Pesaran, 1989, pp. 162–3, 189, 195–6). In this case the FIML estimates either lacked significance or exhibited signs contrary to anticipations, and only the limited information estimates are reported (see next section). Single-equation estimates were obtained for the relationships in this model as follows: equations (1), (2) and (3) were estimated by maximum likelihood, while equation (4) was estimated by instrumental variables (IV)[3] in the absence of serial correlation and ARCH effects. The estimations described above were obtained using software *EViews 3.0*.

Results

Results presented in this section are discussed under the headings "Intrasample results" and "Post-sample results".

Intrasample results

Several points will be emphasized relating to the results for the intrasample period 1983(02) to 1989(12). First, of the estimates of the 12 structural coefficients, presented in Table 7.3, all are of the anticipated sign, and 11 are significant at 5 per cent level of significance (one tail test), while one estimate is significant at 5.2 per cent. These results provide support for the model specification, including the representation of expectations according to the Rational Expectations Hypothesis (REH), although as will be seen below, this does not necessarily imply market efficiency.

Table 7.3 Coefficient estimates: equations 1 to 4

Equation	*Coefficient*	*Variable*	*Estimate*	*Asymptotic* t *value*
1	θ_1	Constant	–28759.86	–3.342
	θ_2	P_t	248817.5	3.906
	θ_3	P^*_{t+1}	–191015.8	–2.885
	θ_4	X_t	7.842	3.099
	Ψ_1	$\sqrt{h_{1t}}$	1.569	3.577
Variance 1	α_0	Constant	18.800	54.865
	α_1	$\left\lvert \frac{e_{1t-1}}{\sqrt{h_{1t-1}}} \right\rvert$	–0.197	–0.763
	γ_1	$\frac{e_{1t-1}}{\sqrt{h_{1t-1}}}$	0.703	3.742
2	θ_5	Constant	–5271.403	–0.307
	θ_6	$(P_t - A_t)$	–466528.9	–3.969
	θ_7	$(P^*_{t+1} - A^*_{t+1})$	635512.1	3.149
	θ_8	GDP_t	185.671	12.914
	Ψ_2	$\sqrt{h_{2t}}$	–4.444	–2.181
Variance 2	α_2	Constant	30.587	6.749
	α_3	$\left\lvert \frac{e_{2t-1}}{\sqrt{h_{2t-1}}} \right\rvert$	0.103	1.149
	α_4	$\left\lvert \frac{e_{2t-2}}{\sqrt{h_{2t-2}}} \right\rvert$	–0.115	–0.878
	α_5	$\left\lvert \frac{e_{2t-3}}{\sqrt{h_{2t-3}}} \right\rvert$	–0.340	–1.730
	β_1	$\ln h_{2t-1}$	–0.420	–2.593
	β_2	$\ln h_{2t-2}$	–0.273	–1.318
	γ_2	$\frac{e_{2t-1}}{\sqrt{h_{2t-1}}}$	–0.041	–0.902
	γ_3	$\frac{e_{2t-2}}{\sqrt{h_{2t-2}}}$	0.014	0.247
	γ_4	$\frac{e_{2t-3}}{\sqrt{h_{2t-3}}}$	–0.085	–1.070
3	θ_9	Constant	–14417.9	0.988
	θ_{10}	P_t	167611.0	2.538
	θ_{11}	P^*_{t+1}	–221183.8	–3.169
	θ_{12}	$r_t (= \sqrt{h_{3t}})$	–1.959	–1.655

Table 7.3 continued

Equation	*Coefficient*	*Variable*	*Estimate*	*Asymptotic* t *value*
Variance 3	α_6	Constant	8.589	2.032
	α_7	$\left\lvert \frac{e_{3t-1}}{\sqrt{h_{3t-1}}} \right\rvert$	0.134	0.973
	β_3	$\ln h_{3t-1}$	0.528	2.244
	γ_5	$\frac{e_{3t-1}}{\sqrt{h_{3t-1}}}$	–0.470	–1.966
4	θ_{13}	Constant	–548.547	–4.783
	θ_{14}	A_t	–1109.290	–1.630
	θ_{15}	A^*_{t+1}	1414.860	2.030
	θ_{16}	ID_t	–78.023	–2.284

Second, the M-GARCH terms in equations (1) and (2) require interpretation. These terms are not necessarily indicative of risk premiums, because the agents, whose behaviour is described in these equations, are hedging. Nevertheless, a risk premium interpretation is not ruled out, because these agents are discretionary hedgers, and their positions contain speculative elements. In equation (1), the estimate of Ψ_1 suggests that short hedgers increase their cover in the presence of increased uncertainty. Alternatively, from a speculative viewpoint, this estimate is consistent with Stein's (1986, p. 53) "net hedging pressure" theory, in which the influence of the risk premium on the futures price may, under certain conditions, be positive. This would imply that in the present model, an increase in the risk premium may have a positive impact on the positions of discretionary short hedgers, who can be seen as attempting to exploit the profit potential of increased volatility. In equation (2) the negative estimate of the M-GARCH term suggests that long hedgers reduce their spot market commitments, and hence their hedge positions, in the presence of increased uncertainty. Alternatively, from a speculative point of view, this estimate suggests that these agents are risk averse in the conventional sense. The estimate of the risk premium in equation (3), of course, is consistent with the conventional view of the risk premium as in Kaldor (1960) and Brennan (1958).

Third, of the terms designed to capture the asymmetric impact of news in the variance equations, only two are significant. These are γ_1 in the variance equation to the short hedging function, and γ_5 in the variance equation to the NSS function. The first of these, however, suggests that the impact of positive news is greater than the impact of "bad" news, while the second suggests the reverse, the latter being consistent with the more frequently observed nature of the "news impact curve" (i.e. the relationship between current news and conditional volatility one period ahead; see Franses and van Dijk, 2000, pp. 148–50; Engle

Table 7.4 Diagnostic tests on residuals

Test Equation	*1*	*2*	*3*	*4*
Ljung-Box Q				
Calculated χ^2_{24}	13.702	25.984	19.242	19.873
Critical $\chi^2_{24}(0.05)$	36.415	36.415	36.415	36.415
Phillips-Perron				
Calculated	–7.646	–7.998	–7.774	–8.154
5% critical value	–2.897	–2.897	–2.897	–2.897
Jarque-Bera				
Calculated	0.632	2.749	0.271	0.367
p-value	0.729	0.253	0.873	0.832

and Ng, 1993). Fourth, in the diagnostic tests on the residuals of the structural equations, reported in Table 7.4, the Ljung-Box test suggests that there is no remaining autocorrelation in the residuals up to lag 24, while the Phillips–Perron test suggests that the residuals are stationary. The Jarque–Bera test, which addresses the null of normality, indicates that there is no evidence to suggest that the residuals are not normally distributed.

Post-sample results

The post-sample forecasting performance of the model is of critical interest in this paper. Table 7.5 provides details of the post-sample forecasts of spot and futures exchange rates by the model, two months ahead, evaluated according to the criteria of correlation coefficient, Theil's Inequality Coefficient (Theil's IC) and per cent Root Mean Square Error (RMSE). It can be seen that, according to all criteria, the better forecast is that of the spot rate. Table 7.6 provides a comparison of the model-based forecast of the spot rate (AS) with two conventional benchmarks, namely a random walk two months ahead (ANAIVE), and a futures rate lagged two months from maturity. Focusing on the per cent RMSE criterion, it is clear that the model outperforms the two rival forecasts, and the difference in per cent RMSE between the model and the random walk is significant, according to the test of Granger and Newbold (1986, pp. 278–9).

The comparison of the forecast of the spot rate by the model with the forecast implicit in the lagged futures rate raises the question of the semi-strong form efficiency of the foreign exchange futures market, because the result reported here suggests that there is information contained in the model which is not impounded in the futures rate.[4] While this outcome may be interpreted as evid-

Table 7.5 Post-sample simulation of exchange rates

Variable	*Correlation coefficient*	*Theil's IC*	*% RMSE*
A	0.9704	0.0078	1.521
P	0.8734	0.0194	4.005

ence against the informational efficiency of the US$/DEM futures market, the critical question is whether this model can be employed to produce risk-adjusted profits, which Rausser and Carter (1983) describe as a sufficient condition for the demonstration of market inefficiency.[5] To address this question the following simulated trading strategy was employed:

- If $AS>P$ this was interpreted as a signal that spot and futures rates would rise, and a long position was taken in the near future (here AS is a one month ahead forecast of the spot rate by the model).
- If $AS<P$ this was taken as a signal that spot and futures rates would fall and a short position was taken in the near future.
- If $AS=P$ this was taken to mean that rates would remain unchanged, and no position was taken.

Although there is not an abundance of information on the holding periods of speculative positions, the information which has become available suggests, predominantly, that such positions are held for a short time. For example, Working (1977, pp. 182, 184) found that 72 per cent of speculators' positions in wheat futures at the Chicago Board of Trade were intraday, during his sample period, while only 35 per cent of hedgers' positions were intraday. He found also that 23 per cent of speculators' positions in wheat were scalping (held for a few minutes only), while in corn futures only 11 per cent of such positions were scalping. Taylor (1992, p. 21), who studied the results of simulated trading in the US$/JPY market, calculated returns as the difference between opening and closing prices on the same day. Some authors, however, have held simulated trading positions for longer periods: for example, Leuthold and Garcia (1992, pp. 66–71), who studied the returns to positions in the live cattle and live hogs futures markets at the Chicago Mercantile Exchange, employed holding periods of one month and longer. In this paper, account is taken of this diversity of views by holding simulated trading positions for seven days, and for one month, in order to make a comparison of the outcomes of these different strategies.

Proportionate returns to each trading position were calculated, and these returns were converted to annual per cent rates of return, assuming weekly compounding for the one-week strategy, and monthly compounding for the one-month strategy. The following adjustments were made for risk:

- Credit risk was taken into account by subtracting the Treasury Bill Rate (TBR) in per cent per annum, to derive Net Annualized Returns (NAR). Many categories of traders, however, are able to lodge Treasury Bills in payment of margin calls, and hence the effect of this adjustment is to make the results more conservative than otherwise.
- Risk of loss due to unfavourable changes in exchange rates was taken into account by dividing the Mean Net Annualized Returns (MNAR) by the standard deviation of NAR, and the null hypothesis was tested that the true MNAR is zero. The method of adjusting for risk by relating the mean return

to the variability of returns is well established in the literature, especially in relation to livestock futures (see Garcia *et al.*, 1988; Leuthold *et al.*, 1989).

Detailed outcomes of these trades are provided in Table 7.8 for the one week strategy and in Table 7.9 for the one month strategy. In these tables, column one shows whether $AS>P$ or $AS<P$, and hence indicates whether a long or short position was taken. Column two gives the proportionate gain for the respective holding period, assuming the position was closed out at the price of the near future one week (one month) later. Column three converts this gain to a per cent Annualized Return, while column four lists the Treasury Bill rate during the relevant holding period, which is subtracted from column three to give Net Annualized Return in column five. The outcomes of the simulated trading positions, of which more than 70 per cent were short, are summarized in Table 7.7, where it can be seen that less than half of the short trades, and most of the long trades, were profitable.

In the case of the one-week strategy, notwithstanding several unprofitable trades, profits more than compensated for losses to such an extent that the Mean Net Annualized Return (MNAR) was not only positive, but also significantly greater than zero.[6] In comparison, although the MNAR for the one-month strategy was positive, it was not significantly different from zero.[7] This result is consistent with previous research, such as Rockwell (1967), who found that large speculators in futures made profits due to their forecasting ability, and with Yoo and Maddala (1991) and Kearns and Manners (2004), who found that speculators in currency futures made significant profits.

This outcome would seem to provide evidence against the Efficient Markets

Table 7.6 Post-sample forecasts of spot exchange rate

Forecast model	*Correlation coefficient*	*Theil's IC*	*% RMSE*
AS	0.9704	0.0078	1.521
ANAIVE	0.6115	0.0262	5.414
P_{t-2}	0.5912	0.0279	5.748

Table 7.7 Simulated trading: summary of results

	7 day positions	*1 month positions*
Trades: total number	35	35
Short positions: number	25	25
Number profitable	10	11
Long positions: Number	10	10
Number profitable	7	8
Mean net annualized return	93.262	16.185
Standard deviation	235.478	58.546
Test statistic	2.309	1.612

Table 7.8 Simulated trading: US$/DEM futures rates of return: 7 day positions*

	Profit/week	*Annualized return*	*TBR*	*Net annualized return*
AS<P	−0.009260818	−38.3567	7.64	−45.9967
AS<P	−0.000681315	−3.4820	7.76	−11.2420
AS>P	0.011342475	79.7665	7.87	71.8965
AS<P	−0.026501174	−75.2576	7.78	−83.0376
AS<P	−0.00373451	−17.6802	7.78	−25.4602
AS<P	−0.011790103	−46.0293	7.74	−53.7693
AS<P	0.006979695	43.6744	7.66	35.9144
AS>P	−0.005211623	−23.7927	7.44	−31.2327
AS>P	0.027311254	305.9816	7.38	298.6016
AS<P	−0.018901622	−62.9274	7.19	−70.1174
AS<P	−0.012131972	−46.9916	7.07	−54.0616
AS<P	0.033034887	441.9752	6.81	435.1652
AS<P	−0.018846042	−62.8180	6.3	−69.1180
AS<P	0.035912039	526.3106	5.95	520.3606
AS<P	−0.023134954	−70.3928	5.91	−76.3028
AS<P	0.012853917	94.2827	5.67	88.6127
AS<P	0.017213842	142.9056	5.51	137.3956
AS>P	−0.002006567	−9.9177	5.6	−15.5177
AS>P	0.008927009	58.7475	5.58	53.1675
AS>P	0.032004197	414.5601	5.39	409.1701
AS>P	−0.013919168	−51.7552	5.25	−57.0052
AS<P	−0.021673387	−67.9992	5.03	−73.0292
AS<P	−0.031738281	−81.3094	4.6	−85.9094
AS<P	0.024113039	245.2157	4.12	241.0957
AS<P	−0.012835093	−48.9184	3.84	−52.7584
AS<P	0.017895255	151.5131	3.84	147.6731
AS<P	−0.019288327	−63.6797	4.05	−67.7297
AS<P	−0.008140887	−34.6269	3.81	−38.4369
AS>P	0.010955373	76.2233	3.66	72.5633
AS>P	0.008328192	53.9215	3.7	50.2215
AS<P	−0.007429421	−32.1433	3.28	−35.4233
AS<P	0.005764094	34.8337	3.14	31.6937
AS<P	0.047639485	1,024.6481	2.97	1,021.6781
AS<P	0.034589732	486.0633	2.84	483.2233
AS>P	0.014832536	115.0344	3.14	111.8944

Notes

* Profit/week is futures rate at end month minus futures rate seven days later divided by initial futures rate. TBR and net annualized return are in per cent per annum.

Hypothesis (EMH), in the very short term, which is removed within the current month. Nevertheless, it is suggested that the EMH should not be rejected, even in the very short run, unless this result can be repeated with other sample periods and other forecasting periods. Moreover, it is possible that some agents may not regard these returns as significant, because they may think that the adjustments for risk made here are inadequate. In contrast, some agents may not require any compensation for risk of loss in this currency futures market, because they are risk neutral, or alternatively, because they may be able to diversify away these

Table 7.9 Simulated trading: US$/DEM futures rates of return: 1 month positions*

	Profit/month	*Annualized return*	*TBR*	*Net annualized return*
AS<P	0.011449739	14.6388	7.64	6.9988
AS<P	–0.006131834	–7.1150	7.76	–14.8750
AS>P	0.009310987	11.7635	7.87	3.8935
AS<P	0.011908755	15.2647	7.78	7.4847
AS<P	–0.022237311	–23.6513	7.78	–31.4313
AS<P	–0.046828296	–43.7589	7.74	–51.4989
AS<P	–0.004441624	–5.2017	7.66	–12.8617
AS>P	0.006159191	7.6466	7.44	0.2066
AS>P	0.034688432	50.5619	7.38	43.1819
AS<P	–0.012894417	–14.4218	7.19	–21.6118
AS<P	–0.002246518	–2.6628	7.07	–9.7328
AS<P	–0.011356844	–12.8084	6.81	–19.6184
AS<P	0.03250591	46.7948	6.3	40.4948
AS<P	0.110109957	250.2612	5.95	244.3112
AS<P	–0.00068646	–0.8206	5.91	–6.7306
AS<P	0.01697822	22.3883	5.67	16.7183
AS<P	0.043614794	66.9101	5.51	61.4001
AS>P	0.042137906	64.0976	5.6	58.4976
AS>P	0.000875197	1.0553	5.58	–4.5247
AS>P	0.042847149	65.4428	5.39	60.0528
AS>P	–0.001844709	–2.1913	5.25	–7.4413
AS<P	–0.032258065	–32.5294	5.03	–37.5594
AS<P	–0.059733073	–52.2455	4.6	–56.8455
AS<P	0.054676701	89.4228	4.12	85.3028
AS<P	0.01039805	13.2166	3.84	9.3766
AS<P	0.012641602	16.2704	3.84	12.4304
AS<P	–0.000831393	–0.9931	4.05	–5.0431
AS<P	–0.031234424	–31.6680	3.81	–35.4780
AS>P	0.044627034	68.8632	3.66	65.2032
AS>P	0.037939543	56.3381	3.7	52.6381
AS<P	–0.056909361	–50.4959	3.28	–53.7759
AS<P	0.017292282	22.8426	3.14	19.7026
AS<P	0.077682403	145.4084	2.97	142.4384
AS<P	0.02745463	38.4050	2.84	35.5650
AS>P	–0.0261563	–27.2436	3.14	–30.3836

Notes

* Profit/month is futures rate at end of month minus futures rate at end of following month divided by futures rate at end of previous month. TBR and net annualized return are in per cent per annum.

risks, if currency futures are held in conjunction with other securities in a portfolio: the latter would be the position suggested by the Capital Asset Pricing Model (CAPM) (for two recent discussions of the CAPM see Perold (2004) and Fama and French (2004)). Ultimately, therefore, what constitutes an appropriate adjustment for risk is a subjective matter.

Given that the gains reported here, for the one week strategy, are significantly different from zero, the question is how can these results be reconciled with the apparent support for the Rational Expectations Hypothesis (REH) in Table 7.3, where the coefficient estimates of the price expectations variables are significant? Two points will be made to resolve this puzzle. First, the EMH is a joint hypothesis, which assumes both rational expectations and risk neutrality. Rejection of the EMH, therefore, does not, in the absence of further tests, indicate which of the joint assumptions has been contravened. In this case, the significant estimate of the coefficient of the risk premium in equation (3) would suggest that there is evidence against the assumption of risk neutrality. Second, the test of the EMH based on post-sample forecasts of the spot price by the model is evidently more powerful than a test of the significance of intrasample estimates of the coefficients of expected price variables.

Conclusions

One and a half decades ago critics claimed that traditional economic models of exchange rates could not outperform a random walk in out-of-sample forecasts. Perceived deficiencies included lack of simultaneity and inadequate representation of expectations. This challenge has not been addressed fully, because, while Goss and Avsar (2000) developed a simultaneous model of the US$/DEM spot and futures markets, which significantly outperformed this conventional benchmark, it has not been demonstrated that this model could be employed to produce risk-adjusted profits. This paper takes up that challenge, and employs the model of Goss and Avsar (2000) as the basis of a simulated trading routine. The model is extended by endogenizing the risk premium, and modified by representing speculators in futures by a net short speculator function rather than by separate long and short functions. The revised model also contains functional relationships for short hedgers, long hedgers and unhedged spot holdings. Expectations are represented according to the rational expectations hypothesis, and agents are assumed to maximize the logarithm of expected utility. The conditional variances of the residuals of the mean equations, of the hedging and speculation functions, are modelled as EGARCH (p,q) processes to capture asymmetries in innovations which are a likely consequence of asymmetries in futures markets. The conditional standard deviations of those residuals enter the mean equations as M-GARCH variables to represent the risk premium demanded by speculators or agents with speculative elements in their market positions. In the unhedged spot equation, however, no evidence of time-varying volatility was found.

Following significant parameter estimates of anticipated sign, the model produced post-sample forecasts of the spot rate which significantly outperformed forecasts by a random walk as well as the forecasts implicit in a lagged futures rate. Indeed the per cent RMSE of the model is 72 per cent less than that for the random walk. The outcome of the comparison of the model forecast with that of the lagged future questions the informational efficiency of the futures market. To investigate whether the so-called "sufficient condition" for inefficiency is fulfilled, a simulated trading program was undertaken, based on the forecasts of the model. The near future was purchased if the spot forecast was greater than the current futures rate, and was sold if the spot forecast was less than the current futures rate. This procedure resulted in 25 short and ten long positions being taken. Returns to these positions were calculated for holding periods of one week and one month, but only the former were significantly different from zero, when allowance was made for the Treasury Bill rate, and mean returns were divided by their standard deviation. It would seem, therefore, that there is some inefficiency in the market in the very short term, which is removed within one month. Nevertheless, the market-efficiency hypothesis should not be rejected even for the very short term, unless these results can be repeated with other sample periods.

The apparent conflict between the demonstration of profits from the one-week trading strategy, and the rational expectations hypothesis, on which price expectations in the model are based, can be reconciled as follows:

- The REH is a joint hypothesis, which embodies the assumptions of risk neutrality and rational expectations. While rejection of the EMH does not, in the absence of further testing, indicate which of these assumptions has been violated, the presence of a significant risk premium in the speculation equation suggests that the assumption of risk neutrality has not been met.
- Comparison of model-based post-sample forecasts of the spot rate with forecasts implicit in a lagged futures rate is likely a more powerful test than a significance test on individual intrasample coefficient estimates.

The main policy implications of these outcomes are first, that while futures prices in the US$/DEM market are less than perfect in their ability to reflect public information in the very short term, this does not imply that agents should have ceased using this futures market for risk management purposes or for forward contract pricing. If traders had maintained their spot positions unhedged, their risks would have been greater, and if they had employed their own price expectations for forward contract pricing, their forecast errors would have been greater, leading to increased misallocation of resources. Moreover, Stein (1986, p. 163) has shown that the magnitude of such resource misallocation is proportional to the square of the forecast error. Second, given the results obtained in this paper, the question arises whether the model can be adapted to provide forecasts into the future, of the US$/EUR futures rate, since the US$/DEM rate no longer exists. While Germany has a major input to the determination of the US$/EUR rate, it is a question for future research whether such forecasts, if obtainable, can yield significant gains via a short-term trading program. If undertaken with daily data, such an extension of the model would likely require an intrasample period of at least six years, and a post-sample forecast period of two years duration. The costs of such a trading program would include not only transaction costs, but also the costs of adapting and maintaining the model.

Notes

1 Research reported in this paper was undertaken when the first author was Reader in Economics, Monash University, Australia. Thanks are due to Dietrich Fausten for assistance with data, and to participants at seminars of the Sydney Financial Mathematics Workshop, Department of Econometrics and Business Statistics at Monash University, and the Melbourne Q Group, for helpful comments. The usual disclaimer applies. A draft of this paper was prepared while the first author held a visiting appointment at LUISS Guido Carli University in Rome. He is greatly indebted to colleagues at LUISS, especially Fabio Gobbo and Gennaro Olivieri, for their hospitality

2 The Deutschemark (DEM) contract at the Chicago Mercantile Exchange (CME) International Monetary Market (IMM) provides for delivery of 125,000 DEM in the months of March, June, September and December. A continuous series of futures prices is constructed by choosing a futures contract which is on average two months from maturity: when the month is December, January, February, the future is March; when the month is March, April, May, the future is June; when the month is June, July, August, the future is September; when the month is September, October, November, the future is December.

3 The instruments employed in the estimation of equation (4) are as follows: U_{t-1}, $A_{t-1,}$ ID_t, $P_{t-1,}$ GDP_t, X_t, H_{t-1}, $L_{t-1,}$ $NSS_{t-1,}$ M_t, AKO_t, $\sqrt{h_{1t-1}}$, $\sqrt{h_{2t-1}}$, $\sqrt{h_{3t-1}}$

4 In deriving these forecasts, the parameter estimates of the model were updated after each forecast, so that the model and the lagged futures rate were on the same informational footing.

5 If the lagged futures rate outperforms the model this is no proof of market efficiency, but may be simply a reflection of a misspecified model.

6 No allowance has been made for transactions costs in the estimation of these returns. Transactions in futures markets comprise costs of order execution, liquidity costs, and the costs of building and maintaining the model. The costs of order execution would include commission and clearing house fees. Kearns and Manners (2004, p. 14) employed a commission upper limit of US$60 per contract, which corresponds to 0.0766% of the value of one futures contract of DEM125,000 at the rate US$/DEM 0.6270 as it was at the end of the post-sample forecast period November 1992. CME Clearing House fees during the post-sample forecast period are not known, but for FX products are currently US$0.14 per round turn, which corresponds to 0.000179% of the value of one DEM futures contract at the end of the post-sample period. CME historical data files do not include ask–bid spreads, but Taylor (1992, p. 106), in estimating returns to trading US$/JPY futures on the CME, made an allowance of 0.2% of the dollar price of futures contracts traded, which included liquidity costs of US$25 per contract round turn, which corresponds to 0.032% of the value of one DEM futures contract at the end of the post-sample period. Deduction of costs of this magnitude is unlikely to have a significant impact on the returns estimated in this paper. The costs of building and maintaining the model will likely be different for a party replicating this exercise, compared with the costs incurred by the authors.

7 A buy and hold strategy in US$/DEM futures, by comparison, produced a Mean Net Annualized Return (MNAR) of 4.637% (standard deviation of 43.024%) for 35 trades held for one month, and a MNAR of 65.388% (standard deviation of 136.730%) if held for seven days. Only the second of these results is statistically different from zero, and in both cases the MNAR values are less than those produced, for comparable holding periods, by trading strategies based on the model.

References

Andersen, T., T. Bollerslev, F. Diebold and C. Vega (2003), "Micro Effects of Macro Announcements: Real-Time Price Discovery in Foreign Exchange", *American Economic Review*, 93(1), 38–62.

Bailey, R.W., R.T. Baillie and P.C. McMahon (1984), "Interpreting Econometric Evidence on Efficiency in the Foreign Exchange Market", *Oxford Economic Papers*, 36, 67–85.

Baillie, R.T. and P.C. McMahon (1989), *The Foreign Exchange Market: Theory and Econometric Evidence*, Cambridge: Cambridge University Press.

Baillie, R.T., R.E. Lippens and P.C. McMahon (1983), "Testing Rational Expectations and Efficiency in the Foreign Exchange Market", *Econometrica*, 51, 553–63.

Banerjee, A., J.J. Dolado, J.W. Galbraith and D.F. Hendry (1993), *Co-Integration, Error Correction, and the Econometric Analysis of Non-Stationary Data*, Oxford: Oxford University Press.

Bilson, J.F.O. (1981), "The 'Speculative Efficiency' Hypothesis", *Journal of Business*, 54(3), 435–51.

Blume, L. and D. Easley (1992), "Evolution and Market Behaviour", *Journal of Economic Theory*, 58(1), 9–40.

Bollerslev, T. and M. Melvin (1994), "Bid–ask Spreads and Volatility in the Foreign Exchange Market", *Journal of International Economics*, 36, 355–72.

Brennan, M.J. (1958), "The Supply of Storage", *American Economic Review*, 48, 50–72.

Dusak, K. (1973), "Futures Trading and Investor Returns: An Investigation of Commodity Market Risk Premium", *Journal of Political Economy*, 81(6), 1387–406.

Engle, R.F. and V.K. Ng (1993), "Measuring and Testing the Impact of News on Volatility", *Journal of Finance*, 48(5), 1749–78.

Engle, R.F., D. Lilien and R. Robins (1987), "Estimating Time-varying Risk Premia in the Term Structure: The ARCH-M Model", *Econometrica*, 55, 391–407.

Fama, E.F. and K.R. French (2004), "The Capital Asset Pricing Model: Theory and Evidence", *Journal of Economic Perspectives*, 18(3), 25–46.

Franses, P.H. and D. van Dijk (2000), *Non-Linear Time Series Models in Empirical Finance*, Cambridge: Cambridge University Press.

Frenkel, J.A. (1981), "The Collapse of PPP in the 1970s", *European Economic Review*, 16, 145–65.

Garcia, P., R.M. Leuthold, T.R. Fortenbery and G.F. Sarassoro (1988), "Pricing Efficiency in the Live Cattle Futures Market: Further Interpretation and Measurement", *American Journal of Agricultural Economics*, 70, 162–9.

Geweke, J. and E. Feige (1979), "Some Joint Tests of the Efficiency of Markets for Forward Foreign Exchange", *Review of Economics and Statistics*, 61, 334–41.

Goss, B.A. and S.G. Avsar (1996), "A Simultaneous, Rational Expectations Model of the Australian Dollar/US Dollar Market", *Applied Financial Economics*, 6, 163–74.

Goss, B.A. and S.G. Avsar (2000), "A Simultaneous Model of the US Dollar/Deutschmark Spot and Futures Markets", chapter 4 in B.A. Goss (ed.), *Models of Futures Markets*, London: Routledge, 61–85.

Granger, C.W.J. and P. Newbold (1986), *Forecasting Economic Time Series*, second ed., London: Academic Press.

Hansen, L.P. and R.J. Hodrick (1980), "Forward Exchange Rates as Optimal Predictors of Future Spot Rates: An Economic Analysis", *Journal of Political Economy*, 88, 829–53.

Hartzmark, M.L. (1987), "Returns to Individual Traders of Futures: Aggregate Results", *Journal of Political Economy*, 95(6), 1292–1306.

Hodrick, R.J. (1987), *The Empirical Evidence on the Efficiency of Forward and Futures Foreign Exchange Markets*, Chur: Harwood Academic Publishers.

Houthakker, H.S. (1957), "Can Speculators Forecast Prices?", *Review of Economics and Statistics*, 39(2), 143–51.

Isard, P. (1987), "Lessons from Empirical Models of Exchange Rates", *International Monetary Fund Staff Papers*, 34(1), 1–28.

Ito, T., R.K. Lyons and M.T. Melvin (1998), "Is There Private Information in the FX Market: The Tokyo Experiment", *Journal of Finance*, 53(3), 1111–30.

Kaldor, N. (1960), "Speculation and Economic Stability", in *Essays on Economic Stability and Growth*, London: Duckworth, 17–58.

Kearns, J. and P. Manners (2004), "The Profitability of Speculators in Currency Futures Markets", Reserve Bank of Australia, Research Discussion Paper, 2004–07.

Klitgaard, T. and L. Weir (2004), "Exchange Rate Changes and Net Positions of Speculators in the Futures Market", *Economic Policy Review*, Federal Bank of New York, 10(1), 17–28.

Lee, C.-F. and R.M. Leuthold (1986), "An Analysis of Investment Horizon and Alternative Risk-return Measures for Commodity Futures Markets", in B.A. Goss (ed.), *Futures Markets: Their Establishment and Performance*, London: Croom Helm, 119–36.

Leuthold, R.M., P. Garcia, B.D. Adam and W.I. Park (1989), "An Examination of the Necessary and Sufficient Conditions for Market Efficiency: The Case of Hogs", *Applied Economics*, 21, 193–204.

Leuthold, R.M. and P. Garcia (1992), "Assessing Market Performance: An Examination of Livestock Futures Markets", in B.A. Goss (ed.), *Rational Expectations and Efficiency in Futures Markets*, London: Routledge, 52–77.

Lintner, J. (1965), "Security Prices, Risk, and Maximal Gains from Diversification", *Journal of Finance*, 20, 587–615.

Lyons, R.K. (2001), *The Microstructure Approach to Exchange Rates*, Cambridge, MA: MIT Press.

McCallum, B.T. (1979), "Topics concerning the Formulation, Estimation and use of Macroeconomic Models with Rational Expectations", *Proceedings of the Business and Economic Statistics Section*, Washington, DC: American Statistical Association, 65–72.

Maddock, R. and M. Carter (1982), "A Child's Guide to Rational Expectations", *Journal of Economic Literature*, 20, 39–51.

Meese, R. (1990), "Currency Fluctuations in the post-Bretton Woods Era", *Journal of Economic Perspectives*, 4(1), 117–34.

Nelson, D. (1991), "Conditional Heteroskedasticity in Asset Returns: A New Approach", *Econometrica*, 59: 347–70.

Perold, A.F. (2004), "The Capital Asset Pricing Model", *Journal of Economic Perspectives*, 18(3), 3–24.

Pesaran, M.H. (1989), *The Limits to Rational Expectations*, Oxford: Blackwell.

Rausser, G.C. and C. Carter (1983), "Futures Market Efficiency in the Soybean Complex", *Review of Economics and Statistics*, 65, 469–78.

Rockwell, C.S. (1967), "Normal Backwardation, Forecasting, and the Returns to Commodity Futures Traders", *Food Research Institute Studies*, 7, Supplement, 107–30.

Sharpe, W. (1964), "Capital Asset Prices: A Theory of Market Equilibrium Under Conditions of Risk", *Journal of Finance*, 19, 425–42.

Stein, J.L. (1986), *The Economics of Futures Markets*, Oxford: Blackwell.

Taylor, M.P. (1995), "The Economics of Exchange Rates", *Journal of Economic Literature*, 33, March, 13–47.

Taylor, S.J. (1992), "Rewards available to Currency Futures Speculators: Compensation for Risk or Evidence of Inefficient Pricing", *Economic Record*, Special Issue on Futures Markets, 105–16.

Working, H. (1953a), "Futures Trading and Hedging", *American Economic Review*, 43, 313–43.

Working, H. (1953b), "Hedging Reconsidered", *Journal of Farm Economics*, 35, 544–61.

Working, H. (1977), "Price Effects of Scalping and Day Trading", in A.E. Peck (ed.), *Selected Writings of Holbrook Working*, Chicago Board of Trade, 181–93.

Yoo, J. and G.S. Maddala (1991), "Risk Premia and Price Volatility in Futures Markets", *Journal of Futures Markets*, 11(2), 165–77.

8 Perceptions of futures market liquidity

An empirical study of CBOT and CME traders

Julia W. Marsh, Joost M.E. Pennings and Philip Garcia

Abstract

Traders' perceptions drive their market behavior, and can influence the dynamics of liquidity. This study surveyed 420 traders on their perceptions of the price path during an order imbalance to better understand the dynamics of liquidity. While most liquidity models assume a linear price path, only 12 percent of traders perceive such a path. This raises questions on the validity of such models. There is considerable heterogeneity in the perceptions of the price path. While trader characteristics are often used to classify traders, trader characteristics do not explain the heterogeneity in perceptions. In contrast, traders of a specific contract are associated with particular perceptions of the price path. This indicates that market microstructure may be the primary driver of traders' perceptions of the price path. Keywords: Liquidity, market depth, market microstructure, trader behavior/perceptions.

Introduction

Adequate liquidity can mean the difference between the success or failure of a futures contract. Speculators flock to liquid markets because of the profitable opportunities and lower transaction costs. Hedgers are also concentrated in the more liquid markets because of lower transaction costs and higher hedging effectiveness. Pennings and Meulenberg (1997) found a strong relationship between hedging effectiveness and market liquidity.

Black (1971) described liquidity as having three distinct characteristics: tightness, depth, and resiliency. Tightness is the cost of the quick purchase and sale of a contract and is often measured by the bid–ask spread. Depth is the number of contracts needed to change prices. Finally, resiliency is the time needed to recover from shocks.

While there is no direct way to measure liquidity, previous researchers have developed various proxy measures. Many of these measures, such as volume and open interest, do not measure the economic cost of low levels of liquidity nor are they directly related to Black's conceptual definition. The economic cost of liquidity is the opportunity cost of not being able to trade one's order at the equilibrium price. This is usually considered one of the intangible components of transaction costs. The bid–ask spread does begin to measure the transaction costs of small orders. However, most futures markets are very tight, meaning that trades of a few contracts are traded within one or two ticks of the equilibrium price.

Market depth is an alternative way to conceptualize and measure liquidity, especially its cost. It is the number of contracts needed to change the market price by one tick (Kyle, 1985). By using market depth, one is able to quantify the economic cost associated with an illiquid market, incorporating the heart of the liquidity definition proposed by Black.

When measuring market depth two important dimensions exist: the rate of price change and the magnitude of price change (e.g. Pennings *et al.* 1998). These aspects are reflected in the shape of the price path, which identifies how prices change as the number of contracts change. Most market-depth measures have not explicitly considered the shape of the price path and simply assumed linearity. The shape of the price path, however, is crucial, as it determines the liquidity costs that traders incur when trading in illiquid markets.

In this paper, we examine traders' perceptions of the shape of the price path during order imbalances. We focus on perceptions as they ultimately drive traders' behavior and their analysis should provide us with a better understanding of the dynamics behind liquidity. Furthermore, a focus on perceptions allows us to investigate whether the current market-depth measures, which assume a linear price path during order imbalances, are helpful when understanding actual market behavior. In addition, studying traders' perceptions regarding the shape of the price path may provide information for exchanges to improve liquidity.

To explain and understand differences in traders' perceptions, we investigate whether their characteristics or characteristics of the market microstructure influence perceptions of the price path. Trader characterization and classification is one of the main tools used by trader behavior models to explain markets. However, if traders' characteristics are the driving force behind perceptions, exchanges have limited tools to enhance liquidity as it is difficult to change these characteristics. In contrast, if market microstructure is the primary factor explaining perceptions, then exchanges have various tools available, including changing their trading system or rules.

To study perceptions, we surveyed traders at the Chicago Board of Trade (CBOT) and the Chicago Mercantile Exchange (CME). The survey allows us to draw conclusions about whether trader characteristics or market microstructure factors have significant relationships with the perceptions of the price path.

The remainder of the paper is organized as follows. First, we examine the current models of liquidity, followed by an explanation of our research design. Then, we examine the relationship between traders' perceptions and trader characteristics, and perceptions and market characteristics. We conclude with implications of our findings and thoughts on further research.

Review of literature

The numerous liquidity measures that have been proposed can be classified into three broad categories: trade-based measures, order-based measures, and market-depth measures (Aitken and Comerton-Forde, 2003).

Trade-based measures

Trade-based proxies generally comprise some of the easiest and earliest measures of liquidity. They consist of measures, such as volume, frequency, trade value, and the open interest. However, none of these measures relates back to Black's definition or captures the economic cost of an illiquid market

While these measures are easily accessible, some research suggests that they do not accurately reflect liquidity. For example, Aitken and Comerton-Forde (2003) tested a variety of liquidity measures using a known liquidity crisis. Their results showed a strong correlation among the trade-based measures, indicating that they were highly reliable. However, this result becomes meaningless when paired with their second finding: the measures demonstrated low validity as they gave the wrong conclusion.

Order-based measures

Order-based measures are some of the most widely used and accepted measures for liquidity. The majority of these measures revolve around the bid–ask spread, which is the difference between the price above (below) the equilibrium at which a contract is bought (sold). Among the order-based measures are Roll's (1984) measure, the covariance of price changes, and Thompson and Waller's (1987) mean absolute price-change squared.

These bid–ask spread proxies only measure tightness which reflects the economic cost of trade for small transactions. An alternative order-based measure is the aggregated daily order imbalance (Chordia *et al.*, 2002) which is the difference between the number of buy and sell orders in the order book. However, many exchanges do not have an open order book, especially open outcry platforms, though there is a move to open books for electronic systems. While this proxy does indicate the possibility of an order imbalance, it does not reflect the economic cost of liquidity.

Market-depth measures

Many market-depth measures are relatively new, because their practical development relies on the availability of tick-by-tick or transaction-specific data. Market depth is the number of contracts needed to move the contract price by one tick (Kyle, 1985). Research on market depth was stimulated by Kyle's 1985 paper. The paper focused on how insider trader information is incorporated into prices and its effects on liquidity. Kyle separated traders into three categories:

the informed trader, trying to maximize the profit derived from his inside information; market-makers (scalpers); and noise traders. Assuming a linear price path, Kyle found that market depth is proportional to noise trading and inversely proportional to informed trading not yet incorporated into price. It is important to note that the structure of the model suggests that liquidity may be driven by the market microstructure. Grossman and Miller (1988), who categorized traders as informed traders and market-makers, further developed market microstructure in relation to liquidity.

Pennings *et al.* (1998) presented an alternative model of market depth, in which the price path due to order imbalances is S-shaped and consists of four phases. They modeled the price path during order imbalances, utilizing the Gompertz S-shaped curve whose parameters can measure the rate of price change and the magnitude of price change. This allows for an easy interpretation of the execution costs of a particular order.

While the recently developed market-depth measures address the execution costs of liquidity, and hence are valuable, they either assume a linear or S-shaped price path. The question then emerges whether this corresponds to traders' perceptions of the price path. If not, traders may react differently to an order imbalance than these models predict. As a result, these models may give inaccurate predictions of the execution costs of trades and/or the level of liquidity.

Market microstructure

The market-depth measures, particularly Kyle's (1985), suggest that market microstructure may influence market liquidity and traders' perceptions. Tse (1999) views market microstructure as the specific trading environment that creates the unique dynamics of a market. In this paper, we describe market microstructure using three dimensions: the composition of traders, trading systems, and trading regulations.

Grossman and Miller's work on liquidity and market structure (1988) discusses the composition of traders. They categorize traders into market-makers and outside customers. They also introduce four general categories to separate the market structure found in the stock market: continuous auction, designated specialist (or market maker), upstairs markets (for trading large blocks), and over-the-counter swap markets. Most trading activity at the CBOT and CME occurs on a continuous auction, but many financial contracts at the CME also allow trading of large blocks of contracts outside of the normal trading pit (e.g. Eurodollars are traded in blocks of over 1,000 contracts). In addition, the CBOT has instituted a designated market maker in the Dow Jones Index contract, which makes it unique among the contracts studied.

A second dimension of market microstructure is the trading system. Different trading systems give the traders access to different information. There are three broad categories that divide trading systems: open outcry only, electronic trading only, and side-by-side trading. Until recently, futures markets have always been open outcry auctions, where individual traders generally do not have quick access to fundamental information. In computerized trading systems, which have become very popular in the last decade, traders have quicker access to fundamental information in the underlying market. Electronic trading systems also usually provide knowledge of the depth of the market through an open-order book, but the knowledge of whom one trades with and other information from the pit, in particular sound, is lost (Pirrong, 1996). Many foreign exchanges have become completely electronic, but the Chicago exchanges are utilizing side-by-side trading, in which both electronic trading systems and open-outcry auctions operate simultaneously (except agricultural contracts, which are open outcry only). However, each exchange's electronic platform varies slightly in design and information revealed. In the contracts studied here, three different trading systems are utilized. Corn futures, corn options, and the soybean complex are traded through open auction. Treasury notes, Treasury bonds, and the Dow Jones Index use side-by-side trading through the CBOT electronic trade system. Finally, Eurodollars and the S&P 500 index use side-by-side trading through the CME electronic trading system.

Finally, trading regulations also help create a market's unique microstructure. The federal government provides basic rules, consistent for all contracts studied here. However, exchanges also dictate rules and regulations that may vary for each contract, such as tick size, price limits, delivery mechanisms, and trading hours. These regulations can help exchanges promote liquidity and maintain order.

Trader behavior

The literature on perceptions in economic models is very limited. Most of the related work examines expectations and beliefs. Since Lucas (1972) developed the macroeconomics implications of rational expectations, researchers have used this concept to investigate how traders behave and react to information and how information is incorporated into equilibrium price. Many of the studies classify traders into different groups, such as informed and uninformed (Grossman and Stiglitz, 1980), noise traders, market-makers, and informed speculators (Kyle, 1985), or hedgers and speculators (Wang, 2003).

Studies by Abarbanell *et al.* (1995) and Yang (1996) have shown that trader beliefs affect reactions to public information announcements. In the presence of heterogeneous trader beliefs and expectations, both their forecasts and their dispersion can affect how the market will respond to public information announcements. While traders' perceptions of liquidity have not been specifically researched, several researchers have incorporated trader beliefs and expectations into their models of liquidity. For example, in contrast to many studies where traders trade in each period, Easley and O'Hara (1992) allow traders the option of not trading based on their expectations.

Research design

To investigate traders' perceptions regarding the price path during order imbalances, we collected data from 420 traders at the CBOT and CME using face-to-face surveys in 2003. We presented traders with five different shapes of the price path due to order imbalances. The shapes (no price change, linear price path, exponential price path, step-wise price path, and S-shaped price path) were selected based on a pre-study conducted with 87 CBOT traders in 2002. In the 2003 survey, we also collected data on traders' perceptions of the number of contracts that cause an order imbalance, how fast prices change during an order imbalance, and when the price hits resistance. In addition, we identified the traders' primary commodities, their trading venues, and market capitalization.

The final survey used was short and concise, so that traders did not have to spend more than ten minutes filling it out. We set up tables adjacent to the trading floor for distribution and collection of surveys. This also allowed for individual interaction with the traders, who could ask questions or make suggestions. Many traders stopped to discuss the survey after completing it; this has enriched the analysis by helping us to better place our findings in context.

Survey design

Labeling of the axes is critical in properly framing traders' responses. Many models put time on the horizontal axis (for example, Grossman and Miller 1988) because they focus on the immediacy of trading. This is how we originally labeled the horizontal axis in the pre-study. However, since our study is concerned with the economic cost of liquidity, the horizontal axis was changed from time to contract number. This interpretation is consistent with the models proposed by Pennings *et al.* (1998) and Bessembinder and Seguin (1993). Note that the contract number was not scaled because the surveys were distributed to traders from many markets with different units of trade. In addition, we added a line showing the equilibrium price. This was done to emphasize how the price path during an order imbalance deviates from the equilibrium price (Figure 8.1).

Additional questions about the price path were used to gain a different perspective on the dynamics of an order imbalance: how many ticks would prices change with a small or large imbalance? How many contracts does it take to create an imbalance? How fast do prices change during an order imbalance? These questions also allowed us to check the accuracy of traders' different perceptions. For example, we hypothesized that a trader choosing the exponential shape to describe the price path due to order imbalances would also indicate rapid price changes during the imbalance.

Results

Descriptive results

Participants in the survey were active traders at CBOT or CME. Over half of the traders worked in the financial markets, while 35 percent of the participants were in the agricultural markets. Only 5 percent indicated that they traded contracts in both financial and agricultural markets.

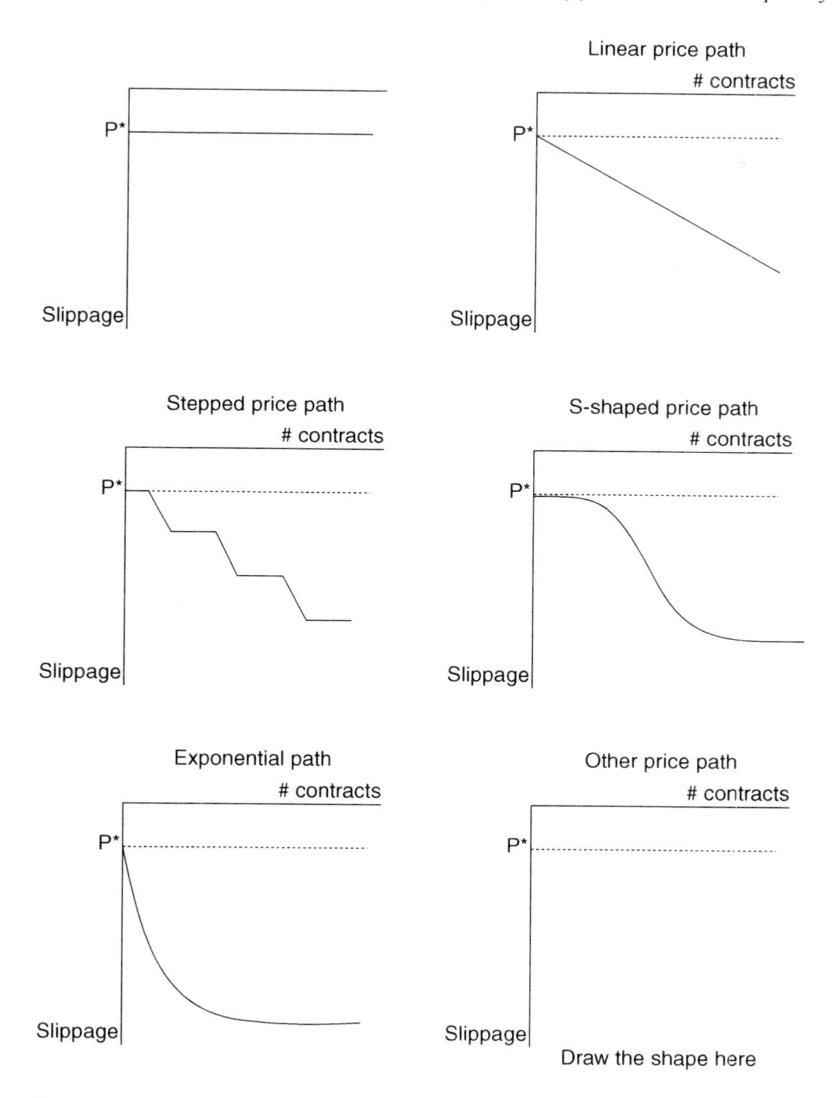

Figure 8.1 Shapes of price path due to order imbalances (slippage).

Type of traders

Traders tended to classify themselves as scalpers (22 percent) or choose multiple answers (22 percent) (Table 8.1). A large number of traders (46 percent) indicated that they hold positions for less than an hour. A chi-squared analysis showed that traders were consistent in their answers. Traders who responded that they held their positions for only seconds tended to classify themselves as

Table 8.1 Types of traders in survey (n=408)

How long do you hold your positions?		*Classify yourself as a trader?*		*What is your primary source of income?*	
Seconds	15%	Broker	18%	Profits from scalping	14%
Minutes	18%	Commercial hedger	1%	Broker salary	12%
Less than 1 hour	13%	Scalper	22%	Broker commissions	16%
Hours	7%	Day trader	8%	Commercial positions	1%
Less than a day	10%	Position trader	16%	Profits from spread trading	17%
Less than a week	11%	Spread trader	13%	Profits from outright trading	29%
Less than 1 month	6%	Multiple answer	22%	Multiple answer	12%
Longer than 1 month	10%				
Multiple answer	10%				

scalpers, while those who answered that they held their position for longer than a month classified themselves as position traders (χ^2=245.889, p=0.00).

The survey also asked, "What is the primary source of your income?" The purpose of the question was to help disentangle some of the multiple answers from the traders' self-classification. Many traders use the market in multiple ways, such as brokering and scalping. While 22 percent of traders classified themselves as scalpers, only 14 percent indicated that scalping profits were the primary source of income. Nevertheless, there was still a significant association between trader classification and income (χ^2=768.657, p=0.00), and between length of positions held and income (χ^2=177.235, p=0.00). Traders who classified themselves as scalpers also indicated that they hold their positions for less than one hour and that their primary source of income is from scalping, while traders who classified themselves as position traders indicated that they hold their positions for a month or longer and that their primary source of income is from outright trading.

Perceptions of the price path due to order imbalance

There was considerable variability in traders' perceptions of the price path. As seen in Figure 8.2, 2.4 percent of the participants perceived no slippage in the price path due to order imbalances, while 12.1 percent perceived a linear price path, 24.7 percent perceived an exponential price path, 26.1 percent perceived a stepped price path, and 20.7 percent perceived an S-Shaped price path. These results demonstrate clearly the heterogeneity in traders' perceptions and suggest that current market-depth measures which assume either a linear or S-shaped price path due to order imbalances may not reflect traders' perceptions.

Perceptions during imbalances

The vast majority (85.7 percent) of traders believe that the price changes vary with the magnitude of the order imbalance. Traders were asked about the differences in the speed of price changes during a small or large imbalance. A wide

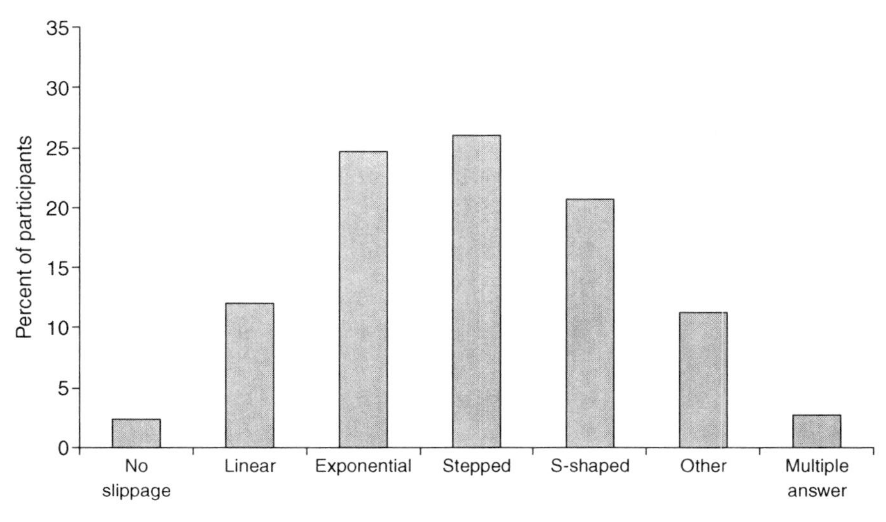

Figure 8.2 Traders' price path perceptions due to order imbalances.

variety of responses was expected on the aggregate level because each contract has its own normal trading activity. The results are shown in Table 8.2 for the contracts with the largest number of traders responding. In general, the results are skewed to the right because of large outliers in the data (e.g. mean>median). In each market, the speed of price changes during a small imbalance is slow (3–4 on scale of 7), while prices move more quickly during large imbalances (5–6).

If traders' responses to the survey are consistent, we would expect traders who perceive an exponential price path also to perceive the fastest changes in price during an imbalance. Table 8.3 shows that traders with exponential perceptions did expect the fastest price changes on an aggregate level. The traders who saw the slowest price changes perceived a stepped price path which reflects a degree of rigidity in price movement.

Perceptions and trader characteristics

We identified considerable heterogeneity in traders' perceptions (e.g. Pennings and Garcia, 2004). Traders' perceptions of price movements during order imbalances may depend on their personal background. Most commonly, traders classified themselves as speculators and hedgers or financial and agricultural traders. However, their education level, as well as the importance they place on execution costs and other factors, may also drive their perceptions. First, we examined whether trader characteristics are associated with particular perceptions of the price path on an aggregate level. Subsequently, traders were segmented by markets (e.g. agricultural, financial) to examine if trader characteristics are associated with specific price paths within a market.

Table 8.2 Differences between a small and large order imbalance

Contract	*Small imbalance*		*Large imbalance*	
	Mean	*Median*	*Mean*	*Median*
	Scale (1 very slow–7 very fast)			
Corn futures	3.8	3.0	5.5	5.0
Corn options	3.1	3.0	5.3	5.0
Soybean complex	3.8	4.0	6.2	6.0
Eurodollar	3.3	3.0	5.4	6.0
10 year notes	3.5	3.0	5.9	6.0
30 year bonds	3.8	3.5	6.1	6.0
S&P 500 futures	4.3	4.0	5.7	6.0
S&P 500 options	3.2	3.0	5.3	6.0
Dow Jones	4.2	4.0	6.0	6.0

Table 8.3 Perceptions of the speed of price changes and shape of price path

Characteristic	*Linear*	*Exponential*	*Stepped*	*S-shaped*	*Other*	*Sig.**
All traders						
How fast does slippage occur during a large order imbalance? (1 very slow–7 very fast)						0.02
	5.5	6.0	5.4	5.8	5.9	

Note

* Based on ANOVA.

When traders were asked which graph accurately describes the price path during order imbalances (Figure 8.2) less than ten participants chose either no slippage or chose multiple answers. Due to the low response rate, these categories were not included in the analysis of trader characteristics.

Initially, the entire sample was examined to investigate whether particular trader characteristics were associated with how traders perceived the price path. The results are presented in Table 8.4. The limited number of significant relationships suggests that trader characteristics are not a driving factor behind traders' perceptions on an aggregate level. At the 5 percent level, the percentage of futures contracts traded is the only significant trader characteristic related to trader perceptions. Traders associated with the highest level of futures trading chose to draw their own price path, while traders who used options perceived a linear price path.

None of the other characteristics were associated with a particular perception regarding the price path during order imbalances at the 5 percent level. However, at the 10 percent level, the type of market the trader uses was significant. Financial traders are more often associated with a stepped perception of the price path, while agricultural traders are associated most with an exponential or

Table 8.4 Price path perceptions associated with trader characteristics

Trader characteristics	*Linear*	*Exponential*	*Stepped*	*S-shaped*	*Other*	*Significance**
Mean						
Age	39.3	40.6	42.3	40.3	39.8	0.354
Began trading	1990.4	1988.1	1987.8	1989.1	1988.9	0.501
Market capitalization	436,964	3,523,974	495,073	22,770,543	447,500	0.464
Average daily volume	1200.9	2104.5	1614.2	1378.8	1553.0	0.691
% Trades that are futures	72.7%	85.3%	78.3%	79.8%	92.2%	0.042
Percent of responses						
Exchange						
CME	14.0	24.8	25.5	21.7	14.0	0.737
CBOT	11.7	27.0	29.1	21.9	10.2	
Market						
Agricultural	9.4	28.2	26.5	28.2	7.7	0.078
Financial	13.3	24.3	27.6	19.0	15.7	
Both	18.8	37.5	37.5	6.3	0.0	
Education level						
None	0.0	0.0	0.0	0.0	100.0	0.579
High school	9.1	36.4	45.5	9.1	0.0	
Some college	12.7	21.8	27.3	21.8	16.4	
College graduate	11.1	26.0	27.9	22.6	12.5	
Some graduate school	13.8	34.5	31.0	17.2	3.4	
Masters degree	21.7	23.9	21.7	21.7	10.9	
Doctorate	0.0	50.0	0.0	50.0	0.0	
Time positions held						
Seconds	12.5	30.4	26.8	14.3	16.1	0.783
Minutes	13.1	27.9	26.2	23.0	9.8	
Less than 1 hour	6.7	20.0	28.9	31.1	13.3	
Hours	15.4	38.5	26.9	11.5	7.7	
Less than a day	12.5	28.1	21.9	25.0	12.5	
Less than a week	16.2	24.3	29.7	16.2	13.5	
Less than 1 month	4.2	12.5	29.2	33.3	20.8	
Multiple answer	10.3	31.0	34.5	13.8	10.3	
Greater than 1 month	18.8	21.9	21.9	34.4	3.1	

Notes

For the variables: age, year began trading, average daily volume, and % of trades that were futures a one-way ANOVA test was performed. For all other factors χ^2 tests were utilized.

S-shaped price path. Informal conversations with financial traders revealed one possible explanation for financial traders' stepped perceptions of the price path. These traders preferred to make trades in specific normal-sized lots (i.e. 100, 500, or 1,000 contract lots). Therefore, traders may perceive a stepped price path, where each step is a different normal lot size with its associated bid–ask spread. Knowing the normal lot sizes may give an indication of where prices will drop, and hence total expected execution costs.

It is interesting to identify some of the insignificant trader characteristics. While many studies of trader behavior divide traders into different trader classifications, there is no relationship between the type of trader (e.g. scalper, spreader, etc.) nor the time traders tend to hold their positions and how one perceives the price path during order imbalances. Neither their self-classification nor their primary source of income are related to the perceived price path. Another non-related characteristic is the futures exchange at which the trader operates. The market–structural differences on an aggregate level between the exchanges appear not to be associated with a particular price-path perception.

Overall, the results from Table 8.4 do not explain to any degree the heterogeneity in observed perceptions. However, they do suggest that it may be useful to study a trader's market to see how the nature of the markets is related to perceptions. The type of market (i.e. agricultural or financial) in which the respondent trades is significant at the 10-percent level, but there is still considerable heterogeneity within the agricultural and financial markets. By aggregating the data, some trader characteristics that are significant on the market level may be hidden. Therefore, traders' perceptions were examined by market segment. The market segments chosen were all agriculture and all financial. In addition, the financial markets were subdivided into exchange rates, interest rates, and stock indexes, because three distinct types of financial contracts are traded in Chicago. Agricultural markets were not subdivided, as grain traders dominate that segment.

As shown in Table 8.5, several characteristics which are relevant at a market level are not significant on an aggregate level. However, only a few characteristics are significant. In the exchange rate and interest rate segments, no characteristics are significant. Trading venue, the importance of execution costs, and contract traded are several characteristics that are significant at the market level. Nevertheless, trader classification still is not related to traders' perceptions about the price path during an order imbalance. In none of the market segments was type of trader (i.e. broker, scalper, spreader, etc.) or duration of holding contracts significant.

Similar to the findings on an aggregate level, the percentage of futures contracts used by the trader is related to traders' perceptions for all financial markets and within stock index markets themselves. In each case, traders that were more active in the futures markets drew their own price path, and traders who were more active in options had a linear perception of the price path during an order imbalance.

In the agricultural markets, the use of electronic trading is controversial and

Table 8.5 Price path perceptions associated with trader characteristics by market

Trader characteristics	*Linear*	*Exponential*	*Stepped*	*S-shaped*	*Other*	*Significance**
All traders						
What percent of trades are futures contracts?	72.7%	85.3%	78.3%	79.8%	92.2%	0.042
Segments						
Agricultural						
What is your trading venue?						0.058
Open outcry	9.1%	28.6%	26.0%	33.8%	2.6%	
Electronic	100.0%	0.0%	0.0%	0.0%	0.0%	
Both, prim. outcry	8.1%	27.0%	27.0%	18.9%	18.9%	
Both, prim. elect.	0.0%	100.0%	0.0%	0.0%	0.0%	
Both, equal	0.0%	0.0%	100.0%	0.0%	0.0%	
Financial						
What percent of trades are futures contracts?	70.3%	86.9%	79.1%	85.2%	93.8%	0.041
How important are execution costs? (1 least important–7 most important)	3.5	4.4	4.7	4.5	4.2	0.065
Exchange rates						
None						
Interest rates						
None						
Stock indexes						
What is your primary contract?						0.013
S&P500 futures	12%	33%	21%	9%	24%	
Russell	33%	0%	0%	0%	67%	
Nasdaq100	0%	0%	50%	50%	0%	
Mid-cap	0%	0%	0%	100%	0%	
Dow Jones	15%	42%	8%	23%	12%	
S&P500 options	55%	18%	9%	18%	0%	
What percent of trades are futures contracts?	68.5%	91.8%	82.9%	79.1%	98.2%	0.087
How important are execution costs? (1 least important–7 most important)	2.9	4.6	5.0	4.1	4.6	0.014

Notes

For the variables: % of trades that were futures and importance if execution costs a one-way ANOVA test was performed. For all other factors χ^2 tests were utilized.

is a discriminating characteristic in explaining the heterogeneity of traders' perceptions. Traders, who only use open outcry, perceive the price path to be exponential (28.6 percent), stepped (26 percent), or S-shaped (33.8 percent), while traders who use electronic systems only perceive a linear price path. These differences may be due to the information available to the traders. Open-outcry traders do not have any statistical data regarding market depth and rely on changes in the bid–ask spread, whereas electronic traders can see part of the order book which could affect their perceptions.

We asked traders to rank the importance of execution costs to their trading activities. This factor is a significant determinant of perceptions for all financial traders (including exchange rate, interest rate, and index traders), as well as for just stock index traders. In each segment, the ranking and perceptions followed a similar pattern. Traders who placed the least importance on execution costs perceived a linear price path while traders who placed the most importance on execution costs perceived a stepped price path. A linear price path would indicate a steady consistent change in prices during an imbalance which makes it very easy to calculate execution costs. A stepped price path, instead, has steep price jumps that may be unpredictable. Therefore, it seems logical that traders with linear perceptions place lower importance on execution costs than traders with stepped perceptions.

In the stock index segment, the specific contract in which the respondent trades is a significant determinant of price path perceptions. Differences in the main three contracts are illustrated in Figure 8.3. Even in the S&P 500 stock index segment, there are large differences between how futures and options traders perceive the price path.

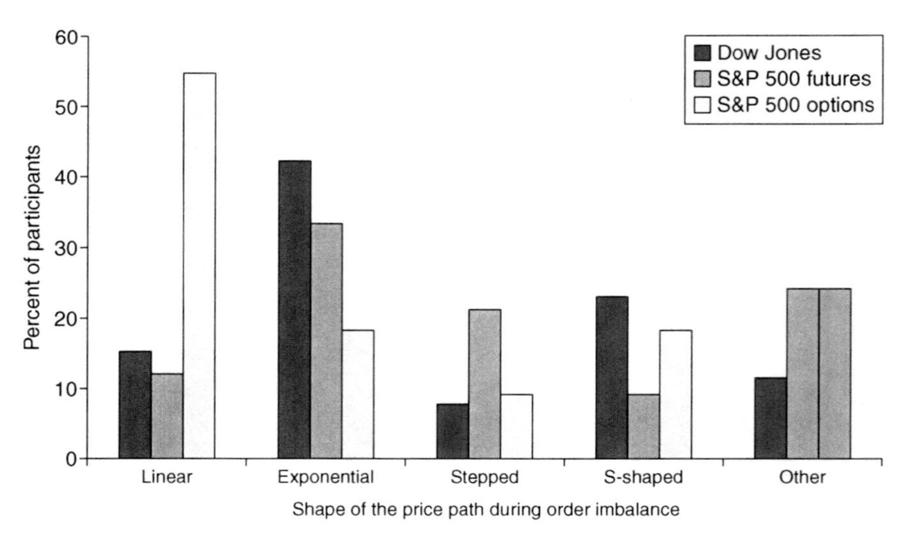

Figure 8.3 Index contract traders associated with perceptions of the shape of the price path.

Overall, trader characteristics, even in the different market segments, do not appear to explain a significant portion of the heterogeneity in perceptions. None of these characteristics is significant in all the different market segments, and those that are statistically significant are not always economically meaningful. For example, while there is an association between the importance of execution costs and perceptions of the price path, there is only a 1.2-unit difference on a 7-point scale between the importance placed on execution costs (this information is not reported here).

The stock index segment indicated that market characteristics, not trader characteristics, may be driving heterogeneity in traders' perceptions of the price path. This suggests that market microstructure and the characteristics of the underlying commodity may be influencing traders' heterogeneous perceptions of the price path.

Perceptions and market characteristics

To this point, we have shown that traders' characteristics do not explain the heterogeneity in perceptions of the price path during an order imbalance. However, there is some evidence that the characteristics of particular markets are related to perceptions. This would indicate that market microstructure and the characteristics of the underlying market are the driving forces behind traders' perceptions.

To investigate this relationship, we examined the ten most commonly used contracts by the respondents; the results are reported in Table 8.6. The specific contract which traders use is associated with their perception of the price path at the 5 percent level. Thus traders' perceptions in a specific market are similar and are likely explained by the market microstructure of the specific market. Recall that the trading system, contract specification, and the market's mix of traders are features of market microstructure which could lead to different and market-specific price paths. Characteristics of the underlying market on which the futures contract is based may also influence traders' perceptions. We discuss the contracts by market type: agriculture, interest rate, and index.

Corn traders are associated with stepped perceptions of the price path, while traders in soybean-complex contracts perceive an exponential price path (see Figure 8.4). Differences in market microstructure may explain the difference in perception between corn traders and soybean-complex traders. Both commodities trade at the same exchange, and use the same trading system.

While sharing many of the same regulations, their contract specifications differ by contract month and price limits. Corn contracts are traded in five months (December, March, May, July, and September), while soybeans are traded in seven months (September, November, January, March, May, July, and August). More importantly, soybeans have a larger daily price limit US$0.50/bu (US$2500/contract) than corn which is US$0.20 cents/bu (US$1000/contract). The composition of the traders also differs between the markets. The soybean complex markets has a high concentration of spread traders (26.9 percent vs. corn 17.6 percent) that trades the three soybean contracts to keep the soybean

Table 8.6 Major contracts and the perceptions of the price path*

Contract	*Linear*	*Exponential*	*Stepped*	*S-shaped*	*Other*
Corn futures	18.2%	15.2%	45.5%	18.2%	3.0%
Corn options	28.6%	0.0%	28.6%	28.6%	14.3%
Soybean complex	7.1%	42.9%	16.7%	21.4%	11.9%
Eurodollar	7.5%	20.8%	30.2%	22.6%	18.9%
10 year notes	11.8%	23.5%	23.5%	23.5%	17.6%
30 year bonds	10.0%	30.0%	30.0%	10.0%	20.0%
30 year bond options	16.7%	0.0%	50.0%	16.7%	16.7%
S&P 500 futures	12.1%	33.3%	21.2%	9.1%	24.2%
S&P 500 options	54.5%	18.2%	9.1%	18.2%	0.0%
Dow Jones	15.4%	42.3%	7.7%	23.1%	11.5%

Notes
*(χ^2=56.462, p=0.016).

crush in proper proportion while the corn market has a high proportion of brokers (32.3 percent vs. soybeans 23.0 percent). In conversations with the traders, many brokers indicated that they were less concerned with liquidity than simply filling customer orders. They may perceive the price path with respect to the batches of orders that they fill which could explain the stepped function. In contrast, soybean traders who trade the spreads in markets may be very sensitive to any changes in the crush margin and may perceive even small changes as having an exponential impact on the price path. Another explanation for the difference in perceptions may be the underlying market. Traditionally, the soybean complex has been considered a much more volatile market than corn which could also explain the exponential perceptions observed in the soybean complex.

The CBOT interest rate futures contracts (Treasury bonds and Treasury notes) face the same trading system, the same regulations, and the same contract specifications, and traders who use the contracts have very similar perceptions. Bond traders perceive an exponential or stepped price path and note traders perceive an exponential, stepped, or S-shaped price path. However, a difference emerges between the CBOT contracts and CME Eurodollar futures contract whose traders predominately have a stepped perception. Several differences in the contract specifications and trading systems between the Treasury contracts and the Eurodollar contract exist which could be related to this difference. First, the Eurodollar has a larger-sized contract (US$1 million vs. US$100,000) and a smaller tick size (US$25.00/contract vs. US$31.25). Second, the Eurodollar is cash settled on the last trading day while CBOT contracts are deliverable. Third, while all of these contracts use side-by-side trading system, the CBOT and CME systems differ. In addition the CBOT contracts trade approximately 90 percent of their contracts electronically, while the Eurodollar trades only about 40 percent of its contracts electronically (see www.cbot.com and www.cme.com). Finally, the CBOT note and bond contracts are long-term interest rate contracts while the Eurodollar is a short-term interest rate contract.

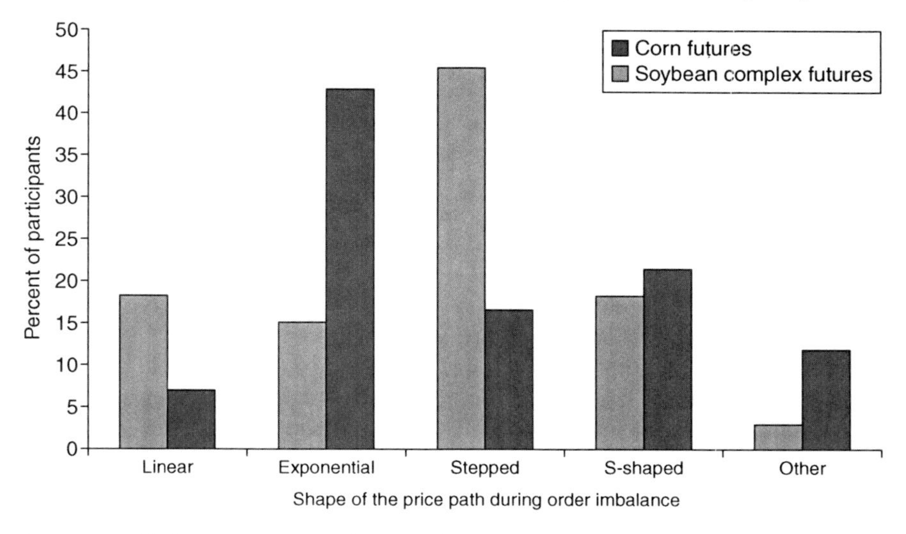

Figure 8.4 Difference in price path perceptions between corn and soybean traders.

In the past two years, the CBOT has instituted a designated market marker to provide liquidity and smooth price movements in the Dow Jones index. However, 42.3 percent of traders perceive an exponential price path during an order imbalance, indicating that traders still believe order imbalances cause prices to drop sharply. Interestingly, traders of the S&P 500 index futures also perceive an exponential price path, suggesting that both groups of traders may be responding to factors characteristic of their stock market index.

While particular markets are associated with particular perceptions of the price path during an order imbalance, they do not explain all of the heterogeneity. For example, equal numbers of traders of the ten-year note contract perceive exponential, stepped, and S-shaped price paths. Additional research is needed to understand the heterogeneity in specific markets and to determine which dimensions in the market-microstructure environment are driving perceptions.

Conclusions

The main objective of this study was to gain a better understanding of liquidity by investigating how traders perceive the price path during temporary order imbalances. Based on the responses of 420 traders from the CBOT and CME a great deal of heterogeneity in perceptions regarding the price path during order imbalances exists. Approximately 2.4 percent of traders perceive no price change due to order imbalances, 12.1 percent perceive a linear price path, 24.7 percent perceive an exponential price path, 26.1 percent perceive a stepped price path, 20.7 percent perceive a S-shaped price path, and 11.3 percent of the traders indicated that none of these price paths describe the price path due to order imbalances. Previous liquidity research has developed models to measure market depth assuming a linear price path, without explicitly considering the shape of the price path due to order imbalances. However, our research indicates that only 12.1 percent of the traders perceived a linear price path during a temporary order imbalance, indicating that these models might not accurately reflect trader perceptions and consequently may be unable to explain and predict trader behavior adequately.

To explain the heterogeneity in perceptions, we first investigated whether trader characteristics were associated with a particular price-path perception. The only characteristic that proved to explain the heterogeneity on an aggregate level was the proportion of futures contracts traded. Disaggregating the responses to market segments shed little additional light on the effects of trader characteristics on the differences in price path perceptions. It appears that trader characteristics which researchers use to classify traders and explain market activity are not related to perceptions of the price path during an order imbalance. However, the particular market or contract traded is a significant factor in explaining the heterogeneity of perceptions during order imbalances. While the market does not explain all of the heterogeneity in perceptions, traders of a particular contract tend to possess similar perceptions. These findings indicate that the market microstructure environment may drive trader perceptions of the price path.

Further research

As the futures industry continues to consolidate and the expansion of electronic trading leads to more global markets, futures exchanges are increasingly worried about improving and/or maintaining liquidity to lower transaction costs. Our study suggests that understanding liquidity and its determinants is challenging and will require researchers to delve into the characteristics of specific markets. While we have demonstrated that perceptions are associated with particular markets, there is a need to study the dimensions' microstructure to determine which factors are most useful in explaining market perceptions. In doing this, attention must be paid to ensure that the markets studied vary sufficiently in liquidity levels and have significantly different microstructures.

In our study, we would have liked to aggregate traders' perceptions in various markets. This would have allowed us to examine if the sum of the different perceptions creates a linear price path consistent with traditional assumptions. However, the survey did not include the information needed to develop the scale for each trader's price path. Future research should consider using computer graphic software so that traders could draw their own price path with the appropriate scale. Market depth could then be represented by a space that is defined by three dimensions: price change, contracts traded, and rate of price change.

In our study, we have examined traders' perceptions. However, this is only the first step to understanding the dynamics of liquidity. Traders' perceptions drive their behavior, but we have little understanding how traders' perceptions are incorporated into their trading strategies. Further research needs to investigate trader behavior – their trader responses and interactions with other traders during temporary order imbalances. Finally, traders' perceptions of the price path need to be tested against transaction-specific data to see whether they are an accurate reflection of the shape of the price path. A challenge for such research is to distinguish a temporary order imbalance from a fundamental shift.

References

Abarbanell, J., W. Lanen, and R. Verrecchia. "Analysts' Forecasts as Proxies for Investor Beliefs in Empirical Research." *Journal of Accounting and Economics* 20 (1995): 31–60.

Aitken, M. and C. Comerton-Forde. "How Should Liquidity Be Measured?" *Pacific-Basin Finance Journal* 11 (2003): 45–59.

Bessembinder, H. and P.J. Seguin. "Price Volatility, Trading Volume, and Market Depth: Evidence from the Futures Markets." *Journal of Financial and Quantitative Analysis* 28 (1993): 21–39.

Black, F. "Towards a Fully Automated Exchange, Part I." *Financial Analysts Journal* 27 (1971): 29–34.

Chordia, T., R. Roll, and A. Svanidhar. "Order Imbalance, Liquidity, and Market Returns." *Journal of Finance* 65 (2002): 111–30.

Easley, D. and M. O'Hara. "Time and the Process of Security Price Adjustment." *Journal of Finance* 47 (1992): 577–606.

Grossman, S. and J. Stiglitz. "On the Impossibility of Informationally Efficient Markets." *American Economic Review* 70 (1980): 393–408.

Grossman, S.J. and M.H. Miller. "Liquidity and Market Structure." *Journal of Finance* 43 (1988): 617–33.

Kyle, A.S. "Continuous Auctions and Insider Trading." *Econometrica* 53 (1985): 1315–35.

Lucas, R. "Expectations and the Neutrality of Money." *Journal of Economic Theory* 4 (1972): 103–24.

Pennings, J.M.E. and P. Garcia. "Hedging Behavior in Small and Medium-sized Enterprises: The Role of Unobserved Heterogeneity," *Journal of Banking and Finance* 28 (2004): 951–78.

Pennings, J.M.E. and M.T.G. Meulenberg. "Hedging Efficiency: A Futures Exchange Management Approach." *Journal of Futures Markets* 17 (1997): 599–615.

Pennings, J.M.E., W.E. Kuiper, F. ter Hofstede, and M.T.G. Meulenberg. "The Price Path Due to Order Imbalances: Evidence from the Amsterdam Agricultural Futures Exchange." *European Financial Management*, 4 (1998): 27–44.

Pirrong, C. "Market Liquidity and Depth on Computerized and Open Outcry Trading Systems: A Comparison of DTB and LIFFE Bund Contracts." *Journal of Futures Markets* 16 (1996): 519–43.

Roll, R. "A Simple Implicit Measure of the Effective Bid-Ask Spread in an Efficient Market." *Journal of Finance* 39 (1984): 1127–39.

Thompson, S.R. and M.L. Waller "The Execution Cost of Trading in Commodity Markets." *Food Research Institute Studies* 20 (1987): 141–63.

Tse, Y. "Market Microstructure of FT-SE 100 Index Futures: An Intraday Empirical Analysis." *Journal of Futures Markets* 19 (1999): 31–58.

Wang, C. "The Behavior and Performance of Major Types of Futures Traders." *Journal of Futures Markets* 23 (2003): 1–31.

Yang, L. "Commodity Futures Market Reaction to Anticipated Public Reports: Frozen Pork Bellies" Thesis, University of Illinois, Urbana-Champaign (1996).

9 Simultaneity and liquidity in US electricity futures

S. Gulay Avsar and Barry A. Goss[1]

Abstract

Previous research on liquidity in securities markets has studied the relationships between liquidity, trading activity and volatility, using single equation methods, mostly with data from US Treasury securities, stocks and foreign exchange spot markets. Such analyses are inadequate, because these relationships are determined simultaneously, and this should be taken into account in empirical research. Moreover, liquidity relationships in futures markets have received little attention, and liquidity in electricity futures markets appears to have been neglected. This paper, which addresses these issues, develops a simultaneous model of cost of liquidity, trading activity and volatility for the California-Oregon Border electricity futures contract. The results show a positive relation between cost of liquidity and volume, which is consistent with a dominant asymmetric information cost and/or increased volatility accompanied by increased volume. The results include also a positive volume–volatility relation (although theoretically ambiguous in sign), and an expected positive cost of liquidity–volatility relation. A comparison is made between the systems and limited information estimates. Keywords: liquidity; electricity futures; simultaneous model. JEL Codes: G13, Q41.

Introduction

Previous research on liquidity in securities markets has studied the relationships between pairs of the three key variables liquidity, and two important determinants of liquidity, namely volume and volatility, using single-equation methods, mostly with data from US Treasury securities, stocks and foreign exchange spot markets (e.g. Bollerslev and Melvin, 1994; Fleming and Remolona, 1999; Bollerslev and Domowitz, 1993; Fleming, 1997, 2003; Andersen and Bollerslev, 1998). Such analyses between pairs of these variables are inadequate, because as pointed out by Andersen and Bollerslev (1998, p. 220) these variables are determined simultaneously, and this should be taken into account in empirical work. Furthermore, liquidity relationships in futures markets have received much less attention than those in spot markets, and liquidity in electricity futures markets appears to have been neglected. There is reason to expect liquidity in futures markets to behave differently from that in spot markets because of the unique asymmetries of futures markets; e.g. futures markets trade on margin, whereas spot markets require full payment, and delivery in futures markets, if possible, is only at seller's option (Goss, 2001, p. 412). Liquidity in electricity futures markets will be of interest in countries in Europe, Asia and Oceania which are deregulating their electricity markets.

The quoted bid–ask spread has been employed frequently in previous research as a measure of liquidity, although as Fleming (2003, p. 85) pointed out, this concept is an appropriate measure of the cost of liquidity only for a small transaction for a short time period. Smith and Whaley (1994) argued that the "effective" bid–ask spread (the difference between the price at which a dealer buys (sells) a security, and the price at which she sells (buys) it) is a more appropriate measure of liquidity, although in the absence of dealer records, no ideal measure of this concept has been found. Market depth is the number of securities that can be traded at given bid–ask quotations, and is an aspect of liquidity which does not suffer from the same limitations as bid–ask spread. Quote size (the quantity of securities to which the bid or offer refers) and trade size (quantity of securities traded at a given price) are measures of market depth, although as Fleming (2003, p. 85) suggests, these measures tend to underestimate market depth. Pennings *et al.* (1998) studied market depth, as represented by the price path due to order imbalance, and found support for the concept of a non-linear price path. Chordia, Sarkar and Subrahmanyam (2003) studied the cross-market dynamics of liquidity and its determinants, between bond and stock markets. They employed order imbalance as a measure of trading activity, and found inter alia that while bid–ask spreads for stocks and bonds are significantly correlated, order imbalance is moderately correlated with liquidity for stocks, and weakly correlated with liquidity for bonds.

Fleming (1997) refers to four components of the bid–ask spread. The first is asymmetric information cost, which represents a compensation to the market-maker for dealing with better-informed traders. Second, the dealer's risk in holding a security is regarded as an "inventory carrying cost" and is thought to be a direct function of volatility. The third component is the market power of the dealer, which will vary inversely with competition among dealers, and fourth there are the direct costs of order execution (see also Wang *et al.*, 1994; Glosten, 1987; McInish and Wood, 1992).

The US electricity wholesale market is largely deregulated: a national electricity grid has been created, and both utilities and independent system operators are permitted by federal law to have access to the national transmission grid. At the retail level, deregulation has progressed further in some states (e.g. California, Pennsylvania and Massachusetts) than others, and consequently the cash market is more developed in some areas. Where wholesale prices are competitively determined, electricity futures contracts provide a risk-management instrument for generators, distributors, traders and consumers. For examples of risk-management strategies for generators, distributors and consumers of electricity, using electricity futures and options contracts, see Avsar and Goss (2001, pp. 480–481). In March 1996 the New York Mercantile Exchange (NYMEX) launched the California–Oregon Border (COB) and Palo Verde electricity futures contracts, which provided for delivery of electricity during on-peak hours, at specified locations in the western part of the country. In July 1998 the Cintergy and Entergy contracts began trading; these contracts referred to Indiana, Ohio and Kentucky for Cintergy, and Louisiana, Arkansas, Mississippi and Texas for Entergy. These contracts were followed by the inception of the PJM contract,[2] which referred to Pennsylvania, New Jersey and Maryland, in March 1999. When these five futures contracts traded on NYMEX they were accompanied by corresponding options on futures.

While the US electricity spot market, especially in California, has attracted significant attention from researchers in recent years, little has been written about the performance of the electricity futures market. Walls (1999) investigated the relationship between volatility and time to maturity for 14 COB and Palo Verde contracts, and found that for 12 of 14 contracts there was a significant negative relationship. Goss and Avsar (2006) studied the relationships between cost of liquidity, volume and volatility, with Palo Verde data, using a single-equation approach, and found these relationships to be positive. Avsar and Goss (2001) studied the extent to which electricity futures prices reflected public information. They found evidence against market efficiency for the period 1996–99, when only COB and Palo Verde contracts traded, but found no such evidence for the period 1998–99 when the Cintergy contract also was trading. Lack of evidence against market efficiency, however, is no guarantee of smooth market operation and consumer satisfaction. Kahn and Lynch (2000) noted that wholesale electricity prices in California in June 2000 were more than seven times those in June 1999, and they argued that shortage of supply was a factor leading to high prices in June 2000. The same authors found that generating capacity in California increased by only 1.2 per cent during the period 1996–99, while peak demand increased by 10 per cent during the same period. Borenstein *et al.* (2002) estimated the extent to which three factors – input costs, scarcity and market power – influenced market outcomes in California during the period 1998–2000. They estimated that rising input prices would have resulted in a three-fold increase in wholesale expenditure on electricity during this period, although they found also that the exercise of market power by suppliers had a significant role in the price increases which occurred. While price behaviour in US electricity futures has received some attention from researchers, the cost of liquidity, which is a major cost of transacting in futures markets (see Ding, 1999, p. 308; Wang *et al.*, 1997, p. 759), has been almost entirely neglected. The objective of this paper, therefore, is twofold: first, to develop a simultaneous model of the relationships between the key variables of liquidity, volume and volatility, and second to estimate these relationships with data from US COB futures. This paper extends the work of Goss and Avsar (2006) by investigating these relationships in a simultaneous framework with data from the most active contract during the most active period for US electricity futures

[1996(04) to 1999(12)]. The remainder of this paper is organized as follows: the next section discusses model specification, while the third section is concerned with issues of data, stationarity and estimation. Results are presented in the fourth section, while some conclusions and policy implications are suggested in the final section.

Model specification

There is a relationship, based on economic theory, between each pair of the three key variables (cost of liquidity, volume and volatility) and each of these relationships gives rise to an empirical equation. Consider first the relationship between the cost of liquidity and volume. As volume increases, it is generally assumed that dealer inventory risk decreases, that unit costs of order execution decrease, and that market power of the dealer decreases with increased competition among dealers resulting from the increased market activity. The effect of changes in these three factors, on the cost of liquidity, therefore, is assumed to be negative. The asymmetric information cost, in comparison, may increase with volume if the dealer perceives that orders are being placed by traders with private information (see McInish and Wood, 1992, pp. 753–54; Wang *et al.* 1994, pp. 838, 843; Copeland and Galai, 1983, p. 1463). Moreover, if increased volume accompanies increased volatility, the increased uncertainty implied by the latter may also raise the cost of liquidity. It is generally assumed that increased volume generates essentially negative influences on the cost of liquidity, and this is consistent with the empirical results of Fleming (1997), Wang *et al.* (1997), Goss and Avsar (1998, 2002) and others. Nevertheless, this relationship, in theory, is ambiguous in sign (see also Hartmann, 1999, pp. 803–5, who puts forward the view that in theory the sign of the relationship between bid–ask spreads and total volume is indeterminate). These influences may be represented as

$$dB=\frac{\partial C}{\partial V}dV+\frac{\partial R}{\partial V}dV+\frac{\partial E}{\partial V}dV+\frac{\partial A}{\partial V}dV \tag{1}$$

where B=cost of liquidity

C=unit cost of order execution, assumed to fall as volume increases

V=volume of futures contracts traded

R=dealer's risk from holding a position in futures; this risk decreases as more traders enter the market

E=dealer's market power, measured by the excess of price over marginal cost; E decreases as competition among dealers increases

A=asymmetric information cost to dealer from dealing with better informed traders, which is assumed to increase with volume; and

$\frac{\partial C}{\partial V}, \frac{\partial R}{\partial V}, \frac{\partial E}{\partial V}<0; \frac{\partial A}{\partial V}>0$, and dB><0.

While Chordia, Sarkar and Subrahmanyam (2003) studied the interdependence in liquidity between stock and bond markets, the cross market dynamics of liquidity between futures and stocks has been ignored. In the empirical representation of the cost-of-liquidity-volume relationship, the value of the S&P 500 Index summarizes a variety of influences in equities upon electricity futures, and represents also common responses of equities and electricity futures to other events. For example, expansionary monetary policy may stimulate demand for equities and electricity futures, so that the relationship between *SP* and *B* would be negative. Alternatively, the share market may be stimulated by new information which makes shares relatively more attractive, so that the relationship between *SP* and *B* would be positive. Hence the sign of this relationship is ambiguous, and the empirical function is:

$$B_t = \phi_1 + \phi_2 V_t + \phi_3 SP_t + e_{1t} \tag{2}$$

Where SP = S&P500 Index

e_1 = error term
t = time in months; and
ϕ_1 = constant; ϕ_2, ϕ_3 >< 0.

Consider next the relationship between volume and volatility. The theoretical foundations of the relationship between price variability and volume have been studied by Epps and Epps (1976), Tauchen and Pitts (1983) and others. In the model of Epps and Epps, with the arrival of new information, the conditional variance of price changes varies directly with volume, through increased disagreement between buyers and sellers (Epps and Epps, 1976, pp. 306–9). In contrast, in the model of Tauchen and Pitts (1983), price variability varies directly with volume, given the number of traders. An increase in the number of traders, however, will reduce the variance of price changes, with the reduction in "inter-trader differences" (Tauchen and Pitts, 1983, pp. 487–90). In the model of Tauchen and Pitts (1983), therefore, the sign of the relationship between volume and volatility is ambiguous. From the liquidity viewpoint, volatility incorporates both new information and the bid–ask spread (Glosten, 1987; Wang *et al.* 1994; Smith and Whaley, 1994). An increase in volatility can be expected to lead to an increase in volume, as investors trade on new information. Nevertheless, if it is perceived that orders are being placed by traders with private information, this represents an increase in the dealer's asymmetric information cost, which will lead to an increase in the bid–ask spread, which will tend to discourage volume (e.g. French and Roll, 1986; Ito *et al.*, 1998). Moreover, the increased uncertainty, which accompanies increased volatility, will increase the dealer's inventory risk, and hence the bid–ask spread, and so discourage volume (McInish and Wood, 1992, p. 754; Wang *et al.* 1994, p. 838, n. 1). The sign of the relationship between volume and volatility, therefore, is ambiguous. This relationship can be represented as follows:

$$dV = \frac{\partial V}{\partial h} dh + \frac{\partial V}{\partial B}\frac{\partial B}{\partial h} dh \tag{3}$$

where h = a measure of volatility

$$\frac{\partial V}{\partial h}>0, \frac{\partial V}{\partial B}<0, \frac{\partial B}{\partial h}>0, \text{ so that}$$

$$dV><0.$$

In the empirical specification of the relationship between volume and volatility, the effect of the general level of economic activity is assumed to be represented by the US Index of Production, and an EGARCH-M term is introduced, following Engle *et al.* (1987), to capture the impact of uncertainty elsewhere in the economy, upon the volume of electricity futures. To capture the asymmetric impact of news on the conditional variance of the residuals the exponential GARCH or EGARCH model of Nelson (1991) has been employed. The empirical function for this relationship is therefore

$$V_t = \phi_4 + \phi_5 h_t + \phi_6 I_t + \phi_7 \sqrt{W_{2t}} + e_{2t} \tag{4}$$

where I = US Index of Production
$\sqrt{W_2}$ = conditional standard deviation of e_2; and
$\phi_5 >< 0$; $\phi_6 > 0$; $\phi_7 >< 0$.

The sign of ϕ_7 also is ambiguous, because increased uncertainty elsewhere in the economy may encourage hedgers to increase their cover, and/or may encourage or discourage speculators from taking further positions in electricity futures.

Third, consider the relationship between the cost of liquidity and volatility. It is generally argued that increased volatility represents increased uncertainty, and will lead to increased dealer risk in holding securities. The increased inventory cost will cause dealers to increase the bid–ask spread, thus raising the cost of liquidity (see McInish and Wood, 1992, p. 754; Fleming, 1997, p. 21, Chordia *et al.*, 2003, pp. 13–14). Moreover, it is often argued that increased volatility is likely to lead to increased asymmetric information costs. This is because volatility is seen as price movements caused by the arrival of information (Fleming, 1997, p. 16), and the subsequent orders are seen, to some extent, as originating from better informed traders (see McInish and Wood, 1992, p. 754; Bollerslev and Melvin, 1994, p. 356; Fleming, 1997, p. 22; and Wang *et al.*, 1994, p. 838). The increased asymmetric information cost also will lead dealers to increase the bid–ask spread. These factors can be represented as follows:

$$dB = \frac{\partial B}{\partial R}\frac{\partial R}{\partial h}dh + \frac{\partial B}{\partial A}\frac{\partial A}{\partial h}dh \tag{5}$$

and

$$\frac{\partial B}{\partial R}, \frac{\partial R}{\partial h}, \frac{\partial B}{\partial A}, \frac{\partial A}{\partial h}>0, \text{ so that } dB>0.$$

The empirical representation of this relationship is:

$$B_t = \phi_8 + \phi_9 h_t + \phi_{10}\sqrt{W_{3t}} + e_{3t} \tag{6}$$

where $\sqrt{W_3}$=conditional standard deviation of e_3, and enters (6) as an EGARCH-M term to capture the impact on the cost of liquidity, of uncertainty elsewhere in the economy; and $\phi_9, \phi_{10} > 0$.

According to the order condition for identification, each of the equations of this model is over-identified, and the rank condition is fulfilled. In the identification analysis the M-GARCH terms, W_2 and W_3 are treated as pre-determined variables, because they are derived from the variance equations associated with the single-equation estimates.

Data, stationarity and estimation

This section discusses issues of data, stationarity and estimation, in turn. This paper employs data for the California–Oregon Border (COB) futures contract.

Data

In some securities markets, such as the New York Stock Exchange (NYSE), there are official market-makers, who simultaneously quote bid and ask prices at which they are ready to deal. Futures markets do not have official market-makers, although in futures markets with open outcry, such as the Chicago Mercantile Exchange (CME), bid and ask prices are provided by open outcry, possibly by different traders, possibly not simultaneously (see Ding, 1999, pp. 308–310). Although futures prices are determined by open outcry on the trading floor at NYMEX, no intraday price data are available for electricity futures contracts, and no bid and ask prices are available on a daily basis for electricity futures. Since no observations are available on bid and ask prices, this implies that bid–ask spreads, as the cost of liquidity, must be imputed from daily price data. Two main classes of estimator have been employed to impute bid–ask spreads from price data: these are the serial covariance estimator (e.g. Roll, 1984), and the absolute price change estimator (e.g. Thompson and Waller, 1988). Bryant and Haigh (2004) reviewed the performance of two examples of each type of estimator, and found that the absolute price change estimators had smaller biases and larger variances than the serial covariance estimators. Moreover, all estimators were found to be likely downward biased (Bryant and Haigh, 2004, pp. 930–931). In this paper the measure of the cost of liquidity (B) employed is the standard deviation of market-clearing prices (Telser and Higginbotham, 1977, p. 970; Telser, 1981, p. 17). While this standard deviation includes both the bid–ask spread and the response of prices to new information (e.g. Wang *et al.* 1994, p. 838), the bid–ask spread is likely the dominant component. For example, Smith and Whaley (1994, pp. 452–453) found that the spread accounted for more than 90 per cent of the variance of observed price changes of S&P 500 Index futures on the Chicago Mercantile Exchange, with intraday data and traded prices for a sample period 1982 to 1987. The measure employed here is closer in nature to the absolute price change estimators than to the serial covariance estimators. In this paper B is calculated as the unconditional standard deviation of daily closing prices, each month, for a COB futures contract two months prior to delivery (which is normally the most heavily traded COB contract). Futures price data were purchased on disk from NYMEX. Volume (V) is the turnover, in number of contracts per month, for a COB futures contract two months prior to delivery. Volume data also were purchased on disk from NYMEX.

Volatility (h) is calculated for the last trading day of each month, using the method of Garman and Klass (1980), which uses information on daily high, low, open and close futures prices, and is shown by the authors to offer efficiency gains compared with alternatives such as squared daily returns (see also Kim and Sheen, 2001, p. 122). Data on S&P 500 are daily observations, on the last trading day of each month, on the Standard and Poor 500 (spot) Index, purchased on disk from the Institute for Financial Markets, Washington, DC. Data on I are monthly observations of the Index of United States Industrial Production (Total), not seasonally adjusted (1995 = 100) obtained from OECD *Main Economic Indicators*.

Stationarity

The behaviour of the residuals of the estimating equations (2), (4) and (6) is of critical interest. In particular, to avoid spurious regressions it is necessary that these residuals are stationary. This condition will be fulfilled, for an individual equation, if all variables in that equation are stationary, or alternatively if two or more non-stationarity variables are integrated of the same order, and are cointegrated. The concept of strict stationarity, which requires that the joint distribution of a process $\{X_t\}$ is unaltered if the series is shifted in time by an arbitrary magnitude K, is difficult to apply in practice. Consequently, in this paper, the concept of weak stationarity is employed. This requires that the process has a constant mean and variance, and that the autocovariances depend only on the lag K.

In this paper three tests for stationarity are employed. The Augmented Dickey–Fuller (ADF) test and the Phillips–Perron (PP) test both address the null of a single unit root, while the test of Kwiatkowski, Phillips, Schmidt and Shin (KPSS) addresses the null of stationarity. Evans and Savin (1981) argued that the Dickey–Fuller test suffers from low power, when the autoregressive parameter is close to, but less than unity. Banerjee *et al.* (1993, p. 113) state that the Phillips–Perron test generally has greater power than the ADF test, although the PP test suffers from greater size distortion than the ADF procedure in the presence of negative MA errors. Nevertheless, all three tests are regarded as having low power, and in this paper the KPSS test is used in conjunction with the ADF and PP tests, for confirmatory analysis, as discussed in Maddala and Kim (1998, pp. 126–127). The level of significance employed is 10 per cent because of the low power of these tests and the small sample size.

Table 9.1 Unit root tests: calculated test statistics

Variable	*ADF*	*PP*	*KPSS*	*Order of integration*
B	–4.8950***	–5.0805***	0.2324	I(0)
V	–3.5250**	–3.5242**	0.2474	I(0)
h	–5.7405***	–5.6983***	0.0866	I(0)
SP	–3.6418**	–3.6950**	0.0425	I(0)
I	–5.9197***	–5.9082***	0.1661**	I(0)$^+$

Notes
*** indicates that the null is rejected at 1% level of significance.
** indicates that the null is rejected at 5% level of significance.
* indicates that the null is rejected at 10% level of significance.
$^+$ indicates that the KPSS test does not confirm the outcome of the other two tests.
ADF is the Augmented Dickey–Fuller test; PP is the Phillips-Perron test; KPSS is the Kwiatkowski, Phillips, Schmidt and Shin test. In the ADF tests for a unit root in the time series for *B* a constant and a one period lag of ΔB, were employed; in the ADF tests for *V* and *h* the estimated model contained a constant but no lags of the dependent variable, while in the tests for *SP* and *I* the model contained a constant and time trend, without lags of the dependent variable. These specifications were determined by general to specific modelling; the tests were conducted for the period 1996(04) to 1999(12).

Table 9.1 presents the outcomes of these tests for the sample period 1996(04) to 1999(12), a total of 45 monthly observations, for the five variables discussed in the preceding subsection. It can be seen that all three tests indicate that the variables *B, V, h* and *SP* are stationary at the 10 per cent level. The US Index of Industrial Production, however, appears to be stationary according to the ADF and PP tests, although the null of stationarity is rejected at the 5 per cent level by the KPSS test. Nevertheless, this variable also is regarded as stationary, first because of the majority verdict of the ADF and PP tests, and second because the graph of this time series (Figure 9.1) suggests that the series is stationary about a deterministic trend. Finally, it is noted that such contradictions are not uncommon in confirmatory analysis (e.g. see Maddala and Kim, 1998, pp. 125–128).

Estimation

The empirical model defined by equations (2), (4) and (6) contains both endogenous and exogenous regressors. There is likely contemporary cross-correlation of the residuals, and the residual of an individual equation may not be contemporaneously uncorrelated with an endogenous regressor in that equation. Under these conditions the Ordinary Least Squares (OLS) estimator will be biased and inconsistent, and three-stage least squares (3SLS) estimates will be consistent. Moreover, financial time series such as futures prices typically exhibit heteroskedasticity, so that the OLS estimator will not be efficient. In this case 3SLS estimates will be asymptotically efficient in the class of instrumental variable (IV) estimators.[3]

In this paper limited information estimates also are produced, first to provide

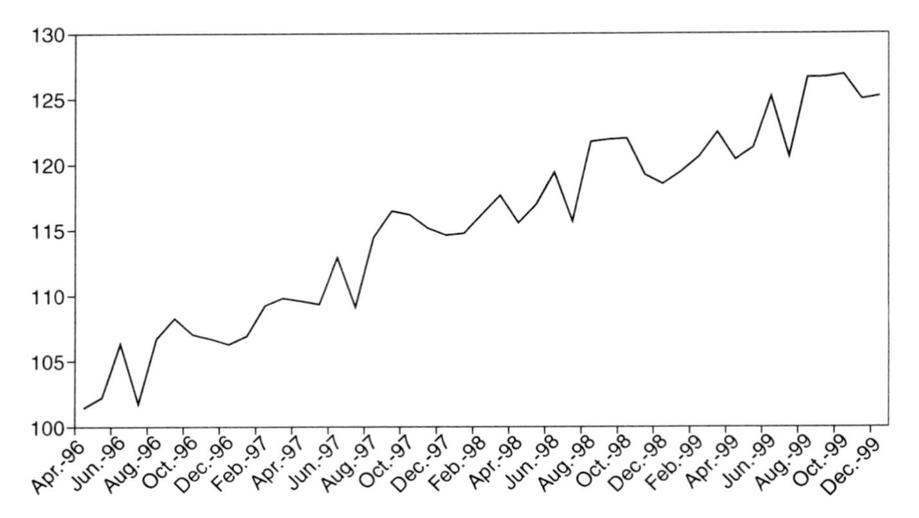

Figure 9.1 The US index of industrial production.

estimates of the EGARCH-M terms which act as proxies for the degree of uncertainty in equations (4) and (6) (these estimates are the square root of the conditional variances of the residuals of the respective single equations). The conditional variance of the residuals of equations (1) and (2) are represented as an EGARCH (1,1) process, while the residuals of equation (6) are modelled as an EGARCH (2,2) process. Second, the single-equation estimates act as starting values for the 3SLS estimates. Third, the single-equation estimates, which are produced by maximum likelihood in each case, form a basis of comparison with the system estimates, although the former will be subject to simultaneous equation bias.

Results

The discussion in this section will proceed in two parts: first the important features of the systems estimates will be discussed, and then the discussion will turn to the relevant features of the single-equation estimates. Table 9.2 presents the 3SLS estimates of the coefficients of equations (2), (4) and (6). First, in the results for equation (2), the negative sign of the relationship between the cost of liquidity and S&P 500 suggests substitutability between shares and electricity futures, given that a positive relation has been found between volume and cost of liquidity. The positive sign of the estimate of ϕ_2 is consistent with dominance of the cost of liquidity by asymmetric information cost, and/or with volatility (and hence uncertainty) increasing with volume. The second explanation is preferred, because the data suggest that volume and volatility tend to increase together in 1997, and fall together in 1999. This suggestion is confirmed by the results for equation (4).

Table 9.2 System estimates: equations (2), (4) and (6)*

Equation	*Coefficient*	*Variable*	*Estimate*	*Asymptotic* t *value*
(2) B_t	ϕ_1	Constant	6.264	2.941
	ϕ_2	V_t	0.001	5.320
	ϕ_3	SP_t	–0.006	–3.785
DW=2.345	ρ_1		0.787	12.914
(4) V_t	ϕ_4	Constant	–5282	–2.147
	ϕ_5	h_t	26364	1.501
	ϕ_6	IP_t	38.302	1.989
DW=2.266	ϕ_7	$\sqrt{W_{2t}}$	2.173	6.807
(6) B_t	ϕ_8	Constant	–2.688	–3.441
	ϕ_9	h_t	20.148	1.549
DW=2.095	ϕ_{10}	$\sqrt{W_{3t}}$	6.363	4.419

Notes
* The sample period is 1996(05) to 1999(12). Estimation is by 3SLS; the instruments employed are listed in endnote 3. DW is the Durbin–Watson statistic.

Second, consider the results for equation (4). The sign of the relationship between volume and volatility, although ambiguous in theory, is here consistent with increased cover by hedgers in the presence of increased uncertainty, and/or an increase in speculation to exploit the opportunities presented by increased volatility. Similar remarks apply to the relationship between volume and the conditional standard deviation, which captures the impact of uncertainty elsewhere in the economy. The estimate of ϕ_7 is significant at 1 per cent, while that of ϕ_5 is significant only at 7 per cent (one-tail test). The relationship between volume and US Index of Production is as anticipated, and is significant at 2.5 per cent.

Third, the results for equation (6) indicate that the sign of the relationship between cost of liquidity and volatility is as expected, although this estimate is significant only at 7 per cent. The EGARCH-M term suggests that increased uncertainty, as reflected in a rise in the variance of financial innovations, is associated with an increased cost of liquidity as expected, and this estimate is significant at 1 per cent. The residuals of equation (2) were represented as an AR(1) process, and there is no evidence of remaining serial correlation in that equation, while there is no evidence of serial correlation in equations (4) and (6).

Turning to a comparison of the systems estimates with those presented in Table A.9.1 (see Appendix) for the individual equations, there are several points of contrast to be noted.[4] First, in contrast with the systems estimate, the positive sign of the coefficient of S&P 500 suggests common responses to liquidity events, in the markets for shares and electricity futures, given that we have found a positive relation between volume and cost of liquidity. Second, the US Index of Production did not perform in the single-equation case, and was replaced by a dummy variable D_t in the estimation of equation (4): $D_t=1$ in June, July and August; $D_t=0$ otherwise. The dummy variable in this case captures the influence of a seasonal peak in demand upon volume, and therefore has

Table 9.3 Diagnostic tests on residuals: equations 2, 4 and 6

Test/Equation	*2*	*4*	*6*
Ljung-box Q			
Calculated χ^2_{20}	22.521	22.301	18.426
Critical χ^2_{20} (0.05)=31.410			
ADF			
Calculated test statistic	–7.596	–6.972	–6.848
5% Critical value	–2.931	–2.931	–2.931
PP			
Calculated test statistic	–7.593	–6.945	–7.000
5% Critical value	–2.931	–2.931	–2.931
Jarque-Bera			
Calculated test statistic	0.1252	0.6054	1.2582
p-value	0.9393	0.7388	0.5331

a positive sign. Third, while the signs of the coefficient estimates obtained by limited information (LI) methods are mostly the same as with 3SLS, the actual values of these estimates are distinctly larger with 3SLS. This applies to the coefficient of volume in equation (2), the coefficients of volatility in equations (4) and (6), and also to the EGARCH-M term in equation (6). By comparison, the coefficient of the conditional standard deviation in equation (4) is essentially similar with both 3SLS and LI estimates. Finally, it should be noted that there is evidence of asymmetry in the variance equation to equation (4), where positive news appears to have a larger impact than negative news, although there is no evidence of asymmetry in the other variance equations. These points of contrast between the two sets of estimates likely reflect the bias of the single-equation estimates.

Table 9.3 reports the results of diagnostic tests of residuals of the 3SLS estimates of equations (2), (4) and (6). These tests indicate that the residuals are not serially correlated up to lag 20, and that they are stationary and normally distributed.

Conclusions

Previous research on liquidity in financial markets has studied the relationships between cost of liquidity, volume and volatility, essentially in single equation frameworks. Empirical research on this topic has been undertaken predominantly with data from Treasury securities, equities and foreign exchange spot markets. The simultaneity, however, in the determination of these relationships has been neglected. Moreover, only limited research in this area has been done with futures markets data, and very little is known about liquidity in electricity futures markets. This paper, therefore, examines the relationships between cost of liquidity, volume and volatility, in a simple simultaneous equations framework, and estimates the model with data from the US California–Oregon Border (COB) electricity futures market.

The empirical results suggest first, that in the case of COB futures, there is a positive relationship between the cost of liquidity and volume. Economic theory predicts ambiguity in the sign of this relation, and this result is consistent with a situation in which decreases in dealer inventory risk, order execution costs, and dealer market power, which accompany increased volume, are dominated by an increase in asymmetric information cost. Alternatively, this result may be explicable in terms of an increase in volatility, which leads to increased volume, at the same time as the increase in uncertainty raises the cost of liquidity. The second explanation is preferred because of the positive relation found here between volume and volatility. Also in the volume-cost-of-liquidity relationship, the S&P 500 Index captures the impact of changes in equities markets upon electricity futures. The negative relationship between cost of liquidity and S&P 500 Index suggests substitutability between shares and electricity futures, given that a positive relation has been found between volume and cost of liquidity.

Second, the results suggest that there is a positive relationship between volatility and volume. This outcome is consistent with increased cover by hedgers in the face of increased uncertainty, and with increased speculation, which aims to exploit the increased profit opportunities presented. Theoretical arguments predict ambiguity in the sign of the volume–volatility relationship, essentially because of the conflicting implications of the information and uncertainty components of additional volatility. The positive sign found here suggests that in this case the information component dominates. In this relationship, the US Index of Production captures the impact of economic activity on the volume of electricity futures, and an EGARCH-M term acts as a proxy for uncertainty elsewhere in the economy.

Third, as anticipated, the results suggest there is a positive relationship between volatility and cost of liquidity, likely reflecting increased dealer's risk and increased asymmetric information cost, as volatility increases. Also in this equation an EGARCH-M term represents the impact of uncertainty elsewhere in the economy, upon the cost of liquidity.

The single-equation estimates of the model, included here for purposes of comparison, indicate first that there is a positive relation between cost of liquidity and the S&P 500 Index, which suggests common responses of stocks and electricity futures to liquidity events, rather than substitutability as suggested in the systems estimates (given the positive sign of the relation between cost of liquidity and volume). Second, the US Index of Production did not perform in single equation estimation, and was replaced by a dummy variable, which captures the impact of peak demand on volume, in the volume–volatility relationship. Third, generally the signs of the single-equation estimates are consistent with those obtained by 3SLS, although usually the latter are larger. The systems estimates are preferred to those obtained by single-equation methods, because in practice key liquidity relationships are determined simultaneously, and single-equation estimates likely will be biased in the environment discussed here.

Further research is required, as a matter of priority, on the relationship between cost of liquidity, volume and volatility, in futures markets, especially with intraday data. In the view of the present authors, this research should preferably be undertaken in a simultaneous-equations framework. In addition, more needs to be known about common liquidity effects between futures markets and other financial markets, such as those for currencies and Treasury securities.

Appendix

Table 9.A.1 Single equation estimates: equations 2, 4 and 6*

Equation	*Coefficient*	*Variable*	*Estimate*	*Asymptotic* t *value*
2 B_t	θ_1	Constant	−1.055	−2.850
	θ_2	V_t	0.00036	7.600
	θ_3	SP_t	0.001	4.578
DW = 2.025	ρ		0.405	5.331
Variance equation	α_0	Constant	0.346	1.712
	α_1	$\left\lvert \frac{e_{1t-1}}{\sqrt{W_{1t-1}}} \right\rvert$	−1.061	−3.549
	β_1	$\ln W_{1t-1}$	0.560	5.181
	γ_1	$\frac{e_{1t-1}}{\sqrt{W_{1t-1}}}$	0.204	0.802
4 V_t	θ_4	Constant	−319.318	−3.650
	θ_5	h_t	10394	6.687
	θ_6	D_t	404.565	4.259
DW = 2.435	θ_7	$\sqrt{W_{2t}}$	2.133	5.047
Variance equation	α_2	Constant	7.336	6.925
	α_3	$\left\lvert \frac{e_{2t-1}}{\sqrt{W_{2t-1}}} \right\rvert$	−0.976	−4.320
	β_2	$\ln W_{2t-1}$	0.479	5.633
	γ_2	$\frac{e_{2t-1}}{\sqrt{W_{2t-1}}}$	1.398	5.208
6 B_t	θ_8	Constant	−1.049	−3.726
	θ_9	h_t	10.620	5.350
DW=1.663	θ_{10}	$\sqrt{W_{3t}}$	3.738	5.885

Table 9.A.1 continued

Equation	*Coefficient*	*Variable*	*Estimate*	*Asymptotic t value*
Variance equation	α_4	Constant	−1.747	−4.775
	α_5	$\left\lvert \frac{e_{3t-1}}{\sqrt{W_{3t-1}}} \right\rvert$	−0.023	−0.233
	α_6	$\frac{e_{3t-2}}{\sqrt{W_{3t-2}}}$	−0.619	−3.057
	β_3	$\ln W_{3t-1}$	0.106	1.922
	β_4	$\ln W_{3t-2}$	−0.660	−9.230
	γ_3	$\frac{e_{3t-1}}{\sqrt{W_{3t-1}}}$	0.079	1.357
	γ_4	$\frac{e_{3t-2}}{\sqrt{W_{3t-2}}}$	0.107	1.194

Notes

* Estimation in all cases is by maximum likelihood. The conditional variance for the residuals of equations (2) and (4) is represented as an EGARCH (1,1) process, while that for the residuals of equation (6) is modelled as an EGARCH (2,2) process. In the selection of model and lag length the Akaike Information Criterion and general to specific modelling have been employed. D is a dummy variable which represents the general level of economic activity in equation (4): $D_t = 1$ in June, July, August, $D_t = 0$ otherwise.

$W_{1t} = var(e_{1t})$, etc.

DW is the Durbin–Watson statistic.

ρ is an AR(1) coefficient.

Notes

1 Research reported in this paper was undertaken when the second author was Reader in Economics, Monash University, Australia. A grant from the Faculty of Business and Economics Research Fund, Monash University, is gratefully acknowledged. Thanks are due to the New York Mercantile Exchange for the provision of data, and to Giulia Iori, Heather Anderson, Joost Pennings and Brett Inder for helpful comments. The usual disclaimer applies.

2 Of these five contracts, only PJM is quoted now by NYMEX, and it is a cash-settled contract. The scope of this contract has been extended to refer to markets in Delaware, Ohio, Virginia and Washington, DC. The Palo Verde contract is now quoted by NYMEX as a Dow Jones Electricity Price Index Futures contract, along with several others of this type.

3 The instruments employed in the production of 3SLS estimates are as follows for all equations: B_{t-1}, V_{t-1}, h_{t-1}, I_t, P_t, PPV_t, WTI_t, (P_t=price of COB futures contract, PPV_t= price of Palo Verde futures contract, each two months from maturity; WT_t=spot price of West Texas Intermediate crude oil; P, PPV and WTI are daily prices at end of month).

4 The expectations of the signs of parameters $\theta_1, \theta_2, \ldots, \theta_{10}$ are the same as the respective expectations of the signs of $\phi_1, \phi_2, \ldots, \phi_{10}$. The variables, however, are not identical in the cases of θ_6 and ϕ_6.

References

Andersen, T.G. and T. Bollerslev (1998), "Deutsche Mark–Dollar Volatility: Intraday Activity Patterns, Macroeconomic Announcements, and Longer Run Dependencies", *Journal of Finance*, 53(1), 219–265.

Avsar, S.G. and B.A. Goss (2001), "Forecast Errors and Efficiency in the US Electricity Futures Market", *Australian Economic Papers*, 40(4), 479–499.

Banerjee, A., J.J. Dolado, J.W. Galbraith and D.F. Hendry (1993), *Co-Integration, Error Correction, and the Econometric Analysis of Non-Stationary Data*, Oxford: Oxford University Press.

Bollerslev, T. and I. Domowitz (1993), "Trading Patterns and Prices in the Interbank Foreign Exchange Market", *Journal of Finance*, 48, 1421–1443.

Bollerslev, T. and M. Melvin (1994), "Bid–ask Spreads and Volatility in the Foreign Exchange Market", *Journal of International Economics*, 36, 355–372.

Borenstein, S., J. Bushnell and F. Wolak (2002), "Measuring Market Inefficiencies in California's Restructured Wholesale Electricity Market", *American Economic Review*, 92(5), 1376–1405.

Bryant, H.L. and M.S. Haigh (2004), "Bid–Ask Spreads in Commodity Futures Markets", *Applied Financial Economics*, 14, 923–936.

Chordia, T., A. Sarkar and A. Subrahmanyam (2003), "An Empirical Analysis of Stock and Bond Market Liquidity", Working Paper, Federal Reserve Bank of New York, July.

Copeland, T. and D. Galai (1983), "Information Effects on the Bid-Ask Spread", *Journal of Finance*, 38(5), 1457–1469.

Ding, D.K. (1999), "The Determinants of Bid-Ask Spreads in the Foreign Exchange Futures Market: A Microstructure Analysis", *Journal of Futures Markets*, 19(3), 307–324.

Engle, R.F., D. Lilien and R. Robins (1987), "Estimating Time Varying Risk Premia in the Term Structure: The ARCH-M Model", *Econometrica*, 55, 391–407.

Epps, T.W. and M.L. Epps (1976), "The Stochastic Dependence of Security Price Changes and Transaction Volumes: Implications for the Mixture-of-Distributions Hypothesis", *Econometrica*, 44(2), 305–321.

Evans, G.B.A. and N.E. Savin (1981), "Testing for Unit Roots: 1", *Econometrica*, 49, 753–779.

Fleming, M.J. (1997), "The Round-the-Clock Market for US Treasury Securities", *Federal Reserve Bank of New York Economic Policy Review*, July, 9–32.

Fleming, M.J. (2003), "Measuring Treasury Market Liquidity", *Federal Reserve Bank of New York Economic Policy Review*, September, 83–108.

Fleming, M. and E. Remolona (1999), "Price Formation and Liquidity in the US Treasury Market: The Response to Public Information", *Journal of Finance*, 54, 1901–1915.

French, K.R. and R. Roll (1986), "Stock Return Variances", *Journal of Financial Economics*, 17, 5–26.

Garman, M. and M. Klass (1980), "On the Estimation of Security Price Volatilities from Historical Data", *Journal of Business*, 53(1), 67–78.

Glosten, L. (1987), "Components of the Bid-Ask Spread and the Statistical Properties of Transaction Prices", *Journal of Finance*, 42(5), 1293–1307.

Goss, B.A. (2001), "The Development and Performance of Financial Markets", *Australian Economic Papers*, Special Issue on Financial Markets, 40(4), 405–416.

Goss, B.A. and S.G. Avsar (1998), "Increasing Returns to Liquidity in Futures Markets", *Applied Economics Letters*, 5, 105–109.

Goss, B.A. and S.G. Avsar (2002), "Concentration and Liquidity in Mature Markets: Evidence from the US Dollar/Yen Futures Market", *Australian Economic Papers* 41(4), 577–591.

Goss, B.A. and S.G. Avsar (2006), "Liquidity, Volume and Volatility in US Electricity Futures: The Case of Palo Verde", *Applied Financial Economics Letters*, 2, 43–46.

Hartmann, P. (1999), "Trading Volumes and Transaction Costs in the Foreign Exchange Market: Evidence from Daily Dollar–Yen Spot Data", *Journal of Banking and Finance*, 23, 801–824.

Ito, T., R.K. Lyons and M.T. Melvin (1998), "Is There Private Information in the FX Market: The Tokyo Experiment", *Journal of Finance*, 53(3), 1111–1130.

Kahn, M. and L. Lynch (2000), *California's Electricity Options and Challenges: Report to Governor Gray Davis*, 41, accessed at: www.cpuc.ca.gov/published/report/GOV_REPORT.htm.

Kim, S-J. and J. Sheen (2001), "Minute-by-Minute Dynamics of the Australian Bond Futures Market in Response to new Macroeconomic Information", *Journal of Multinational Financial Management*, 11, 117–137.

McInish, T. and R. Wood (1992), "An Analysis of Intraday Patterns in Bid/Ask Spreads for NYSE Stocks", *Journal of Finance*, 47(2), 753–764.

Maddala, G.S. and I-M. Kim (1998), *Unit Roots, Cointegration and Structural Change*, Cambridge: Cambridge University Press.

Nelson, D. (1991), "Conditional Heteroskedasticity in Asset Returns: A New Approach", *Econometrica*, 59, 347–370.

Pennings, J.M.E., W. Kuiper, F. ter Hofstede and M. Meulenberg (1998), "The Price Path due to Order Imbalances: Evidence from the Amsterdam Agricultural Futures Exchange", *European Financial Management*, 4(1), 47–64.

Roll, R. (1984), "A Simple Implicit Measure of the Effective Bid–Ask Spread in an Efficient Market", *Journal of Finance*, 23, 1127–1139.

Smith, T. and R.E. Whaley, (1994), "Estimating the Effective Bid/Ask Spread from Time and Sales Data", *Journal of Futures Markets*, 14, 437–455.

Tauchen, G.E. and M. Pitts (1983), "The Price Variability–Volume Relationship on Speculative Markets", *Econometrica*, 51(2), 485–506.

Telser, L.G. (1981), "Why There Are Organised Futures Markets", *Journal of Law and Economics*, 24, 1–22.

Telser, L.G. and H.N. Higginbotham (1977), "Organised Futures Markets: Costs and Benefits", *Journal of Political Economy*, 85(5), 969–1000.

Thompson, S.R. and M. Waller (1988), "Determinants of Liquidity Costs in Commodity Futures Markets, *Review of Futures Markets*, 7, 110–126.

Walls, W.D. (1999), "Volatility, Volume and Maturity in Electricity Futures", *Applied Financial Economics*, 9, 283–287.

Wang, G.H.K., R.J. Michalski, J.V. Jordan and E.J. Moriarty (1994), "An Intra-day Analysis of Bid-spreads and Price Volatility in the S&P 500 Index Futures Market", *Journal of Futures Markets*, 14, 837–859.

Wang, G.H.K., J. Yau and T. Baptiste (1997), "Trading Volume and Transaction Costs in Futures Markets", *Journal of Futures Markets*, 17(7), 757–780.

Index

adjustment for risk 153–4, 163, 164
agricultural markets 6, 46, 87–8, 176; decreased government involvement in 75; seasonality of futures 61
Amsterdam Agricultural Futures Exchange 92
Anderson, H. 6
Anderson–Darling test 131, 134, 140
arbitrage: on forward premium 153; on spot premium 153
Arteta, C. 22
Asia: foreign debt unsustainable in 33–4; growth generated by high investment and saving 19; macroeconomic instability in 20–1; private capital flows to 21–2
Asian crisis: and contagion 112–14; empirical analysis of 31–4; evidence of 18–42; impact of 134–6, 141; tequila effect 112; warning signals 18–42, 126
Asian currencies, overvaluation of 31–3
asymmetric information cost 11, 192, 203; increasing with volume 200
augmented Dickey–Fuller test 131, 156, 198–9
Avsar, S.G. 88, 150–66, 165, 193

backwardation 6, 80
Baillie, R.T. 151
Barrucci, E. 7
Beijing Commodity Exchange 55
Berwald, D.K. 87
Bessembinder, H. 84
bid-ask spread 6–7, 12, 90–3, 151, 171–2, 182, 192, 195–7; absolute price change estimator 197; effective 10–11, 192; components of 11; intraday 92; nominal 10–11
Black, F. 90
Bollerslev, T. 125, 191
Borenstein, S. 193
Brennan, D. 80
Brorsen, B.W. 79
Brownian Motion 28–9, 30, 106, 129

California, wholesale electrical prices in 193
California–Oregon Border (COB) 14, 193, 198, 202–3
Calvo, S. 113
capital asset pricing model (CAPM) 152, 164
Caramazza, F. 114
Carter, C. 161
Chan, K.C. 68
Chang, H. 55
Chicago Board of Trade 13, 48, 58, 68, 88, 161; soybean prices on 66
Chicago Mercantile Exchange 8–9, 11, 88, 127, 155, 161, 172, 197–8
China: bilateral trade agreement with US 53; concern with national food security 48; evidence of seasonality in exchange trading 61–3; official national standards in 67; opening of futures markets in 53–8; pattern of trading in 58–63; price efficiency on futures markets 63–8; soybean futures market in 66; soybean producing provinces in 51; volume of trading in 48–58, 61
China National Cereals: Oils and Foodstuffs Import and Export Corporation (COFCO) 48, 53
China Securities Regulatory Commission (CSRC) 54–6, 69
China Zhengzhou Commodity Exchange (CZCE) 4
Chinese futures market: copper 4–5; recent developments in 4–5; soybeans 4–5

Clay, J. 77
cluster: volatility 13, 115, 123
cointegration 81, 156
Commodity Futures Trading Commission (CFTC) 86, 151; Washington DC 155
consumption; increasing at time of falling productivity 36
contagion 105, 126; and Asian crises 112–4; cross-border 113; fundamental-based 113; non-symmetric nature of 119
copper 46–7; futures on Shanghai Exchange 57, 61
cost: asymmetric information 11, 192, 194, 196, 200, 203; dealer inventory 11; inventory carrying 192, 194
Crámer–von Misses test 131, 134, 140
crisis: Asian 18–42; currency 20; debt 20, 27–31; financial 18, 126–7; interactions of types of 34–42; warning signals of 18–42
Crook, F. 49, 50–1
currency crisis 25–7; resulting from unstable macroeconomic policies 20
currency futures: forecasting in 9–10, 160–5; profits in 9–10, 162–5; volatility during 1997 East Asian crisis 103–19

Dalian Commodity Exchange 4, 47, 54–5, 56; soybean contracts 63; soybean futures on 58; soybean prices on 66, 68; specializing in agricultural products 68
data: high-frequency 6–8, 103, 125, 129; low-frequency 7; tick-by-tick 106, 124, 127
debt: crisis 20, 27–31; and currency crisis 25–7; excess 3; in Latin American countries 28; optimal 1–14, 27, 29, 30
deficit: current account 21; fiscal 21
diffusion: processes 104; stochastic 129; temporal behaviour of coefficient 109; volatility 136
Dutt, H.R. 89–90

efficiency 81–2; of foreign exchange futures market 160; hypothesis 151; pricing 82
Efficient Markets Hypothesis (EMH) 162–3, 165, 166
EGARCH 157, 165, 200
EGARCH-M model 196–7, 200, 201, 203
Egelkraut, T.M. 75–94
electronic trading 5, 87–8, 175, 182–3, 188; liquidity 88; and market depth 92–3; volatility 88
Ellis, L. 117
empirical analysis of Asian crises 31–4
empirical research on foreign exchange markets 151
Epps effect 104
Epps, M.L. 12, 195
Epps, T.W. 12, 195
exchange rate: equilibrium real 24–5; nominal 35; real 27, 31–3

Federal Reserve Bank of New York 152
financial crisis: in East Asia 18–42; and capital flows 126–7; postwar 18
Fishe, R.P.H. 89
Fleming, M.J. 2, 10, 192
Fleming, W.H. 29
Forbes, K.J. 113
forecast: currency futures 9–10; error 166; model-based 160; short-term 155–6; volatility 6
forecasting 150–66; performance of traditional economic models 150; post-sample 160
foreign debt, unsustainable 21–3, 27, 33–4
foreign exchange market, empirical research on 151
Fourier analysis 106–12; application of 103–19; with high frequency data 6–8
Fourier coefficients 106–7
Fourier–Féjer inversion formula 107
Frenkel, J.A. 151
Friedman, M. 115–16
Fung, H.G. 66, 68
futures market liquidity, perceptions of 171–89
futures exchange, pervasive Chinese characteristics of 58
futures markets 11, 150; agricultural 46; for AU dollar 124, 127; experimental 54; hedgers in 151–3; opening in China 53–8; and price discovery 84–5; survey of performance 5–6

Gale, F. 48–9
GARCH 8, 103, 114, 124–5, 154
Garcia, P. 75–94, 81
Gilmour, B. 49
Gompertz curve 92
Goodwin, B.K. 85
Goss, B.A. 1–14, 88, 150–66, 165, 193
Granger, C.W.J. 4, 8
Gray, R.W. 5
gross domestic product (GDP) 22; ratio of external debt to 3; reduced by bad shock 28

Guo, X. 58

Hainan China Commodity Futures Exchange 56
Hanson, S.D. 77
Hartzmark, M.L. 89
hedge ratio: optimal 76; risk minimizing 77; utility maximizing 77
hedger: in futures market 151; large corporate 86; long 152–4, 159, 162; operational 153; selective 153; short 152–3, 159, 162
hedging: behaviour 75–9; cross-hedging 76; dynamic 76–7; selective 77
Heston, S.L. 110
high-frequency data 103, 125, 129; non-homogenous nature of 108
high-frequency exchange rate dynamics 125
Holt, M.T. 81
Holthausen, D.M. 76
Hong Kong, growth rate of 42
Hsu, H.H. 48
Huang, J. 48
hyperbolic absolute risk aversion (HARA) 154
hypothesis: Efficient Markets (EMH) 162–3, 165–6; of normality 134, 136, 140; rational expectations (REH) 153, 157, 165

Index of United States Industrial Production (Total) 198–9, 203
information: private 151, 195; public 151
insurance programs 75
intertemporal budget constraint (IBC) 29
interest, open and margins 89
interest rate 19; uncovered parity theory 26
international capital markets 23–4
international financial statistics 32
International Monetary Fund 21, 23–4
interpolation: linear 104; previous-tick 104
intra-daily sampling frequency 128, 130
intraday data 7–8, 106, 124–5, 127
intraday trading pattern 124
intraday volatility pattern 125
Iori, G. 7, 103–19
Irwin, S.H. 81, 86

Jarque–Bera test 131, 134, 140, 160
Jiang, G.J. 108
Johansen maximum eigenvalue test 156

Kahn, M. 193
Kamara, A. 81
Kaminsky, G.L. 126
Kansas City 91
Kazakhstan, wheat futures in 5
Ke, B. 66–7
Kearns, J. 152
Kendall, S. 83
Kenyon, D.E. 77
Klitgaard, T. 152
Koontz, S.R. 85
Korea: industrial policy in 34; warning signals in 33
Kuhn, B.A. 89

Lagrange Multiple test 157
Lence, S.H. 79
Leuthold, R.M. 75–94
Lewis, E. 117
Li, M. 58
Lim, G.C. 2, 18–42, 126
liquidity 5, 10–14, 90–3; appropriate measure of cost of 192; depth 171; dynamics of 188; economic cost of 172; electronic trading 88; key variables in determination of 10; market 90, 128; and price volatility 91; relationships 10–14; resiliency 171; and stock/bond markets 194; tightness 171; in US electricity futures 191–205; and volume 91, 194–5, 201
Liu, D. 68
Ljung-Box test 160
logarithmic realized standard deviation 123–6, 130; and realized variances 131–4
logarithmic utility function 154, 165
London International Financial Futures Exchange 11
Lynch, L. 193
Lyons, R.K. 6

M-GARCH model 157, 159, 165
McKenzie, A.M. 81
macroeconomic instability: in Asia 20–1; as cause of currency crisis 20
Malliavin, P. 7, 104, 108, 117
Mancino, M. 7, 104, 117
Manners, P. 152
margin: changes as endogenous to system 90; effect of on market behaviour 89–90; and increasing or decreasing volatility 89; and open interest 89; and trading volume 89
marginal convenience yield 79–80

market: agricultural 6, 87–8, 176; anticipations 23–5; computerized bund (DTB) 91–2; developed cash 4; effect of margins on behaviour 89–90; heterogeneity 182; illiquid 172; inversion 80; liquid 90, 128; microstructure 174–5, 185; mungbean 56; open outcry Bund (LIFFE) 91–2; power of dealer 192, 194; soybeans 46–53; stock 174; US electricity 191–205; wheat 46–53
market characteristics and traders' perceptions 174–5
market depth 10, 92, 172–4; and electronic trading 92–3; time dimension 93
Mathews, K.H. 76
Mattiussi, V. 103–19
Mean Net Annualized Return (MNAR) 162
measure: liquidity 173–4; market-depth 173–4
Meese, R. 9
microstructure: friction 128; market 174–5
Miller, S.E. 76
misalignment 20; measure of 27
mungbean market 56; Zhengzhou Commodity Exchange contract on 56

Natural Real Exchange Rate (NATREX) 2, 18, 20, 24–5, 27, 32, 42
New York Mercantile Exchange (NYMEX) 193
New York Stock Exchange (NYSE) 8, 11, 197

open outcry 11, 197
optimal debt 1–14, 27; ratio 2–3, 30–1
option pricing model, validity of 8
option-price-based model 125
order imbalance 174, 185, 187; affecting traders' perceptions of price path 178–9; and liquidity relationships 10–14; temporary 189

Paladino, G. 23
Palo Verde 193
Park, A. 49
Pearson correlation estimator 111–12
Peck, A.E. 5, 46–70
Pennings, J.M.E. 13, 77–8, 174, 192
Pesaran, M.H. 155
Philips–Perron test 131, 156, 160, 198–9
Pirrong, C. 92
Pitts, M. 12, 195
Poon, S.H. 4, 8
Precup, O. 7
price: efficiency 63–8, 82; linkages 85; risk 79; simultaneous dynamics 85; spot 127; variability 86; volatility 63, 79–84
price discovery 84–6; and futures markets 84–5
price path: exponential 17; linear 171, 176, 184; perceptions of 178; S-shaped 176, 182, 187; step-wise 176; stepped perception of 180, 185
price-spikes in US electricity market 13
productivity 32; falling increasing consumption 36

Rajan, R. 42
rational expectations hypothesis (REH) 153, 157, 165
Rausser, G.C. 161
real exchange rate 27, 31–3
realized standard deviation 140
realized variance distribution 134
realized variance estimator 141
realized volatility 103–4, 124–5, 127, 140
regressor: endogenous 199; exogenous 199
Reinhart, C.M. 113
returns 136–41; leptokurtic density 138; raw 138; standardized 136–42
Rigobon, R. 113
risk: adjustment for 153–4, 163, 164; attitude 78; perception 78; reduction 153; and volatility 3–10
risk management 5, 6; and marketing strategies 75–9; strategy 78
risk premium 79, 82–3, 159; in portfolio framework 82–3; time-varying 81
risk-adjusted profit 82
risk-return ratio 82
Rockwell, C.S. 151
Rogoff, A. 9
Rozelle, S. 48, 49
Rutledge, D.J.S. 5, 94

Sanders, D.R. 87
Schieck, V. 123–42
Schroeder, T.C. 85
seasonality of agricultural futures: in Chinese exchanges 61–3; in US trading 62–3
Seguin, P.J. 84
Shanghai Cereals and Oils Exchange 54–5
Shanghai Futures Exchange 4, 47, 56, 61; aluminium futures at 57–59; copper futures at 61; copper prices on 68; specializing in industrial products 68

simulated trading 165
simultaneity in USD/DEM futures 150–66
simultaneous-equations framework for liquidity of US electricity futures 191–205
Singapore currency 42
Siregar, R. 42
Sorensen, C. 80
soybeans 46–7, 77, 185, 186; absence of strong seasonality of trading 62; producing provinces in China 51; tariff-rate quotas for 53; Tokyo Grain Exchange futures for 58
soybean futures at Dalian Commodity Exchange 4–5, 58, 66
speculative bubble 28
speculator 159, 175, 179; position holding period 161
spot premium: arbitrage on 153
standardized returns 136–42
stationarity 152, 156–7, 197–200, 198–9
Stein, J.L. 2, 18–42, 23, 126, 159, 166
stochastic optimal control/dynamic programming (SOC/DP) 20, 24–5, 29

Tauchen, G.E. 12, 195
Thalmaier, A. 108
Thomakos, T. 130, 141
tick-by-tick data 106, 124, 127
trader: access 174–5; behaviour 175; informed 175; market-maker 175; noise 86–7, 174, 175; stock index 184; uninformed 175
trader perceptions 171–2; aggregate 188; heterogeneity of 184; of liquidity 175; of market characteristics 174–5, 185–7; of market microstructure 185; of order imbalance 174
trading: Chinese pattern of 58–63, 69; electronic 5, 11, 87–8, 175, 182–3, 188; environment 84–93; pit 87; regulations 175; volume in China 48–58
transaction cost 80, 166; in agricultural futures 90; of small orders 172

Vahid, F. 6
volatility 10, 191, 198; clustering 13, 115, 123; during 1997 East Asian crisis 103–19; diffusion 136; early-morning 128; electronic trading 88; forecast 6; and government programs 84; historical 111; implied 8; as latent variable 3; realized 8–9, 103–4, 130; reconstructing trajectories of 105; relationship with volume 11–12, 193, 195, 203; seasonality as determinant of 83; spillover 114; in capital flows 21–2; transmission of changes 113
volume 10, 191; expected 84; and liquidity 194–5, 201; and margins 89; relationship with volatility 11–12, 193, 195; shocks 84; of trading in China 48–58; unexpected 84

Walls, W.D. 193
Wang, H.H. 66–7
Wang, T. 130, 141
Wang, X. 55
warning signals: of Asian crises 18–42, 126; components of 20; in Korea 33; objective 36; traditional 20–5; used by international market 24
Wein, I.L. 89–90
Weir, L. 152
wheat 46–7, 56; absence of strong seasonality of trading 62; Chinese national standards for 52; tariff-rate quotas for 53
wheat futures 49–53; at Zhengzhou Commodity Exchange 57–8; in Kazakhstan 5
Williams, J.C. 80
Working, H. 153
Wright, B.D. 80

Yamey, B.S. 5
Yao, L. 54
Yoon, B. 79

Zhao, J. 66
Zhengzhou Commodity Exchange 47, 53–6, 61; mungbean contract 56; specializing in agricultural products 68; wheat futures at 57–8
Zhengzhou Grain Warehouse Market (ZGWM) 49, 53–4